CENTRED ON LEARNING

CENTRED ON LEARNING

Academic Case Studies on Learning Centre Development

Edited by
Edward Oyston

ASHGATE

Published by
Ashgate Publishing Limited
Gower House
Croft Road
Aldershot
Hants GU11 3HR
England

Ashgate Publishing Company
Suite 420
101 Cherry Street
Burlington VT 05401-4405
USA

British Library Cataloguing in Publication Data

Centred on learning: academic case studies on learning centre development
1. Academic libraries – Great Britain – Aims and objectives
2. Instructional materials centres – Great Britain
I. Oyston, E. 027.3

Library of Congress Cataloging-in-Publication Data

Centred on learning: academic case studies on learning centre development
edited by Edward Oyston.
p. cm.
Includes bibliographical references.
ISBN 0-7546-0805-0 (alk. paper)
1. Instructional materials centers – Great Britain. 2. Academic libraries – Great Britain.
1. Oyston, E.

LB3044.74.G7 C46 2002
027.7'0941–dc21
2002074455

ISBN 0 7546 0805 0

Printed on acid-free paper

Typeset in 10pt Century Old Style by Tradespools, Frome, Somerset
Printed and bound in Great Britain by Antony Rowe Ltd, Chippenham, Wiltshire

Contents

Contributors

Claire Abson, Information Specialist, Learning Centre, Sheffield Hallam University

Phil Bannister, Research Assistant, Learning and Teaching Institute, Learning Centre, Sheffield Hallam University

Graham Bulpitt, Director, Learning Centre, Sheffield Hallam University

Sue Clegg, Professor of Educational Research, Learning and Teaching Research Institute, Sheffield Hallam University

Philippa Dyson, Support Manager, Learning Resources, University of Lincoln

Katherine Everest, Planning and Marketing Manager, Learning Support Services, Leeds Metropolitan University

Sheona Farquhar, Help Desk Services Manager, Directorate of Information Systems and Services, University of Aberdeen

Madeleine Freewood, Research Assistant, Learning and Teaching Institute, Learning Centre, Sheffield Hallam University

Julie Hanson, Research Assistant, Learning and Teaching Institute, Learning Centre, Sheffield Hallam University

Roger Hines, Information Specialist, Learning Centre, Sheffield Hallam University

Alison Hudson, Head of the Centre for Multimedia in Education, Educational Research Coordinator, Learning and Teaching Institute, Learning Centre, Sheffield Hallam University

Meg Message, Learning Centre Manager, Learning Support Services, Leeds Metropolitan University

Kay Moore, Information Specialist, Learning Centre, Sheffield Hallam University

Jo Norry, Deputy Learning Centre Manager: City Campus, Learning Support Services, Leeds Metropolitan University; formerly User Services Manager, Learning Centre, Sheffield Hallam University

Edward Oyston, Head of Technical Services and Development, Learning Centre, Sheffield Hallam University

Sadie Parr, Research Assistant, Learning and Teaching Institute, Learning Centre, Sheffield Hallam University

Philip Payne, Head of Learning Support Services, Leeds Metropolitan University

Linda Purdy, Senior Information Adviser, Learning Centre, Sheffield Hallam University

Marie Scopes, Deputy Learning Centre Manager: Beckett Park, Learning Support Services, Leeds Metropolitan University

John Steel, Research Assistant, Learning and Teaching Institute, Learning Support Services, Learning Centre, Sheffield Hallam University

Norma Thompson, Learning Centre Manager, Beckett Park, Leeds Metropolitan University

Liz Waller, Skills for Learning Consultant, Learning Support Services, Leeds Metropolitan University

Stephen Wan, Research Assistant, Learning and Teaching Institute, Learning Centre, Sheffield Hallam University

Alison Ward, Information Specialist, Learning Centre, Sheffield Hallam University

Dilys Young, Head of the Library Learning Centre, Rotherham College of Arts and Technology; formerly Academic Services Manager, Learning Support Services, University of Lincoln

Introduction

◼

Academic libraries and other services are driven by institutional strategies and priorities, and demands for greater efficiency, effectiveness and responsiveness. They do it in different ways, according to the character of their parent institution and their role within it. As the title of this book indicates, our focus is the response of academic services to one particular aspect of institutional strategy: learning and teaching. We also concentrate on one specific approach to this agenda, which can be called: *the learning centre*.

The learning centre concept is a distinctive, learner-centred, response to supporting and improving the quality of student learning. It has a relatively uncontroversial starting position – that library and information services are more than just about supporting student information needs – but goes beyond this to take a wider view of student learning support than is normally associated with academic library services, taking into account other services, such as IT and media production. However, the real distinctiveness of the learning centre concept lies in its holistic approach to student learning. It is not just resource-based or even service-based, but is activity-based, concerned with supporting a range of learning styles and student interaction with these resources and services. It also has the potential to extend beyond just supporting existing student needs, to influencing learning development and thus shaping the student learning environment.

That is the theory. The purpose of this book is to explore what this learning centre approach can mean in practice. It does so by examining how academic services in four universities have developed to meet the particular learning needs of their students, with a view to drawing out from their experience the elements that contribute to the learning centre approach. All have undergone radical change in terms of role, organization, range and nature of service provision. The extent to which each has adopted a learning centre approach varies according to institutional character.

On the basis of this experience, what does the learning centre approach mean in practice?

The essential characteristic of the learning centre approach is that it is actually 'centred on learning': its fundamental *raison d'être* is institutional teaching and learning strategy, not information provision or technological convergence, although these are likely to be important parts of the equation. This approach will be evident in the vision statement, mission and objectives of the service, which will seek to place it firmly in the context of the organization's teaching and learning agenda. It may go even further, to project a learning development, not just a support role for the service.

Organizational arrangements supporting a learning centre approach must facilitate joint working between academic services units to enable them deliver the learner-centred vision. In practice, this is likely to be reflected in some organizational convergence of these units, driven by the recognition that different services need to be managed together to contribute effectively to institutional strategy; marriages of convenience do not qualify. The exact mix of services constituting the learning centre organization will undoubtedly vary; library and information services are essential, together with at least the academic user services part of IT provision. The addition of media production services, particularly when they provide multimedia capability, broadens the contribution of the service to teaching and learning. They can also generate information resources for the learning centre environment and can provide additional opportunities to engage with teaching staff. The most significant inclusion could be educational development services, which have the potential to add a different dimension to the role of the learning centre organization, making it more of a partner in the development of student learning and encouraging more effective exploitation of its resources and services. Whatever the mix, there must be a sense of the different parts working together across boundaries, in an integrated way, rather than just coexisting within an organizational structure.

The organization underpinning service provision is largely irrelevant to students. The distinctiveness of the learning centre approach for them is that it seeks to meet their learning needs as a whole – not just their information or IT needs. This will be evident through, for example, integrated access, both physical and virtual, to a broad range of information, IT and learning resources. Physical accommodation should combine access to these resources with facilities to support various learning styles, both group and individual.

The nature of interaction between learning centre staff and students will also be distinctive, based on a sound understanding of academic programmes and learning styles. Staff roles are likely to integrate information and IT support. While their role in providing learning support may still be developing, the need for such a role is accepted. Some learning centre staff will engage with students outside the traditional support role, with information-based teaching programmes properly integrated into academic programmes and ideally part of their assessment. Operational convergence and new models of teaching and learning will be reflected in different staff roles that challenge traditional professional boundaries and will need to be supported by more flexible management structures and working practices.

The role of learning centre staff will be recognized as integral to the institution's teaching and learning agenda. They will work in partnership with academic colleagues in course development and management, including membership of the boards of schools of study and course forums. A good measure of this could be the range and extent of their involvement in the development of virtual learning environments. The wider contribution of learning centre staff to the institutional academic agenda will also be recognized through active participation in institutional academic-quality arrangements.

In supporting the student learning experience, learning centre buildings will certainly contain an extensive range of facilities – networked PCs and associated facilities such as printing, video playback, perhaps satellite broadcasting – although these may not be significantly different from any modern academic library service. Their use, however, will be more distinctive, targeted explicitly at meeting learning, not just information needs. Learning centres are likely to be the principal location for open-access IT facilities. Networked PCs will provide access not just to information resources but to general purpose and often more specialist software, and to learning materials and programs; they are regarded as powerful but standard tools, not something needing special treatment. As a result, they are likely to be physically integrated with other study facilities and information resources. In accommodating different styles of learning, group study facilities will not just be more extensive but will be accepted as integral, not just as an add-on to individual quiet study. As a consequence, the general study environment will be markedly different: there will be a greater acceptance of 'noise' as the sound of students collaborating on work, not just enjoying a social chat, and tolerance of some eating and drinking, in line with the working environments that students will encounter in their subsequent careers.

This general approach is not for everyone, but elements of it are relevant to academic services everywhere.

The academic library service is at the heart of the learning centre concept. Of all academic services, it has been the one that has focused most directly on supporting student learning. It has prided itself on its user orientation and its close relationship with the academic life of the institution. Library buildings have always been the most important public learning space on campus. However, while academic libraries are crucial to the learning centre concept, they are not sufficient in themselves to deliver it. This argument is developed in Chapter 1 in the context of the changing sectoral and institutional environment and taken forward in the remaining chapters, which examine experience from the organizational perspective, then from those of staff, students and the learning environment. The final chapter draws these different strands together and looks ahead to further developments that the future will bring.

The underlying aims of the book are to capture existing innovative practice and to stimulate thinking about new approaches to supporting student learning needs.

Edward Oyston

1 The changing picture of higher education

Claire Abson

INTRODUCTION

The learning centre approach is a particular response to the changing teaching and learning landscape within higher education, which in turn is driven by wider educational and societal developments. Some higher education institutions have used the challenges and opportunities presented by these developments to rethink the role and purpose of their academic support services. This chapter examines the place of academic libraries in the learning landscape, so as to provide a starting point from which the remaining chapters will draw out the distinctive features of the learning centre concept as one approach to developing their role.

In the interests of clarity, the chapter will look first at the wider national and international developments that have changed the picture of higher education in the UK over the last two decades of the twentieth century. Precisely what these developments have meant for institutions and their students will add additional layers to this picture. The issues raised for academic libraries will complete a complex picture of change and development.

ECONOMIC, POLITICAL AND SOCIAL DEVELOPMENTS

THE CHANGING EMPLOYMENT PROFILE

Changes in the employment picture in the UK over the last 20 or 30 years have undoubtedly had an impact that has been felt by higher education institutions. The general shift in the skills requirements of the workforce has gone some way towards creating demand for higher level qualifications. Increasing opportunities in the service sector, alongside declining manufacturing and industrial careers, have dictated an emphasis on 'graduateness' and the importance of graduate-level skills. This shift has increased opportunities in small and medium-sized enterprises for graduates. The difficulty in providing formal training programmes in smaller companies and organizations and the reliance on the individual, increasingly mean that new graduates need to 'hit the ground running'. It is also the case that, as the Dearing Report points out,

> the pace of change in the workplace will require people to re-equip themselves, as new knowledge and new skills are needed for economies to compete, survive and prosper. A lifelong career in one organization will become increasingly the exception (NCIHE, 1997, p. 9)

Definitions vary as to what constitutes these core skills that are so in demand, but Harvey and Mason (1996, p. 17) outline the five broad areas that emerged from their study as being of major importance to employers, namely:

- knowledge
- intellectual ability
- ability to work in a modern organization
- interpersonal skills
- communication skills.

Arguing that the graduate must be a 'reflective practitioner', they go on to state that, 'the combination of reflection, transformation and the acquisition of the high-level skills of critique, analysis and interpretation, forms the basis of the reflective practitioner' (ibid., 1996, p. 27). Many older students returning to education are doing so because they, or their employers, have identified the need to develop these skills and see higher education as the means to do this.

Working has also become more flexible for many people and can fit more easily around other areas of their lives. In research published in 2001, it was found that more than half of all workers either work away from the office or are employed for variable hours outside the standard 9 to 5. In addition, more than 20 per cent of employees work less than 30 hours per week, with many firms allowing staff to work some form of flexitime, and thus have some control over the hours in their working week (Behar, 2001, p. 1).

TECHNOLOGICAL DEVELOPMENTS

In a general sense, technological developments have had a far-reaching impact on the population and this has been felt by higher education. In the UK 38 per cent of households now own a PC, almost triple the proportion for 1985. In addition, 45 per cent of adults have accessed the Internet at some stage, the majority (59 per cent) doing so from home (*Social Trends*, 2001, p. 233). Technological capabilities, such as Internet and email access, and developing mobile phone technologies have been key factors in the increasing numbers of people working from home, thus affording them greater flexibility with their time. Learning is much more accessible, and the means are there to generate an interest in knowledge and learning without necessarily leaving the home. It is arguable whether it is the accessibility of knowledge that has created the demand for flexible learning routes, or vice versa; but the demand is clearly there.

Equally, technological change has impacted on the workplace. Ability to use and exploit information technology is a highly valued skill, underpinning the five core skills areas outlined above. It is a key aspect of well-developed communication skills and forms an integral part of the modern organization, the adaptation to which is so prized by employers.

THE GOVERNMENT AGENDA FOR HIGHER EDUCATION

Lifelong learning

Official encouragement for those considering returning to study has also been an important factor. The business of continuing learning through life was seized on by the new Labour administration in 1997 as a priority issue, culminating in the publication of the green paper, *The Learning Age*, in 1998. This consultation document outlined plans for making learning more accessible and more relevant, to encourage more people to remain in, or return to, education at all levels. It tackled adult learning at a basic level, focusing on literacy and numeracy skills, and at a more advanced level by providing an additional 500 000 places on higher education courses by 2002. The expectation outlined in the green paper was that more than half of these additional places would be taken by mature students without traditional A-level or Scottish Higher qualifications.

The launch of the University for Industry (now LearnDirect) picked up the key issue of business and industry support for their employees in continuing their learning and development. The focus was on using, 'modern communication technologies to link businesses and individuals to cost-effective, accessible and flexible education and training' (*The Learning Age*, 1998). In other words, learning would happen when and how the individual wanted, possibly via a combination of different mediums and locations – physical and virtual, for example, TV, radio, a CD-ROM package, or in the workplace. The emphasis was on lifelong learning, which the paper defined as, 'the continuous development of the skills, knowledge and understanding that are essential for employability and fulfilment' (ibid.).

This 'fulfilment' element cannot be ignored. The issue of increased leisure time has already been noted; the *Learning Age* document firmly places this aspect on the government agenda alongside the more tangible economic aspect of enhanced employability for individuals.

The financial burden: funding for higher education

The shift of the cost of higher education away from the policy makers and the tax payer, and directly onto students and institutions, has had a huge impact on who is studying, what, why, and what their expectations of their period of study are. Levels of funding for institutions, relative to student numbers, have fallen dramatically since the late 1970s. Indeed, figures for funding per student show a 40 per cent drop since 1976 (NCIHE, 1997, p. 45). As a result, higher education institutions need to find alternative ways of raising revenue. These routes have included increasing research commitments, thus gaining access to research council funding, and development of postgraduate continuing professional development courses where there is a demand and where income generation is not limited by the capping of fees (as it is with undergraduate courses). In addition, the franchising of courses to overseas institutions has become increasingly common, raising questions over the quality of delivery, student attainment and student support.

There have been recent injections of targeted funding into higher education. Public money has been made available for much needed estates and infrastructure developments, for staffing (following the findings of the Bett Committee) and for other initiatives – for example, the development of teaching and learning strategies. However, there has been no real sign of sectoral funding to support additional student numbers. Universities UK (formerly the Committee of Vice-Chancellors and Principals) has estimated that £10 billion will be needed to meet government expansion targets in the sector.

The then Education Secretary's recent letter to the chairman of the Higher Education Funding Council for England highlights the key financial and other issues as viewed by the present government (Morris, 2001). The letter focuses on the need for educational bodies and institutions to collaborate on widening participation in higher education and to link in with local communities and local businesses to embed vocational skills ever more widely in higher education courses. It is noted that only one in five young people from lower socio-economic groups currently enter higher education, compared with half of young people from the middle classes. The announcement of 8000 New Opportunity Bursaries to be made available for students with particular pressures or from low-income backgrounds highlights this focus on wider participation and on student retention. The letter stresses the need to use access and hardship funds to support these same students to keep them in higher education.

The financial burden: student finances

The abolition of the student maintenance grant and the introduction of fee payment have clearly had an impact on young people entering higher education and their motivations for study when they do. Tuition fees were introduced in the 1998/99 academic year (although subsequently abolished in Scotland in 2000). The maintenance grant was gradually eroded from the mid-1980s onwards, before finally being abolished with effect from the 1999/2000 cycle. Applications for higher education courses remain high overall, but it is interesting to note that recent research at South Bank University found that six out of ten students from a sample of 2000 claimed to have friends who had been deterred from entering higher education because of the financial implications (Judd, 2000, p. 1).

Long-term financial reward and job satisfaction cannot be applied across the board as a motivation for study but the average 18-year-old, as well as the average mature student, is arguably more focused in this area than perhaps they may have been 15 or 20 years ago. The vast majority of students are now making a personal financial investment in their education and want to see a good return on that investment. This investment extends to the way in which they choose to study. Even where education doesn't need to fit around other commitments, such as family responsibilities, many students now need to work to avoid carrying through an unmanageable amount of debt into their graduate careers.

A student hardship survey conducted by the National Union of Students in 1999 found that 41 per cent of full-time undergraduates had jobs during term-time, working an average of 13 hours per week (Watkins, 2001, p. 1). Full-time students are often not really full-time any more, and part-time students may not come on to campus more than once a week. Some may choose to study in their home town, or perhaps live at home and commute, further isolating themselves from their institution of study. These motivations have impacted on the ways in which courses are taught and supported.

The boundaries have changed and are continuing to change, and higher education institutions have had to respond to this. In some cases, this personal investment and these time pressures have made the student more focused in their studies. In others, the service demands they are making of their institution of study can be likened to the demands they might make of a service provider in the high street. There is an expectation that the institution will be flexible enough to respond to the conflicting demands on student time and personal resources.

The quality agenda

The quality of provision and standards of awards in higher education, and also how they are assessed are high on the national and institutional agendas. The introduction of Teaching Quality Assessment to the higher education sector in 1994, followed by a change to Subject Review in 1998, was met in a positive way by higher education institutions, who wished to see maximum points scored in all six aspects of academic subject provision:

- curriculum design, content and organization

- teaching, learning and assessment
- student progression and achievement
- student support and guidance
- learning resources
- quality management and enhancement.

The resulting cycle of external audits of subject provision has done much to change the nature and profile of academic work. One consequence of the requirement to provide evidence of quality and high standards in teaching and learning has been a substantial administrative load for academic staff. There is a clear need for assessment of the quality of provision, and the future of quality assessment in higher education is undecided at present, but the issue of who supports this is a key one. Paperwork and committee work, often driven by internal and external quality requirements, now take up an ever increasing proportion of staff time which can only impact on their teaching and research activity.

THE IMPACT ON HIGHER EDUCATION INSTITUTIONS AND THEIR STUDENTS

Student numbers

It is clear from Table 1.1 that more students are staying on at school, or attending college, in order to gain a place in higher education.

The Dearing Report stated that, 'forecasts suggest that, if current patterns of participation continue, more than half of today's school leavers will experience Higher Education at some time in their lives' (NCIHE, 1997, p. 18). A large number of these additional students are from less educationally-oriented backgrounds, where they will probably form the first generation of the family to go into higher education. Nonetheless, these increases alone cannot account for the dramatic rise since the mid-1980s. Table 1.1 illustrates the sharp rise in students in higher education during the 1990s, and crucially this rise has occurred not only on standard full-time courses but in part-time study as well. The relative proportions of full-time to part-time students has not altered significantly as of 1996, when part-time students made up 28 per cent of the total, the same proportion as they had in 1980 (Higher Education in the

Table 1.1 Students in higher education, 1989–2000

	Students in HE	Full-time	Part-time
1989/1990	1,004,900	689,100	315,800
1994/1995	1,813,300	1,153,900	659,400
1999/2000	2,024,100	1,259,700	764,400

Source: Annual abstract of statistics (1993, 1998, 2001) HMSO

Learning Society, 1997). However, the fact that so many more people are choosing to study in this way is significant. As is evident from Table 1.1, in 1999/2000 there were more part-time students in the UK than there had been full-time students ten years before. This brings the issues highlighted in the *Learning Age* document into sharp focus. Many employers are releasing workers part-time for study to enhance their skills or to develop themselves in given areas. Equally, part-time study is popular as a leisure or personal development activity for many people with other commitments.

The student profile

In addition to these increased numbers of part-time students, there has been a dramatic increase in mature, or over 21s, students. The figures from one of the very steep periods of growth in numbers speak for themselves. Applications for undergraduate courses from under 21s increased by 66 per cent during this period, but applications from over 21s increased by 215 per cent (Blackstone, 1997, p. 1). Nearly 60 per cent of all students in higher education are now over 21.

Another key development has been the increased participation in higher education of school leavers from lower social classes and swelling numbers on postgraduate courses. The majority of students still come from professional backgrounds, and, as we have seen, increasing higher education participation rates in the lower social classes is a priority of the present government. However, those whose background would be classified as class III, IV or V are catching up, particularly in the post-1992 universities (Blackstone, 1997, p. 1). Postgraduate numbers have grown fastest in relative terms, comprising 12 per cent of total student numbers in 1979/80 and 14 per cent in 1995/96.

The student experience

So, what are the motivations of these students for entering higher education? What has made them choose a path that their parents, their older siblings, or even themselves as teenagers, would never have considered? At least part of the reason, for many, is because they can. The availability of access courses and the recognition of prior learning and experience have made higher education accessible for many without the need to return to school or college and sit for A-level or Scottish Higher qualifications. Personal satisfaction, and for some the increased leisure time in which to pursue it, is clearly a factor. As we have seen, the demands of prospective, or current employers, and the opportunities that higher education affords for a better quality of life are crucial across the broad spectrum of students. However, this kind of motivation can impact on the way that these students study, which in turn impacts on the way they are taught and supported by their institution of study.

7

Growth in postgraduate study has been largely in vocational courses or courses tied in to continuing professional development. It could be argued, in fact, that the assertion, or assumption, that higher education engenders the development of those core skills (knowledge, intellectual ability, ability to work in a modern organization, interpersonal skills and communication skills) has necessitated careful examination of how they are developed in higher education programmes.

Opportunities for the development of such skills are certainly made more explicit in degree programmes than they once were. There is a recognition of the need for skills that higher education can provide. Students recognize the value of a degree in the market place, that while it can't guarantee them a good job, it can certainly add value. With the advent of tuition fees, in addition to the demise of the student maintenance grant, it could be argued that the average student is more mercenary in their approach to higher education. As Elaine Martin has argued:

> the newly-expanded generation of university student does not, on the whole, come to university to question and develop theoretical ideas. They, increasingly, seek an education where the emphasis is on future employment. (Martin, 1999, p. 9)

Equally, Michael Scott places a question mark over the ability and motivation of a large proportion of recent and current undergraduate students to really take on independent study. Students, he points out, are having to return to the old concept of 'reading' for a degree instead of simply being taught, even if this reading takes the form of accessing materials electronically, but 'to "read" for a degree demands an element of motivation and intellectual maturity with which not all are blessed' (Scott, 1997, p. 1). This, he argues, is the basis for the shift from the concept or 'reading' for a degree to the idea of coming to higher education to be 'taught' a subject. So what does it take for a student to work in a 'student-centred', or self-motivated and independent, way yet still be taught? One of the answers must be a supportive environment in which to learn.

This shift in motivation, driven by a number of factors, should not in itself indicate the academic quality, or personal motivating characteristics, of any given student. Harvey and Mason (1996, p. 27) have argued that independent study can equip students with the very skills that employers are looking for and that their subject of study provides a backdrop for the development of their critical, reflective and analytical skills, and their ability to communicate effectively. Motivation to 'get a degree' may be high, but for many, perhaps, the subject of study is increasingly irrelevant, which will arguably impact on this motivation in a negative way.

The student needs the motivation and the ability (and the comprehension of what they are being asked to do) to make the most of the opportunities available to them. An emphasis on independent work without a safety net may be an appropriate method for a vocational postgraduate course, but is it a sensible model for the 18-year-old undergraduate who wants to experience higher education and come out equipped to get a good job at the end of three or four years of study? The safety net is key, as the average student will require support on hand in and around their place of study.

Financial pressures on students may drive their education and long-term ambitions. Whatever their motivations for studying for a degree, the fact that they will almost certainly come out from the experience with a substantial amount of debt can alter the way they view their institution as a service provider. As Professor Norma Reid, the Vice-Chancellor of Plymouth University, stated, 'facilities and access become more important to students if they're going to act as independent learners, rather than be spoon-fed with knowledge' (cited in Sandy 1998, p. 2). Indeed, some students seem to be viewing higher education in the same way that they would view service provision in any other area of their life and judging the service provision by the same standards.

The institutional experience

How have these wider developments and their impact on the student profile and student motivations impacted on higher education institutions? How has their role, and the way they conduct their business, changed over the last two decades? The Dearing Report (NCIHE, 1997) paints a very clear picture of the state of higher education in the mid-1990s and the emerging issues at that time. This picture provides an interesting parallel with the developing student profile previously outlined and the student concerns that have emerged.

Technological developments have clearly had an impact on the way that higher education institutions are functioning at the turn of the century. Developments in electronic access to information will be picked up in more detail in the way that it has impacted on academic libraries. However, access to information via the Internet has impacted on all areas of academic life, none more so than recruitment. The institution's web page now plays an important role as a marketing tool in the battle to win students, but the availability of other information outside its control, for example Quality Assurance Agency reports, can balance this out.

Computer-based information systems have been integral to institutional manage-ment for many years. They are increasingly being regarded as 'mission critical' and are being developed as strategic business tools, central to the drive for greater efficiency and effectiveness and to an institution's competitive position. The most significant current development is the managed learning environment, which integrates previously independent systems – from the management of student records and student tracking, to the delivery of teaching and learning materials. At the same time, technology is being subordinated to the information it carries, as part of information strategy.

Perhaps the most crucial issue, which impacts on all other areas, is that of staffing. The traditional picture of higher education teaching is of lectures supplemented by one-to-one or small group tutorials and seminars. In some senses this picture hasn't changed a great deal. However, lectures to 200 instead of 50 students, and tutorials for 20 instead of half a dozen have not only placed an additional burden on staff but have caused many to question the effectiveness of their teaching and how much of it is getting through to the students. Elaine Martin quotes a senior chemistry lecturer as stating that,

> I now teach a first-year class of 300. Around 15 years ago I used to teach similar subject content to a class of 30 – and was concerned even then that the students found the concepts difficult. (Martin, 1999, p. 8)

There is also an expectation that academic staff will engage in research in addition to teaching, in addition to their increased teaching load. This is not the only additional demand on their time. According to the study that informed the Dearing Report, which consulted over 800 academic staff in higher education institutions, more than half of those engaged in research were doing it in their own time (NCIHE, 1997, p. 31). This may mean that they are stretched and overworked, but there are other factors taking them away from teaching and learning activities.

A recent article in the *Times Higher Education Supplement* highlighted the experience of an academic at a new university, who left her job to escape the bureaucratic burden. She stated:

> the growing teaching burden and the administrative burden made me think about the pointlessness of it all. There were the mindless meetings, timesheets, justifying every lecture on the basis of aims and outcomes rather than having the freedom to occasionally just go into a lecture theatre and talk freely about any given subject. (Greenhalgh, 2001, p. 1)

Recent developments in the formulation of teaching and learning strategies have formally acknowledged a lot of these changes taking place in teaching in higher education. The availability of funding to implement coherent and well thought out strategies has been an incentive to institutions producing plans for tackling the most common problems they are facing. These include the strains placed on conventional teaching methods by increased student numbers and declining resources, increasing diversity in student backgrounds and prior learning, and increased assessment loads. Some economies of scale exist with formal lecturing. It may be different, and perhaps less effective, lecturing to a class of 300, but it doesn't necessarily require additional work from the tutor. Assessment for 300 rather than 50 students, however, requires considerably more work, and the opportunities for investigating alternatives, such as computer-based assessment methods, are very valuable.

Sending students away to work independently or work in small groups would seem to be a way of dealing with the problem of numbers. It could also be viewed as a means of killing two birds with one stone, providing a way, if handled appropriately, of developing those all-important 'core skills' outlined above. How better to develop interpersonal and communication skills, for example, than to have students engage in group work, with its incumbent need for effective negotiation and collaboration, in order to produce a report and make a joint presentation at the end? According to the Dearing Report, 60 per cent of lecturers involved in the study said they were setting more group work for their students. In addition, 61 per cent said they were setting more individual project work.

There is certainly an academic justification for a lecturer to spend less time with his or her students, aside from expediency: send them away to learn independently and they will develop the skills they need for their future careers. However, independent and group study still require support, and this support requirement – and the question of who is responsible for it – is an increasingly problematic one for many institutions.

The Dearing Report also tells us that 59 per cent of teaching staff surveyed are using more and more multimedia in their teaching, which raises similar skills issues. It may be more economical to use computer software, for example, to give students problems to work through, or to test their progression in a particular module. However, if they are uncomfortable with the software and have not had adequate instruction, or have fallen behind their peers, the strategy for dealing with larger numbers is failing individuals from the outset.

Packages such as Web-CT and Blackboard, which allow for the creation of a complete, virtual learning environment for a student on a particular course or module of study, are being seized on by large numbers of institutions. Used innovatively, and with substantial support for staff new to teaching in this environment, virtual learning environments of this kind can add considerable value to the student experience, particularly in terms of allowing for flexibility. The tutor can be contacted for feedback, ideas can be exchanged with fellow students, and course material can be accessed, all via one portal. However, one concern is that the rapid take-up of virtual learning environments may signal a desire to use them to solve the problem of the ratio of students to staff, and that the quality of the student experience may suffer. A sound virtual learning environment can change the form of teaching, but only where the teacher is actively engaged with it.

In addition, the question has been raised of whether or not virtual learning environments, used correctly or incorrectly, encourage more or less development of independent study skills in students. There would appear to be a fine line. Gareth Davies argues that, while there is much to be gained from such innovations as using discussion boards, where students can help each other, there is also a point at which students need to go away and find out for themselves, rather than be directed to the relevant resources, be they electronic or print-based, by the tutor.

> A large part of the point of going to university must be learning to be independent, including in study. This means doing your own research and answering your own questions. If you do not learn this you can still get good grades, but you are ill-prepared for life beyond. (Davies, 2001, p. 1)

He goes on to highlight the quandary facing many institutions in an increasingly competitive environment. A course can be marketed on good IT facilities, for example, but, 'marketing on the basis that "we won't help you and as a result you will learn", is rather harder to see' (ibid., p. 2).

Support issues are raised either way. Extensive use of computer packages raises skills and support issues, as we have seen. Sending the students away to find out for themselves can have a similar impact on support staff and, as the next section will highlight, library staff are amongst those in the frontline.

THE IMPACT ON ACADEMIC LIBRARIES

THE SCENARIO

The Follett Report includes an outline of a typical day for an undergraduate student, an academic and a librarian in the year 2001. The student checks her daily schedule on-line, considers skipping a lecture to be beamed in live from Strasbourg, which she will be able to pick up later on the campus video review channel. She goes on to make changes to an electronically 'marked' draft essay returned by her tutor, and downloads a journal article with a swipe of her credit card. The academic takes a seminar with a dozen students, only four of whom are based on campus. The seminar is conducted in an audio-visual studio and network connections are set up for virtual simulations of an experiment for the remote students. The librarian spends his day meeting with academics to plan electronic packages of materials for course support, and delivers an 'information discovery' seminar. Library staff are involved in consortium projects and cataloguing is done with a swipe of the barcode when the book is received from the publisher. (HEFCE, 1993).

We aren't quite there yet and in some respects probably never will be. However, this crystal ball gazing has achieved its purpose in sketching out a radically different learning environment and projecting a new role for the academic library service. How well-equipped is it to fulfil it?

ORGANIZATIONAL ARRANGEMENTS

Students are not very interested in the organizational structures that underpin support for their learning needs. They do, however, need information, IT and learning facilities, and materials, preferably managed more as an integrated resource. Service provision must not be compromised by departmental barriers and demarcation lines. Even if they do not lead to organizational convergence, these very basic requirements challenge service management arrangements.

Institutional strategies for information and teaching and learning can also challenge the autonomy of the academic library service and push it from centre stage; it is merely one component in a much broader framework. If it is to remain an active partner in strategy formulation and delivery, it must as a minimum collaborate closely with other academic and administrative units. Some institutions, including the four examined in Chapter 2, have decided that the contribution of the library service to this agenda is best made in the context of organizational convergence with other academic support services, based either on an information- or a learning-centred model.

THE LEARNING ENVIRONMENT

The growth of electronic collections will undoubtedly slow down demand for physical collection space and eventually reverse it; the networked information environment is already reducing the number of visits to many libraries and thus occupancy of reader spaces. However, the library building still remains a core part of the campus. (Indeed, one outcome of the Follett Report was a recommendation for a £140-million building programme to provide 49 000 additional study spaces in higher education libraries across the UK.) The underlying questions really are: for how much longer this will be the case, and how must the library develop its role to keep pace with changing demands?

While buildings are undoubtedly important, the relevance of free-standing academic libraries to the new learning environment is certainly open to question. Do they contain the breadth of facilities and resources to attract students? Can they accommodate a different balance of learning styles? Are they equipped to support the way that technology is increasingly embedded in student learning?

The academic library model is not seriously challenged by technological developments related to information provision; all academic libraries are making greater provision for technology, principally in the form of large numbers of PCs. However, its ability to respond effectively to the integration of communications and information technology (C&IT) into student learning is much more open to question. The facility to word process assignments, use spreadsheets and databases, access e-mail and computer conferences and, increasingly, to access computer-based learning materials is a basic expectation. These developments have led to a blurring of academic support boundaries. The technologies for the storage, manipulation, delivery and presentation of information have converged, and for many institutions it has become increasingly inappropriate to provide sophisticated means of accessing information but no means of translating and manipulating that information without going elsewhere in the institution and finding another PC.

In many cases, the kind of student experience examined in Chapter 4 needs more than an information-based library building. They have incorporated the academic library into a different kind of building, with a broader role and often with a different name – 'learning centre', for example. On the basis of the experience of the case study institutions described in Chapter 6, it is evident that they do offer the facilities, resources and services necessary to satisfy student learning needs for the foreseeable future.

The new frontier is the virtual learning environment. There is a ready made, resource-based role for the academic library in its development. Perhaps that is enough, but it is likely to lead only to a peripheral role. There are, however, exciting opportunities for much greater involvement, although the library service cannot grasp these alone. Its staff need to be regarded as partners in multi-disciplinary development teams. The case studies in Chapters 5 and 7 illustrate some promising initiatives in this direction.

STAFF SUPPORT

The electronic library is not breaking news in the early years of the twenty-first century. Quality controlled electronic information resources have certainly had a significant impact on information provision, in terms of access, range and power of retrieval. Service users have had to develop new, often quite sophisticated, information skills. However, this development does not in itself demand a significant shift in the role of the academic library or its staff. The acceptance of the Internet as a key information resource represents a bigger challenge, both in terms of the quality of information and the seduction of its search engines, but one that is tailor-made for the librarian's skills and which has been grasped with enthusiasm and some success, through, for example the Resource Discovery Network subject gateways, bringing together strong, evaluated resources.

Nevertheless, new approaches and skills are required where frontline support for independent study goes beyond the boundaries of information into learning and technical support.

Learning support

Library and information services (LIS) staff have a long and successful tradition of supporting student learning and are well-placed to develop their role further. They go outside the library to meet students and to work closely with academic staff. They spend a lot of time observing student learning in the library and so know what students are doing: not just the books on the reading lists but the ways they study – the group work, their presentations.

The role of LIS staff is now far more proactive. It has to be. The volume of students coming through the doors and the profile and prior experience of these students necessitates outreach to train them to be effective and independent users of information from the very beginning of their programme of study. LIS staff encourage student independence, but also welcome those needing help and have become the first port of call for many who need support. A model of support that not just allows but encourages students to be independent, is an important part of contemporary teaching and learning methods. However, this independence needs to come with a safety net. Twenty years ago the safety net might have been a personal tutor; today, a more robust system capable of supporting large numbers of students is crucial. This is arguably where library provision is changing the most and where a learning centre approach to provision enters into its own.

The nature of this support does raise questions regarding the true role of LIS staff. The role is clearly, and rightly, extending beyond what might be thought of as library support, but the blurring of boundaries in terms of resource provision is mirrored in this area of staff support for users. What are the limits of appropriate learner support? How much of it can be encompassed within established library roles? When do LIS staff become teachers? This definition of learner support and the establishment of boundaries for library staff are complex issues. The Fielden Consultancy sought ways to address this in its report, but the issue has become more pertinent since then, as student remoteness from teaching staff has increased. The wide-ranging definition that the report settled on, of 'the activities within library/information services that exist to support individual learners' (John Fielden Consultancy, 1993, p. 24) is perhaps too vague to be of much assistance, accurately describing as it does the accepted librarians' role. However, the report goes on to dissect learner support into a grid of activities (see Figure 1.1).

The grid divides learner support, both structured and unstructured, into competencies weighted towards library and information services and those weighted towards academic work. It provides a means of measuring how much closer learner support offered by LIS staff is moving towards support offered by lecturing staff. The further to the right the work sits, the more closely aligned it is with the role of teaching staff. Changes since the publication of the Fielden Report have moved learner support gradually from predominance on the left-hand side to that on the right.

LIS staff need new skills to fulfil this role successfully. Its success will also depend on them developing new relationships with academic staff and processes. In addressing these issues, Chapter 5 argues that the most effective support for students comes through an in-depth understanding of, and engagement with, the whole academic process, based on a broad, preferably integrated, approach to academic support.

IT support

The same issues arise with regard to support for IT, which clearly lies outside traditional library roles. With the current rapid and wide-ranging take-up of virtual learning environment software by a large number of institutions, this issue is particularly pertinent. Here, the question is where to draw the line. One response is to keep it separate, either by retaining a separate staffing base for library and IT

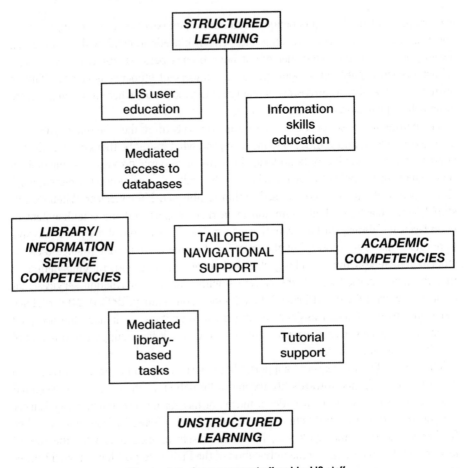

Figure 1.1 Learner support offered by LIS staff
Source: John Fielden Consultancy and HEFCE, 1993, p. 25

support, or a separate location for IT equipment, or by LIS staff only dealing with a specific type of enquiry. However, students who are struggling with the technology need sufficient support in its use to allow them to make the most of the learning opportunity that it affords, and the issue of who provides this support is key, although of little interest to the student. The four case study institutions have adopted a different, integrated, approach that certainly blurs and most likely breaks through, professional boundaries. The impact of this approach on staff skills and roles is examined in Chapter 3.

CONCLUSION

The picture of higher education as we enter the twenty-first century is one of rapid change. Higher education institutions must respond to wider societal and educational changes with unprecedented speed. The size of the student body has increased dramatically over the last 15 years, without a commensurate increase in the numbers of staff to teach and support those students. Equally, the student profile has altered, most noticeably in terms of age, prior learning and experience, and mode of study.

The world of graduate work is one that demands a high level of existing skills from its recruits. Technological developments and government intervention have made learning more accessible at all levels but students, who are in many cases making considerable financial sacrifices in order to study, are entering institutions which are themselves under financial pressure.

Educational rationale and financial pressures combine to produce new models of teaching and learning, including a greater emphasis on resource-based and independent learning approaches. One of the consequences of these additional pressures on staff and students in higher education has been something of a vacuum where support for student learning should be. Non-standard entry into higher education has made it even more difficult to make assumptions about prior skills development. The traditional student, coming straight from school at 18, may or may not have had the necessary study skills, IT skills and so on, but at least there were grounds for confidence that they had recent experience of education and of study. New students coming from employment may have these skills in abundance, or they may have none of them. Increasingly, there are students who need support simply to get them to the stage where they can make best use of the learning opportunities available to them. As a tutorial group might typically contain 30 students, responding to individual student needs has become increasingly difficult for academic staff.

There are immense opportunities for the academic library if it can engage with this agenda. However, it is the argument of this chapter and of the book as a whole, that it cannot fulfil this potential on the basis of its present role within the institution, its current skills base and the range of resources and facilities at its disposal. Some progress can undoubtedly be made within the service itself but alliances and partnerships with other academic stakeholders are also needed. The learning centre concept developed in the later chapters of this book and summarized in its Introduction is one particular way to achieve this. For some academic library services, it can provide a climate within which they can develop their role as a major contributor to the development and implementation of teaching and learning strategy.

REFERENCES

Behar, D. (2001), Millions shun the 9–5 routine [CD-ROM]. *Daily Mail*, 25 September.

Blackstone, T. (1997), Open all hours for the masses [CD-ROM]. *Times Higher Education Supplement*, 17 October.

Davies, G. (2001), Caught in a web of click to learn [CD-ROM]. *Times Higher Education Supplement*, 9 March.

Greenhalgh, T. (2001), Academic quits over rise in bureaucracy [CD-ROM]. *Times Higher Education Supplement*, 19 October.

Harvey, L. and Mason, S. (1996), A quality graduate, in J. Tait and P. Knight (eds), *The management of independent learning*. London: Kogan Page.

Higher Education Funding Council for England et al. (1993), *Joint Funding Councils' Libraries Review Group: Report* (Follett Report). Bristol: HEFCE.

John Fielden Consultancy (1993), *Supporting expansion: a report on human resource management in academic libraries for the Joint Funding Council's Libraries Review Group*. Bristol: HEFCE.

Judd, J. (2000), Student debts have trebled in four years [CD-ROM]. *The Independent*, 21 December.

The Learning Age: a renaissance for new Britain. DFEE [online]. Last accessed on 27 September 2001 at URL: http://www.lifelonglearning.co.uk/greenpaper/

Martin, E. (1999), *Changing academic work: developing the learning university*. Buckingham: Open University Press.

Morris, E. (2001), *Higher education funding and delivery to 2003–4*. Press release, 29 November 2001. HEFCE [online]. Last accessed on 13 December 2001 at URL: http://www.hefce.ac.uk/news/hefce/2001/fund.htm

National Committee of Inquiry into Higher Education (NCIHE) (1997), *Higher Education in the Learning Society* (Dearing Report). Bristol: HMSO.

Sandy, P. (1998), Designs on a student's life [CD-ROM]. *Times Higher Education Supplement*, 3 April.

Scott, M. (1997), Bespoke tuition for today's new readers [CD-ROM]. *Times Higher Education Supplement*, 2 May.

Social Trends (2001). London: HMSO.

Watkins, K. (2001), Earning versus learning: the great student juggling act [CD-ROM]. *London Evening Standard*, 4 September.

2 Organizational frameworks

Edited by Edward Oyston

Contributors:

University of Aberdeen	Sheona Farquhar
Leeds Metropolitan University	Philip Payne
University of Lincoln	Dilys Young
Sheffield Hallam University	Edward Oyston

INTRODUCTION

The learning centre concept draws on the expertise of information, IT and learning development staff; its buildings provide access to a similarly wide range of facilities, resources and services that have previously been managed separately. However, organizational convergence of these academic service units is certainly not a prerequisite. In some higher education institutions, the teaching and learning agenda is driven strategically by means of a high-level committee that brings together key players from across the institution, and on the ground by formal and informal collaboration. Indeed, it may be considered unduly restrictive to cross-institutional collaboration to try to put an organizational box around some of the key contributors.

Nevertheless, more than half of UK higher education institutions have decided that organizational convergence of academic services is necessary to optimize their contribution to institutional strategies. The nature of this organizational convergence can be seen as a strong statement of institutional intent. The predominant characteristic of convergence to date has been that it has been information-centred, supporting institutional strategies, including teaching and learning, by bringing together library and IT services. The case study institutions represented in this chapter present a different perspective. Three of the four are either predominantly learning-centred, or at least give equal prominence to this focus, which is evident in the titles adopted for their converged services: Learning and Information Services (Leeds Metropolitan University), Learning Support (University of Lincoln) and Learning Centre (Sheffield Hallam University). Their organizational models can be

19

compared with that of the University of Aberdeen's Directorate of Information Systems and Services, which demonstrates how the institutional teaching and learning agenda can be taken forward in what is primarily an information-centred model of convergence. The different approaches adopted by each institution are examined in terms of rationale, organizational model and vision, mission and objectives.

RATIONALE

Whether they operate with converged services or not, most higher education institutions have considered that this is an issue worthy of serious consideration. If they are so inclined, there are plenty of reasons to support a decision to converge.

STRATEGIC DRIVERS

Institutional learning and teaching strategies

The growing emphasis placed on independent and student-centred learning moves academic services to the centre of institutional academic life, giving them a higher strategic profile and more of a shared agenda. The application of communications and information technology (C&IT) to teaching and learning provides further impetus to this trend. The developing virtual and managed learning environments represent crucial strategic investments for many institutions and require the active and collaborative involvement of information, IT and learning development services.

Strategic information management

Information is a strategic resource and needs to be managed as such. As is made clear by the Joint Information Services Committee guidelines for developing information strategies (JISC, 1995), this approach 'is concerned with the ways in which a higher education institution makes major decisions about the future of its teaching and research'. All academic services therefore need to own the institution's information strategy and to collaborate in its delivery. In the electronic environment especially, information provision and use will not necessarily conform to existing academic service boundaries and can therefore challenge organizational arrangements both within and between services.

Strategic planning and resource allocation

The growing centrality of academic services to institutional strategies and their interdependence requires a response to planning that goes beyond coordination, to require close collaboration. Institutional senior management may also wish to see competing, and possibly duplicated, demands for resources prioritized before being presented to them. It may be that agreement can best be reached executively, by a senior officer who has not just an overview of services, but also managerial responsibility for them.

Representation

One consequence of the focus on information is an acceptance that it needs to be represented and championed strategically at the most senior level in the institution.

MANAGERIAL DRIVERS

Information services management

It is evident that the delivery of information content is increasingly dependent on the underlying technical infrastructure and that the information systems themselves are interrelated. Integrated management of the medium and the message may therefore be considered to be the most effective approach to optimizing performance and service.

Resource management

Organizational convergence is often a response to the need to deal with continued pressure on the deployment of resources. An integrated department may allow for more efficient service delivery through reductions in the number of service points, adopting common administrative and financial systems, and coordinating liaison with schools of study. Furthermore, integrated management of what will be a significant budget has the potential to support a more ambitious developmental agenda.

Service management

From the perspective of the service user, the need for clarity of responsibility and consistent, seamless service delivery and support might best be achieved through unified management.

Staff management

The overlapping agendas of academic services mean that staff with different professional backgrounds need to work closely together; in some cases collaboration across departments on just a project basis is not enough. Furthermore, the increasing overlap in staff roles through, for example, web development may suggest that staff expertise can be managed most productively through reconfigured management.

OPERATIONAL DRIVERS

Physical learning environment

One of the strongest drivers for organizational convergence is where services are brought together operationally. Where they are co-located physically in new or refurbished accommodation, coherent service provision can benefit from unified operational management. The case is even stronger where facilities and resources are physically integrated.

Virtual learning environment

Integrated desktop services bringing together information access and office software may blur the boundaries between libraries and IT services; the development and delivery of virtual learning environments is an even stronger driver for convergence. The much broader range of information and IT skills required in both library and IT services might also be most effectively and economically acquired through operational convergence, rather than each meeting its skills gap separately.

UNIVERSITY OF ABERDEEN

Strategic drivers

The Directorate of Information Systems and Services was formed in 1996/97 by the integration of the formerly separately managed University Library, Computing Centre and Administrative Computing. The creation of the Directorate was a response to the view that:

- in the long term the University would benefit from integration of the management of all information systems, printed or electronic, academic or administrative;
- the availability of new technology would enable increased electronic provision in teaching and learning, both local and at a distance, and allow shared access to library resources via electronic media to researchers across the world;

- wider scope for development of innovative delivery of teaching, learning and research would be allowed by a focused strategy spanning all information services and modes of delivery; and
- the University would be well positioned to attract funding from government and other sources to develop this vision further.

Integration followed consideration of the strategic options for the University and wide consultation within the University community. It received strong support from senior management at the time, on the basis that close coordination of the three disparate services, Library, Computing and Administrative Computing, would provide better value for money and give the University strategic advantage over its competitors.

The platform of integration following the creation of the Directorate in 1996/97 made possible the development of a coherent Institutional Information Strategy in 1998/99 (http://www.abdn.ac.uk/central/infostrat/index.hti) covering the interrelationships of resources, technology and service delivery.

Managerial drivers

The Directorate plan produced in 1997 was to support a strategy that:

- 'individuated' the student through maximum support to student-centred learning;
- recognized the student as producer as well as consumer within the interactive learning process;
- enabled a focus on scholarship, learning and research;
- established a framework for distance learning which extends the operating horizon of the University regionally, nationally and internationally; and
- provided an infrastructure that facilitates an effective and efficient institutional organism.

Operational drivers

The main implications of the above strategy were:

- a need for increased access to a multiple media resource;
- increased and planned investment in learning centre facilities, resources, training and the information infrastructure;
- the criticality of sharing the development and measurement of forward strategy between the Directorate and the teaching, learning and research community within the University;
- a reconfiguration of information resource provision 'plant' (space, buildings, equipment) to optimize availability whilst minimizing the risk of 'IT/IS isolation' for its user community; and

23

- a cultural shift which embraced the devolution of management to departments and would respond actively by translating this commitment into operations which support and contribute to corporate objectives.

LEEDS METROPOLITAN UNIVERSITY

Strategic drivers

The first stage of organizational convergence at Leeds Metropolitan University took place towards the end of 1992. A new converged service, Learning Support Services, was created from a merger of what had been Library and Learning Resources and the Computing Services Units. However, some initial organizational convergence already effectively existed in that the former Library and Learning Resources Unit was responsible for both library and media services. The primary driver for this first stage of convergence was the shared agenda of the two units to support the academic work of the faculties and schools of study, and the growing recognition of the need for greater coordination between these services. Prior to this time, the two units each reported through to a different Deputy Vice-Chancellor.

The Follett Report of academic libraries, published in 1993, recommended that every institution should have an information strategy, to ensure that it had a proper planning framework for the development of its library and computing facilities. Academic Board charged the new Director of Learning Support Services to establish a University information strategy. The first draft of a strategy appeared in 1994 and covered information infrastructure, information production, information sources and access, information technology, and information skills.

A second and more radical phase of convergence and restructuring took place in 1997. A review of Information Services had been carried out in 1996, following a consultancy by Professor Peter Ford of Nottingham University, the main reason for which was the apparent overlap in information services provided by Computing Services (within the former Learning Support Services), by the separate Management Information Services Unit (responsible for administrative computing), and by the faculties and other functional areas. The resultant report recommended the establishment of a new division managed by a Director of Information Services that brought together IT technical services currently within Learning Support Services and Management Information Systems. It also recommended that a high-level Information Services Strategy Group should be established to bring forward an information strategy to the University's Executive Board.

The focus of the Ford review was very much upon computing. However, the subsequent consultation across the University broadened out the discussion and it was clear that the faculties felt that more radical change was needed if the new division was to adequately support the academic community. Many senior managers within the former Learning Support Services division (especially within the former Library Services) supported this broader agenda, as it was felt that the existing organizational structure could not fully cope with the management of converged facilities or facilitate new developments such as services for off-campus learners.

An Information Strategy Development Group, chaired by a Deputy Vice-Chancellor, was established in 1996 and produced an information strategy for the University in 1997. Although the production of this information strategy actually pre-dated the Learning, Teaching and Assessment Strategy, it was informed by developments taking place across the University in learning and teaching. The production of this document influenced the organizational structures for the individual departments within the new Learning and Information Services division in that it made clear the priorities for development of information services and systems.

The Learning and Information Services division was created in 1997 with three departments: Computing and Communication Services, Learning Support Services, and Learning Technology Services.

All of this coincided with planning for a brand-new learning centre at the University's City Campus. The development provided an opportunity for senior colleagues across the University to consider what they required from a learning centre and how it could contribute to meeting strategic objectives, especially those relating to students' learning. The University saw the new learning centre as: 'the physical core of a widening learning support system which recognises an increasingly diverse student body with different support needs'. The learning centre would effectively act as a hub for learning support both for students on campus and for those studying off-campus.

Basically, the development of the learning centre concept was based upon the following underpinning learning context:

- *Autonomous learning*: moving from teaching to independent learning
- *Open and flexible*: giving students more choice of where, when, and how they study
- *Resource-based*: greater use of learning resources in the delivery of the defined curriculum
- *Peer-based*: facilitating learning from one another through group work
- *Lifelong*: opening up higher education access to a wider variety of students; more emphasis upon continuing professional development; greater diversity in student population with greater variation in competencies and support needs; more focus on off-campus learning including distance learning and work based learning
- *Skills development*: supporting the development of the information literacy and other key skills that students need to be effective learners.

This strategic thinking relating to the learning centre clearly influenced the structure within the new division. This was especially the case for Learning Support Services with responsibility for the management of the learning centres.

Managerial drivers

The first stage of convergence was very much an evolution rather than a revolution. In particular, it had little impact upon the roles of most staff other than amongst senior managers of the new Unit. However, it did achieve the goal of a more coordinated approach to the development of learning support and closer working between library, media and computing colleagues. It also meant that there was greater coordination and control across academic support services in respect of budget monitoring and review, capital investment, and greater consistency in processes and procedures.

The second stage of convergence led to a much more fundamental restructuring, including a redefinition of the responsibilities of the respective departments and a complete review of staffing. The new Learning Support Services department, for example, was much more than a reincarnation of the former Library Services, as the responsibilities of the new department now extended into IT support and a greater emphasis was placed upon the development of electronic services. Senior managers in the new Learning Support Services department put in place a significantly more radical structure, which provided the opportunity to redefine staff roles to meet the changing needs of the University. As far as the learning centres were concerned, this meant establishing a structure that would support integrated learning support facilities available both on and off campus. Almost every post had a new job title to reflect the converged service and therefore none of them included the word 'librarian'. New job descriptions and employee specifications were drawn up with considerable emphasis upon multi-skilling.

Operational drivers

Although there were no fundamental changes to staff roles, the initial restructuring in 1992 provided the impetus for convergence in areas other than organizational and staffing convergence. The new Unit was better able to support technological convergence. Developments such as the implementation of CD-ROM networking and the initial provision of access to the Web through the libraries were implemented at this time. The new Unit sought to present itself to the faculties and to its clientele as a single entity: a common house style enabled publicity material and documentation to be uniformly branded with the Unit's name; induction for staff and students was handled in an integrated way; and a *Learning Support Services Newsletter* was published which informed faculty staff of new developments across the Unit.

Within the new Unit a considerable focus was placed upon working closely with the faculties. A Learning Support Strategic Forum was created to ensure that there was synergy between the development of the new Unit and the strategic plans of the faculties. A user group was established as a forum for academic staff to comment on the services provided by the new Unit. A service-level agreement was established between Learning Support Services and the faculties based upon the one that had been negotiated and agreed with the faculties for Library Services.

Opportunities for physical convergence were exploited so that library and IT facilities were co-located in the same security envelope. A major development at this time was the creation of a learning centre at Beckett Park, where the former Beckett Park Library was completely reconfigured while continuing to operate. However, when the new learning centre opened in October 1996, it represented a complete metamorphosis, as the former library had been transformed into a multimedia learning centre. The learning centre included multimedia collections, self-access IT workstations, IT laboratories, facilities for individual and group study, audio-visual playback facilities, over-the-counter media loans, and video editing. This was the first time that the term 'learning centre' had been used but it more accurately reflected the range of resources and facilities available to support learning and teaching. The term 'learning centre' was then extended to the University's other co-located libraries/IT facilities at Calverley Street and Brunswick.

The second stage of convergence in 1997 coincided with planning for a brand-new learning centre at City campus. Lessons were learnt from the design of the first learning centre at Beckett Park and the new learning centre was designed to provide fully integrated access to facilities and resources irrespective of whether these resources had previously been considered to be in the library, computing or media domains. The focus was now on the 'learner' and providing ready access and good support to a range of facilities and resources to support learning. These developments in the physical learning environment proved to be a major driver for change and for full organizational convergence.

UNIVERSITY OF LINCOLN

Strategic drivers

In 1992, the Library and Media Services department at the then University of Humberside was expanded to include end-user support for IT and a new department of Learning Support was formed. A new Computing and Network Services department was also created to manage the IT infrastructure for the University. This was a strategic response to:

- changes in learning and teaching within the University;
- the need to focus on providing a more student-centred service (by separating end-user support from the technical infrastructure); and
- the need for a closer alignment of learning resource provision between the department and academic subjects.

As the University expanded and diversified (becoming the University of Lincolnshire and Humberside in 1996 with the addition of a new campus in Lincoln to those already existing in Hull and Grimsby), there was a recognized need to develop new information and learning and teaching strategies, as well as reviewing the mechanisms for strategic planning, resource management and the underpinning importance of information at strategic, tactical and operational levels. A new Learning Development Unit was formed to lead the development of learning and teaching within the University and the role of the Director of Learning Support was seen as pivotal to these developments. In 1998 he led the development of a new institution-wide learning and teaching strategy. This became a blueprint for each faculty and academic department to develop their own strategy, which identified the ways in which they contributed to the overall University learning and teaching strategy.

Managerial drivers

With a decreasing unit of resource being allocated to Learning Support and year-on-year cuts in stock and journal budgets, it became increasingly important to develop a converged approach to information and resource management. In 1995, the new Director and existing management team undertook a structural review of the Department. This resulted in a new staffing structure which identified the need for multi-skilling as a way of equipping staff with the skills and competencies required to support users over the full range of Learning Support services (IT, library, media and modern languages support). A competency framework was developed which identified the behavioural, knowledge and skill competencies required to undertake a role within the new structure successfully. This enabled the Department to achieve economies of scale, as staff worked across different helpdesks supporting users in a range of Learning Support centres.

Operational drivers

Convergence of services within Learning Support began in a small way with the opening of the Hooper Learning Support centre in September 1992, under a new operational management structure. The rest of the Department remained operationally separate with Site Librarians and Computing Centre Managers running a range of Learning Support centres, each offering a different range of services. Cooperation and the development of a collaborative style of working were encouraged, although it was not until the appointment of a new Director of Learning Support in February 1995 that greater moves towards full operational convergence began.

The split between IT infrastructure and end-user support which occurred in 1992 required the development of a range of new cooperative and collaborative systems so that the two new departments (Learning Support, and Computing and Network

Services) could work together to provide a seamless service to end users. This included decisions concerning the development of a common desktop, operating systems, system support and fault reporting, and resulted in the development of a service-level definition to ensure the effective operation of key service targets. Increasingly, the liaison between Learning Support and academic departments was reflected in a greater collaboration with the Learning Development unit as new learning and teaching initiatives were developed within the faculties.

Since 1992 the physical learning environment has changed dramatically, not only through the reconfiguration of services within existing Learning Support centres and the opening of a new centre at Lincoln, but also in the range of services and facilities offered. These now included a much greater number of PCs in Learning Support centres (with an overall ratio of PC:FTE student of 1:11), the provision of a range of study areas and increases in group study rooms, new services for off-campus and distance learners, the development of closer links with partner colleges and consequent increase in resource entitlements for students in regional centres, extended opening hours to enable greater access to resources, and the changing balance between holdings and access to resources. These have been mirrored by changes in support systems, including new job roles and the increased use of technology to provide information during unsupported access hours.

The development of a University virtual learning environment (the Virtual Campus) was pioneered by the Learning Development Unit and greatly utilized the liaison mechanisms developed within Learning Support for consultation and information dissemination with the Faculties. Here the role of the Learning Adviser has been of particular importance and there have been a number of initiatives championed within academic subjects through the technical expertise held by Learning Support staff. This has enabled these developments to be integrated within the curriculum and enhanced the reputation of Learning Support as a department within the University. The skills and knowledge of staff within the department have also been developed, and the quality of information coming back from the faculties improved.

SHEFFIELD HALLAM UNIVERSITY

Strategic drivers

The impetus to organizational review was provided by the University's learning and teaching strategy, particularly:

- its mission to increase access to students and to provide programmes of study that offered flexibility;
- the trend towards student-based work rather than classroom-based lectures, the increasing use of information resources and the emphasis on students developing

their personal skills, including learning, information handling and communication skills; and

- the need to investigate new approaches to programme delivery that would enhance the quality of students' experience in a cost-effective way.

Developments in C&IT were recognized as important enabling factors, particularly the convergence of technologies for the storage, manipulation, delivery and presentation of information. The University also wished to exploit the potential of C&IT for teaching and learning.

The University's response to these drivers included strategic priorities of direct relevance to academic support services:

- to create the physical learning environments to support learning (this approach was taken forward through a major building programme – see Chapter 6);
- to develop new virtual learning environments to transform learning; and
- to put in place organizational arrangements that would support, and in some respects lead, development.

The last of these priorities was taken forward in 1996 to coincide with the opening of a new building at the city-centre campus, the Adsetts Centre. A working group with University-wide representation was established to examine the future context and structure of academic services provision across the University and to recommend any necessary operational and/or structural changes.

The brief of the working group was to consider the different roles and functions of service providers, ranging from infrastructure development, through information services to pedagogical innovation. While consideration was given to the balance between School and central provision, the principal services under review were, however, the central ones: Corporate Information Services (academic computing services, administrative computing and infrastructure support); Library and Learning Resources (library services and media production); and the Learning and Teaching Institute (innovation in teaching and learning, educational research).

The starting point for the review was that, although academic support services had independently secured substantial infrastructure and developmental investments, and had also undergone separate reorganizations they had, arguably, failed to consolidate their potential shared strengths with respect to customer expectations of coherence and complementarity, in response to curriculum change.

Managerial drivers

In examining how these central services should be organized and managed, the working group asked several basic questions. Should the existing configuration of independent services led by relevant professionals be retained, or would a reconfiguration, with the possibility of leadership change, offer benefits? If the latter, should teams be clustered with respect to their functional skills focus, their customer focus, and/or their 'product' development focus? Staff and service management arrangements in the Adsetts Centre were a significant influence.

Operational drivers

The principal influence here was the user experience in the new city campus learning centre. As will be seen in Chapter 6, the building would provide access to, and support for, a very wide range of facilities, resources and services, integrated into an open-plan environment. The chosen organizational framework would need to deliver seamless, user-focused service provision.

Operational, and to some extent management arrangements were informed by extensive consultation with staff and students across the University, as part of the work of the review group:

The voice of users Schools of study commented from management, quality and subject perspectives. The areas of resourcing, staff development, IT infrastructure and links between central departments and the schools were the major concerns of all user respondents. Each of the three departments was acknowledged as specialist and these specialisms were considered valuable and not to be compromised. However, greater integration at the user-support level was generally favoured. Academic staff and students identified an overriding need for clarity, consistency and communication, delivered in a service culture. More information was required about the availability of services, more assistance needed in the production and use of resource-based learning materials (staff), and in support for independent learning (students).

The voice of providers Academic services staff met as departmental teams, focus groups and staff groups. They acknowledged the overlap of activities within the three areas under review, but generally perceived a range of difficulties in going beyond current practice; this was attributed to different traditions and the differing impact which each area had on school activities, in particular the different contributions of the three areas in terms of service delivery and development work. Delivering service, supporting innovation in teaching, learning and research, and direct engagement with developmental work with academic colleagues were the main areas of work for each department. In addition there was the responsibility for infrastructure. The balance between these areas was different for each service. There was a general view that specialist expertise would continue to be necessary to enhance the user experience. All were agreed that the focus of attention should be the consumer of the service.

ORGANIZATIONAL MODELS

COMPOSITION

There are several basic models of convergence, with numerous variations:

- Early converged models demonstrating a focus on teaching and learning can be seen particularly in the polytechnics, where the linking of library and information services to media production services (TV, Graphic Design, Photography, Audio-visual services and more recently multimedia production) was common. Part of the underlying rationale for this approach was that the converged service could produce the learning resources it was not able to buy.

- More recently, the emphasis has shifted to the convergence of information and the underlying C&IT infrastructure. Here, the simplest convergence is that between library services and IT services. Within this, there is variation as to which aspects of IT are included: academic support certainly, perhaps infrastructure, quite often business systems, occasionally Management Information Services. In some cases, the emphasis on unified technology management can extend to other services such as telephony.

- The addition of learning development services to these converged models is a potentially significant development, in that it can change the role of academic services from vitally important support services to being properly integrated into an institution's academic management and development.

The breadth of convergence can be further extended through a more holistic approach to the student experience, by including a broader range of student advisory and support services.

STRATEGIC POSITIONING

At the strategic level, services may operate independently but have some degree of coordination through a common reporting line to a senior academic or administrative post as part of a broader portfolio of responsibilities. Alternatively, more-focused strategic management may be provided by organizational convergence under the direction of a senior manager with a title such as Director of Information Services, or Director of Learning Support. This post can report through an intermediate manager, as above, or be positioned more strategically and report directly to the Vice-Chancellor or Principal – as is sometimes the case with the Chief Information Officer role common in the United States.

MANAGEMENT ARRANGEMENTS

To what extent are traditional service boundaries valid? Within the converged service, it may be that the previously independent services are kept intact and operate to a considerable degree independently, each with its own professional head of service. Beyond this, there are varying degrees of boundary shifts – from, perhaps, merging systems support, to taking a cross-departmental functional approach that breaks down previous departmental and professional barriers. At this end of the spectrum, the professional background of managers becomes less important than their leadership and generic management skills.

SERVICE MODEL

Perhaps the biggest challenge is the extent to which it is possible or desirable to blur or remove traditional boundaries at the operational level. The best opportunities for integration arise with new buildings. Here, facilities and resources, services and user support can be integrated to varying degrees. The opportunities for the most radical approach are, however, independent of buildings. The real challenge arises from bringing together staff with different specialisms into multi-disciplinary teams focused around the needs of particular user groups, rather than on the basis of function or professional speciality.

UNIVERSITY OF ABERDEEN

Composition

The Directorate of Information Systems and Services integrates an extensive range of academic support services, encompassing library, academic and administrative computing, audio-visual services, learning technology support and development.

Strategic positioning

The senior management reporting line for the Directorate of Information Systems and Services is from the Director to the University Secretary, who is the principal officer of the Court and is responsible for ensuring that it acts within its powers and follows proper procedures. He or she is head of the University's administration.

The Information Management Committee is responsible for University policy and strategy in the area of C&IT, Library and Information Services, and associated matters of information management. As part of its remit, the Committee makes recommendations to the appropriate internal agencies, retaining strategic oversight of expenditure on relevant matters.

The Committee has two sub-committees: the Information Systems Users' Committee and the Library Users' Committee. Each draws membership from every faculty, and the Student Representative Council, as well as a Convenor; appropriate staff from the Directorate (the Consultancy and Client Liaison Division Manager and the Library Division Manager, respectively), are also in attendance.

In addition, there are Faculty Information Groups or IT User Committees attended by representative academic members of staff and Faculty Information Consultants and Faculty Computing Consultants who are members of staff within the Consultancy and Client Liaison Division of the Directorate.

Management arrangements

The director and eight divisional managers form the Directorate Management Group, responsible for forming Directorate strategy. As well as regular Division Meetings for Service Managers there are other Management groupings, such as Technology Development Group and Library Forum, where appropriate cross-division and service managers meet to coordinate day-to-day issues and advise the Directorate Management Group.

Service model

The Directorate management structure, developed in response to strategy requirements, comprises eight Divisions:

1. *Applications Support Division*: responsible for the procurement, licensing, installation, development and support of applications software.

2. *Consultancy and Client Liaison Division*: manages the relationship of the Directorate with its clients, to ensure the delivery of effective services to support the needs of the University. Areas of responsibility are Liaison, Consultancy, Training, Student Teaching, Documentation, Helpdesk Services, Client Administration, Web Management, Learning Technology Support and Development, and Audio-visual services.

3. *Corporate Systems Division*: responsible for all aspects of the University's management of information systems. This includes planning, development, procurement, installation, implementation, upgrades, and continuous support of corporate hardware/software and management of its applications.

4. *Enterprise and Business Unit*: provides services in the areas of Photographic, Reprographic and Binding; identifies, negotiates, implements and maintains other income-generating projects and agreements both within and outwith the

University; incorporates the maintenance and provision of the Business Information Service.

5. *Historic Collections*: manages large collections of rare books and manuscripts dating back to the twelfth century, anthropological and archaeological collections along with substantial and important art and photograph collections, to maximize their use for the benefit of the University and education in general, and to protect and enhance them for future generations.

6. *Infrastructure Systems Division*: maintains, supports and manages the information processing, data storage and data transmission resources within the University.

7. *Library Division*: serves the University's teaching, learning and research communities and external users beyond the campus, providing and managing site-based counter and reference services, learning resources and subject consultancy, and collaborating as an information provider with other institutions in the public and private sector.

8. *Management Services Division*: serves the other seven divisions of the Directorate in the provision of finance and procurement functions, staffing, personnel and secretarial services and logistics; acts as a central, coordinating point for training, staff development, and safety and security for the Directorate; contributes to many externally-oriented functions in the areas of equipment and resource provision and in the operation of the departmental devolved budgetary system.

Service integration

The Consultancy and Client Liaison Division is where formerly separate services meet and where the biggest changes to staff responsibilities and relationships are found. An integrated Helpdesk Service supports all aspects of the Directorate's services. Staff who work in this team are trained to give information and advice on the full range – library resources (paper and electronic), IT applications, software installations, hardware faults, the University's VLE, student records, and so on. Former Faculty Librarians have evolved into Faculty Information Consultants who liaise with and advise academic staff on the use of information resources and services, working closely with a partner from the Applications Support Division (the Faculty Computing Consultant) when specialized technical input is required. Student teaching embraces both IT and information skills and is delivered through partnership of the Faculty Information Consultants with the IT Trainers.

The establishment of the Learning Technology Unit within this division was another pulling together of formerly disparate strands. Staff and resources that had been spread thinly across the faculties were brought together in a single unit with the remit to promote and support the use of learning technologies within the University.

Applications continue to be developed in collaboration with academic staff but, as part of the Directorate, Learning Technology Unit staff have ready access to the expertise and assistance of their colleagues across the Directorate, leading to more coordinated and practical development and design.

Staff in the Web Management Team design and manage the University's central web pages, working with University administrators to deliver the 'business' information for Student Recruitment, PR and External Relations, and with academic staff to provide a corporate look and feel to departmental web sites and instruction on web authoring and maintenance. Through their strategic positioning within the Directorate, the Web Team can deliver these services in harmony with the technical provision, ensuring applications are realistic and practical and informing technical development to meet genuine corporate needs.

LEEDS METROPOLITAN UNIVERSITY

Composition

The Learning and Information Services division that was created in 1997 had three departments:

1. *Computing and Communication Services* (now called *Computing Services*): responsible for voice and data networks, corporate information services, servers, and PC purchase, installation and support.
2. *Learning Support Services*: responsible for learning centre services, development of academic services to support the needs of off-campus learners, information resource access policies and strategies, information literacy development, and for developing academic partnerships with the faculties.
3. *Learning Technology Services*: responsible for media production, reprographics, audio-visual support and loans, technology in support of learning, development of academic staff to ensure the exploitation of technology in support of learning.

A small central Resource Management Team led by a Resources Manager supports the three departments.

The responsibilities of these departments have evolved and grown further since restructuring in 1997. Learning Technology Services has taken on responsibility for the University's web development and for the implementation and management of Web-CT as the University's virtual learning environment. Learning Support Services picked up responsibility for the development and promotion of Skills for Learning (a set of print and web-based resources to support the development of key skills) and is involved in work on computer-based diagnostic testing and development of students' IT skills. Learning Support Services has also taken the lead role in the implementation of Campus Pipeline as a student information portal. Additionally, all the departments have assumed responsibility for services to the Further Education Faculty based at Harrogate following the merger of Harrogate College with Leeds Metropolitan University in 1998.

Strategic positioning

The Director of Learning and Information Services reports to a Deputy Vice-Chancellor. The Director is a member of the University's Executive Board, which consists of the Vice-Chancellor, the three Deputy Vice-Chancellors, the Deans of the Faculties, the University Secretary, the Academic Registrar, the Director of Finance, the Director of Human Resources, and the Director of Facilities. Executive Board advises the Vice-Chancellor on strategy and policy issues.

The Information Strategy Steering Group is a subcommittee of Executive Board. Chaired by a Deputy Vice-Chancellor, it is responsible for annual review and updating of the information strategy, determination of an annual operational plan, and for monitoring progress towards agreed outcomes. The Deputy Vice-Chancellor responsible for teaching and learning is a member of the Group and there is representation by senior managers from the faculties and from central services. The Director of Learning and Information Services is an ex officio member and the Head of Learning Support Services is also currently a member. The information strategy provides essential underpinning of the key educational strategies relating to learning, teaching and assessment, and to widening participation and lifelong learning.

Management arrangements

The Director of Learning and Information Services has overall responsibility for the services provided by the Division. The Director, Deputy Director, the three Heads of Department, and the Resources Manager form the Divisional Management Group that provides a strategic framework for policy- and decision-making. However, much of the responsibility for implementing overall policy and developing policies specific to a particular service rests with the management of one of the three departments of the Division. Learning Support Services, for example, has a Management Team including the Learning Centre Managers, Senior Learning Advisers and the Electronic Services Development Manager.

Service model

Learning Support Services has overall responsibility for services within the learning centres, including user support for all library and IT facilities. However, Learning Technology Services are responsible for media loans and video editing/presentation facilities. The faculties have responsibility for their own faculty-specific IT facilities which reside in the learning centres.

Computing and Communication Services is responsible not only for the PCs in the learning centres but also for the installation and operation of servers and for the University's network upon which the learning centres are critically dependent. The responsibility for printing and photocopying in the learning centres rests with Learning Technology Services.

A partnership approach with the academic community is at the core of the service model. Each school in the University has a designated Learning Adviser who is responsible for working with them and can advise them as to the facilities and resources available, and how these can be exploited in students' learning. The Learning Advisers also act as a conduit for feedback from the schools as regards academic developments, needs, and issues. In addition, there are a number of forums to solicit views of the academic community about Learning and Information Services and their development. These include:

- *LIS Academic Liaison Group*: which is attended by the Director of Learning and Information Services and the three Heads of Department, and which provides feedback from the user community
- *IT Consultative Group*: which advises on the development of the student/staff desktops and the availability of applications software
- *Skills for Learning Advisory Group*: which advises on the development and uptake of the Skills for learning resources.

The service has a strong customer focus and the views of the clientele are crucial to service development. Learning Support Services, as the front-end for many of the Division's services, has been particularly proactive in seeking the views of customers. Mechanisms include representation by Learning Advisers on course committees, undertaking surveys and focus groups, and encouraging customer comments.

Service integration

The new learning centre at City campus is situated at the very front of a building that truly provides a gateway to learning. The learning centre offers fully integrated library, media and IT facilities to support students' learning. The design and delivery of the project involved colleagues from across the whole of the Division working together to create a 'one-stop shop' that would meet the changing needs of learners. Although the management and operation of the learning centre predominantly rests with Learning Support Services, the department is critically dependent upon support from its sister departments.

The emphasis within the Division is upon providing a service that is as seamless as possible to the end user. This is based upon the premise that the user is not interested in the organizational structure of the division but in the quality of the service provided. In order to achieve this seamlessness, Learning Support Services is highly dependent on a good working relationship with other parts of the Division. Inevitably, staff in the learning centres often act as the front-end for services provided by other parts of the division. Similarly, Learning Advisers field comments and complaints relating to all parts of the Division. Being part of the same organizational structure undoubtedly helps; however, first class communication is required to ensure that these people at the front-end are fully briefed when services are disrupted or there are changes to services. Differences in ethos, and sometimes language, between colleagues in different departments can be significant barriers to achieving that communication.

UNIVERSITY OF LINCOLN

Composition

As with many new universities, the earlier organizational model comprised Library and Media Services, with educational technology support being provided through the Media arm of the Department. The move towards increased convergence began in 1992 with the addition of end-user IT support, as the two new departments of Learning Support and Computing and Network Services were formed. The model was further developed in 1995 following a structural review of the former. The earlier convergence of services in the city centre at Hull was viewed as the way forward. Professional consultants were brought in at the start of the process to focus it and to facilitate the development of the business objectives. The review therefore made recommendations about new staffing structures and conditions of service as well as the range of Learning Support services to be brought together.

Strategic positioning

The Director of Computing and Network Services, along with the Directors of the Management Information Support Service and Estates and Facilities reported to the same Pro Vice-Chancellor, thus providing a single strategic positioning of all infrastructure departments. The Director of Learning Support, on the other hand, reports to the Deputy Vice-Chancellor, along with the Deans of Faculties. The department is therefore firmly established as being part of the academic process within the University.

Management arrangements

Within Learning Support, a new team of three managers was formed with functional responsibilities for Customer Services, Academic Services and Resources.

- *The Customer Services Manager* leads the teams of service staff (Service Advisers) who are based in Learning Support centres throughout the University.
- *The Academic Services Manager* leads the team of Learning Advisers and Technical Advisers. Learning Advisers work in locations wherever their subject is delivered, thus spanning the three campuses of the University, whilst the Technical Advisers provide a service that is centrally based but also requires a campus presence.
- *The Resources Manager* holds no line management responsibility but has overall responsibility for budgets, staff training and development, and the implementation and evaluation of the Progress Review scheme, which uses objective setting as a mechanism for determining staff progress towards the competencies required by their new job roles.

Service model

One outcome of the 1995 restructure was a recognition that what had been a traditional staffing model with a few enhancements intended to reflect an additional broadening of responsibilities was not sufficiently robust for large-scale, departmental convergence. A further dimension was added to this convergence with the development of the new role of Learning Adviser. In order to facilitate their closer integration with the academic process, Learning Advisers were required to spend up to 40 per cent of their time with academic colleagues, developing and supporting the curriculum in new areas to complement the more traditional ones of resource provision and user education.

The Departmental review of 1995 redefined a service ethos as the most important success factor for Learning Support in supporting students and the wider University mission. Students were defined as the main 'customers', with academic staff as partners. Other service departments were defined as the suppliers of specialist services to Learning Support in order to provide services to end users. An example of this is the service provided to Learning Support by Computing and Network Services. In this relationship Learning Support provides end-user support and first-line technical fault reporting. Second-line technical support plus all infrastructure support, procurement and IT development is provided by Computing and Network Services to the University. The relationship between the two departments is defined by a Service Level Definition and liaison between them takes place on a regular basis at strategic, tactical and operational levels.

The refocusing of service delivery to promote a more customer-led approach was widely welcomed within the University, and the development of the new learning environment in the Lincoln Learning Support centre was deliberately slanted to enable students to feel more like customers and consumers of the Learning Support service. Examples of the strategies used included:

- the naming of the building as a Learning Support centre rather than a library, to reflect the growing range of learning resources available;
- the mix of staff backgrounds within the team structure to provide converged services and support the learning process more effectively;
- the emphasis placed on staff customer-care skills;
- the setting up of a range of new feedback mechanisms, including student panels and suggestion boxes, as well as a wide-ranging annual satisfaction survey;
- the decision that students should be able to bring food and drinks into the centre to enable them to study at their own pace and over long periods of time;
- the provision of a range of different learning environments in the building, including teaching as well as learning space; and
- the empowering of staff within the new staffing structure to problem solve and develop new approaches to student learning needs.

The new Learning Support centre therefore provides a new concept of student learning support at the University of Lincoln. Whilst developing a new and broader range of services, delivered from one building by staff working within a converged service and staffing structure, it is firmly based around a new concept of learning that puts the student first. Structures aimed to develop student independence in managing their own learning process and services are therefore supported not only by knowledgeable staff but also by a range of newly developed learning materials.

The underlying ethos also encompasses a new partnership approach between Learning Support and the academic community. Learning Advisers play an increasing role in developing more effective relationships with subject teams, in order to support students' learning needs more effectively. This includes the provision not only of appropriate learning materials, but also of more active support of the curriculum through course development and delivery, underpinned by a range of Learning Support workshops to support generic learner-support skills in information retrieval and the effective use of C&IT and media technology.

The Learning Support centre at Lincoln also plays a wider role in the teaching process as it encompasses the Media Production Centre for the Faculty of Arts and Technology and a range of teaching spaces which include lecture and seminar rooms used by students on all courses. This has raised the profile of the Learning Support centre as a facility in which a wide range of learning opportunities is available. Being closer to the academic curriculum has also resulted in closer integration of Learning Support staff with academic colleagues, which in turn has enabled many joint initiatives to be developed. The integration of a range of learning resources and skills development opportunities into the learning experience of students has been made easier by the establishment of the new Learning Support centre and has been built on over the years as a wider view of learning has developed within the University.

Service integration

The development of the Lincoln campus from 1996 onwards provided the opportunity to develop a Learning Support centre that would support a full integration of services. This required a rethink of the key business processes of Learning Support, in order to align them with a new vision for the University that encompassed the major development of the Lincoln campus.

A small learning support centre was opened in 1996 within the main academic building on the new campus and this was extended to a purpose-built centre for the 1998 academic year. It contains a range of facilities, including: integrated library, IT and media facilities; group and individual study spaces; IT labs and open access areas; printing and photocopying; audio and video playback; language laboratories; books, journals and media resources in hard-copy and electronic formats; specialist hardware and software for disabled students; a number of service points including circulation, media equipment and short loans; information points and access to subject specialist staff on a drop-in and appointments basis.

SHEFFIELD HALLAM UNIVERSITY

Principles

The review of academic services considered four options, ranging from just building on good practice by retaining existing structures and responsibilities, to the much more radical one of meeting the distinctive needs of individual user groups by devolving services to Schools.

The organizational model chosen was based on the principle that academic services should be organized around three integrated customer service areas: technical infrastructure, service delivery and research and development. In its purest sense, this implied a single service with three divisions, aligning closely but not identically to existing service structures. It assumed a single reporting line to one Pro Vice-Chancellor. The application of this model to SHU academic services meant that:

- technological capability would be led principally by Corporate Information Systems;
- information capability would be led principally by Library and Learning Resources;
- pedagogic capability would be led principally by the Learning and Teaching Institute.

The key decision was that a one-service model was not the best way forward to address the University's strategic priorities. The preferred approach was to abstract the principles underpinning this model and to develop existing services against them – but not to embrace full convergence. The outcome was two separate departments,

Corporate Information Systems and the Learning Centre, which brought together Library and Learning Resources and the Learning and Teaching Institute. For the Learning Centre, the central driver was the University's teaching and learning agenda. The view was taken that the technological convergence on which this would need to be based did not require organizational convergence. While Corporate Information Systems was undoubtedly part of this teaching and learning agenda, its technological development role was better served acting collaboratively but independently and in some senses would be a distraction for the new Learning Centre. Corporate Information Systems, therefore, remained a separate department, with responsibility for infrastructure support, academic and administrative computing. Each department was represented separately at a senior level in the University.

Composition

It was recognised that a wide range of staff skills and expertise was needed to support the learning centre concept: information, IT, media production, curriculum development, and educational research. The make-up of the new Department ensured that all of these areas were brought together:

- *Library and information services* (renamed *Information Services*), with front-line responsibility for information and IT services and support.
- *Media production units* (collectively called *the Studio*), including the TV, photographic and graphics units, and audio-visual provision.
- *Learning and Teaching Institute*, including the Learning and Teaching (Research) Institute. The LTI retained its identity within the new department. The Centre for Multimedia in Education, including a production capability, was based within the Learning and Teaching Institute.
- *Open access IT provision*, based initially on the existing Corporate Information Systems City Campus open access IT facility and machines transferred from the Campus Library. Planning for the development of a learning centre on the University's second largest campus had already begun.
- *Sheffield Hallam University Press*, the University's publishing house.

Strategic positioning

The place of the Learning Centre is firmly set within the University's teaching and learning framework. Its reporting line is directly to the Pro Vice-Chancellor (Academic) and it is represented on University academic-related committees. Learning Centre staff are also members of school-based committees and boards. The Director of the Learning Centre is a member of the University's Executive Group, along with school directors and other senior staff.

Corporate Information Systems now report to a different Pro Vice-Chancellor.

Management arrangements

Three senior staff who have distinct responsibilities but are encouraged to work collaboratively across the Department support the Director of the Learning Centre. They have complementary remits:

Head of LTI is responsible for:
- identifying the key educational issues which will make the University successful, and devising strategies to:
  - shape University policies
  - stimulate innovation
  - promote best practice and high professional standards
  - stimulate research.

Head of Academic Services and Development is responsible for:
- monitoring developments in the University's teaching, learning and research activities, and ensuring that the potential of information resources is realized
- overseeing the operation of information services
- developing appropriate strategies for the department's staffing and staff development.

Head of Technical Services and Development is responsible for:
- monitoring developments in information technology and identifying those which will contribute to the University's success
- overseeing the department's planning arrangements, and the allocation, use and monitoring of resources
- overseeing the work of central teams, and the Studio
- developing commercial and external activities, including the University Press.

It was decided that the team-based approach that had been adopted in the Library and Learning Resources department should form the basis for the structure of the new department. The emphasis on this approach was consistent with the increased need to facilitate working partnerships across the Department that crossed formal functional boundaries. Each member of staff was able to identify themselves with a functional unit within the Department, with a designated line manager, but was encouraged to work directly across the department, rather than to necessarily go up one hierarchy and down another.

44

Service model

Operationally, it was decided that, within learning centres, Learning Centre staff would manage all user services and Corporate Information systems would provide technical support. IT facilities outside learning centres would continue to be managed by Corporate Information Systems. For the Learning Centre, this organizational arrangement means that it manages all of the resources and frontline services for which it is likely to be held accountable. It has the additional benefit of facilitating their integrated development.

The new range, scale and complexity of Learning Centre C&IT operations and their dependence on the University network infrastructure meant that this arrangement for technical support was the only feasible option. In addition to managing University systems and network infrastructure on which the Learning Centre depended, Corporate Information Systems also allocated a dedicated technical support team, based in the Adsetts Centre, to provide technical support to the Department.

The media production services were brought together in the Adsetts Centre, to facilitate joint project working, to take advantage of the potential of digital technologies and to draw them more closely into teaching and learning developments. They also provide specialist support to students, especially with video editing. The work of audio-visual services has developed, as IT-enabled teaching facilities have developed across the University.

Service integration

Integration was a driving principle in establishing the Department's service philosophy. It encompasses:

- *the physical learning environment*, within which facilities and resources were integrated (see Chapter 6);
- *the virtual learning environment*, where the principle of integration was applied to the networked student desktop, combining previously separate systems to deliver a full range of software and information resources through a single interface (this approach has been extended by using the integrative potential of Blackboard, the University's virtual learning environment); and
- *user support*, extending beyond integrated information desks that provide both information and IT advice to include integrating the support itself through developing staff with both information and IT skills (see Chapter 3).

Nomenclature

New nomenclature was needed for a variety of reasons. For the Department, the name Learning Centre was chosen to reflect its wider role and, most importantly, to emphasize the department's work rather than its resources. Its buildings were called Learning Centres, rather than Learning Resource Centres, for the same reason – as places where the activity of learning was supported and stimulated.

While the expertise of librarians was still at the heart of the Department's work, the title of Librarian not only did not reflect the breadth of work but also would have been inhospitable to other professions. Subject Librarians were redesignated Information Specialists; Assistant Librarians, Information Advisers; and Library Assistants, Information Assistants (see Chapter 3).

VISION, MISSION, STRATEGIC OBJECTIVES

Unless the newly converged service is just an administrative convenience, its senior staff will want to achieve some break in continuity with the past and to communicate its new identity and role across the institution and within the service itself. A new statement of vision, mission and values can encourage the academic community to regard the new organization as something more than just the sum of its individual parts and to exploit it as such.

Convergence can bring together staff groups with different service values and priorities, and different degrees of enthusiasm for the new arrangements. This can go beyond difficulties of identifying with the new organization, perhaps to feelings of resentment that one group has been taken over by another. Within the service, a new statement of vision, mission and values can encourage ownership and commitment from all staff groups – providing that it is genuinely a new statement and not just an updating of the vision, mission and values of one of the constituent parts.

UNIVERSITY OF ABERDEEN

In its mission statement, the University of Aberdeen 'aims to create, develop, apply and transmit through the work of all its members, knowledge, skills and understanding at the highest levels of excellence'.

The development philosophy against which the Directorate of Information Systems and Services developed its strategic plan was in the context of:

- a working environment of mass higher education;
- a university identity as an extended community of learning;
- institutional aims for academic excellence, uniqueness and competitive advantage; and
- the prevailing and forecast political and financial climate for higher education.

46

In support of this and to optimize the University's potential and productivity as an effective and efficient higher education institution, the Directorate aims to:

- provide collections of first resort in all media by preserving, developing and promoting written, printed, aural, visual and digital resources within its care and at its disposal;
- identify and secure technological solutions for the generation, processing, and communication of information and knowledge vital to the academic and business processes of the University; and
- actively support, guide and train the University community in the exploitation of information resources and systems as essential components of the teaching, learning, research and business programme.

The likely outcomes of this approach for the University community that the Directorate serves are:

- student reliance on resources rather than mass teaching demands;
- improved resource provision and management;
- an increase in one-to-one or (more realistically) one-to-few tutor–student relationships;
- increased time for research arising from release from mass knowledge transfer;
- increased satisfaction for academic staff, derived from more diverse and more focused teaching;
- an enriched student experience and better-quality, more self-reliant graduates;
- a position of strength on a regional, national and international level where collaborative development will attract investment and cooperation without threat to competitive advantage;
- a corporate systems infrastructure which, within a strategic institutional business, enables the effective devolution of management to individual departments; and
- reorganization of space and equipment into more effective modes of use.

LEEDS METROPOLITAN UNIVERSITY

The vision of Learning and Information Services is to create an information environment that inspires students to learn, empowers staff to meet the challenges and opportunities of technology-supported learning, and enables the University to operate efficiently and effectively. Leeds Metropolitan University sees itself as a 'university of applied learning' and its mission reflects this positioning. Service delivery and development within Learning and Information Services are informed by the University's mission and the strategies and strategic plans pursued by the University to realise that mission.

The information strategy, in particular, is central to the development of services and systems by Learning and Information Services. So, for example, the major focus of the information strategy at the present time is to achieve a managed learning environment through effective integration of access to a range of electronic services and systems. At the heart of this strategy is the implementation of Banner as the University's student record system, Web-CT as the virtual learning environment, and Campus Pipeline as the student information portal. The vision is to create a single authenticated access route to the range of information and resources that students need for their particular courses and modules. This will include on-line access to the emerging On-line Learning Centre (now called 'Learning Centre On-line'), which will provide access to information resources, help and support, and (through Skills for Learning) access to materials to support the development of key skills. Teams involving colleagues across the Division (and beyond) are engaged in various projects that will help to realize this vision.

The emphasis placed upon the information strategy means that there is great stress at divisional level upon teamwork, project management, quality procedures, and working closely with clients and customers. Much of the responsibility for operational services rests with the individual departments. The underlying philosophy of the Learning Support Services department, spelt out at the time of restructuring, is upon: customer focus, partnership with faculties and schools, empowering our clientele through skills development, continuous quality improvement, team building, commitment to the development of staff, and exploiting IT.

UNIVERSITY OF LINCOLN

The University mission – 'To provide our students world-wide with the best employment prospects and equip them to become lifelong learners' – was echoed by a new vision for Learning Support: 'To create an environment that inspires students to learn.' This, in turn, was supported by the following new objectives:

- To nurture lifelong learning by:
  - promoting, developing and supporting the acquisition of transferable skills;
  - assisting subject staff with curriculum development and delivery;
  - supporting research and scholarly activity.

- To supply end user support to learners by:
  - providing effective and efficient support for users accessing the University's information sources; generic C&IT; media and modern language facilities
  - developing, within a stimulating and caring environment, services that are relevant to the University's local, regional and international student communities
  - supporting the delivery of units and named awards.

- To deliver quality services by:
  - striving to continuously improve the quality of services delivered by the department.

- To provide value for money by:
  - providing selective services that are well managed and relevant to the work of the University.

- To communicate effectively by:
  - continuously improving communications within the department
  - promoting the department within the University and in the wider academic community.

SHEFFIELD HALLAM UNIVERSITY

A new vision was especially important to communicate the distinctiveness of the Learning Centre, particularly its combination of service and developmental roles. If it was to fulfil its potential to be integral to learning and teaching, leading some academic development and not just acting in a support role, it needed to be accepted as a partner in academic development. The new vision was therefore developed partly to stimulate key university staff into thinking about future learning landscapes and the potential of the Learning Centre to contribute to them. Another of its aims was to engender a sense of ownership of learning centre buildings among academic staff, encouraging them to see them as resources to be used as an extension of their teaching.

The Department's vision is, therefore, proactive: to contribute to the University's success by providing a high quality service, which stimulates student learning and enhances the professional lives of teachers.

The means to achieving this were identified as:

- building on the existing strengths of the Department, which provides an integrated and flexible learning environment, supporting a wide range of approaches to teaching and learning to meet the changing needs of students and staff;
- collaborating with schools of study to develop innovative approaches to teaching and learning based on best practice and underpinned by rigorous evaluation;
- continuing to develop high-quality services which focus on meeting the needs of users and which are provided by well-trained staff;
- developing its network of external partners and adopting a proactive approach to income generation; and
- increasingly developing service to the University's targeted research areas through current awareness, electronic resources and inter-library collaboration.

The character of the Department is also evident in its strategic objectives:

- To develop effective and efficient approaches to course delivery which focus on student learning and the exploitation of communications and information technology.

- To increase the strength and autonomy of educational research groups and reinforce the scholarship that underpins education innovation.

- To develop and maintain learning environments and services which meet the changing requirements of staff and students on and off campus by refining the Learning Centre model and by building an electronic learning environment.

- To maintain an innovative approach to the purchase, production and management of information resources, which exploits the potential of new media and ensures maximum value for institutional investment.

- To develop roles that enable Learning Centre staff to contribute fully to course development and learner support, and which anticipate changing patterns of study.

- To develop global links with external partners to exploit educational innovation, to share expertise and to improve access to information to benefit the region.

- To actively promote the full range of Learning Centre provision within the University, to support the University's widening access agenda and to seek new external markets which will broaden our income base.

- To maintain a clear focus on meeting user needs through adopting quality frameworks and professional standards within which to develop staff and services.

CONCLUSION

How effective have the different organizational models been in supporting a learning-centred approach?

UNIVERSITY OF ABERDEEN

It has taken time for the Directorate to embed and establish itself partly because the University has not had the focus of a new building. At the strategic University management level and at Directorate management level the new organization was an immediate reality. Within the Consultancy and Client Liaison Division formerly separate services were brought together and new working relationships were quickly established. However, for many, both within the Directorate and for staff and student clients, there has been minimal apparent change. Library and computing service activities and staff continue to be located in separate buildings.

The pressures of rising demand and costs, and of a budget that has declined in real terms have resulted in a potential budget shortfall in recent years. In order to address this deficit, the Directorate has undergone a further major restructuring exercise during 2001–02, with a view to identifying further efficiencies. The main elements of the restructuring exercise were: identifying core services to be funded institutionally and charging directly for specialist services required by small numbers of users; identifying services and activities that are no longer relevant or cost-effective; and exploring options for outsourcing a range of C&IT services.

Overall, integration of the management of information has made it possible to spread a smaller number of staff across all services, and save on management and administration costs. The efficiencies achieved since the creation of the Directorate have allowed the development of new initiatives and services with almost static staff numbers. These include high-value services such as the Learning Technology Unit, the Web Design Unit, an integrated Help Desk for library and C&IT functions which is open to students as well as staff, and appointing, in place of Faculty Librarians, Faculty Information Officers who are able to coordinate and plan for all the information needs of Faculties, regardless of the medium in which they are delivered.

LEEDS METROPOLITAN UNIVERSITY

The benefits of the underlying LMU model have been at both the divisional and departmental level:

- Learning and Information Services is a large division with a high profile within the University. This means that the Director is centrally involved in key strategic discussions within the University.

- There is a very close integration between the strategic development within the Division and the University. The University's information strategy is the major driver for development of information services and information systems in the University. The strategy is developed through the Information Strategy Steering Group with a membership of senior managers from across the University. Learning and Information Services undertakes most of the projects that are required to realise the strategy.

- The breadth of responsibilities of the new Division means that the potential for close working across professional boundaries is considerable. This offers much more scope for 'joined-up thinking' to achieve strategic objectives. It is also easier to put in place and manage projects involving colleagues with computing, library, and media professional backgrounds. This is evidenced by recent work on implementing a student information portal: Learning Support Services is taking the lead, Computing Services are responsible for the server and the links with the student record system, and staff from Learning Technology Services are responsible for the integration with Web-CT as the virtual learning environment.

• Organizational convergence has fundamentally supported the management of change and created an environment that is supportive of further change. Implementation of a new staffing structure for the Division was at times slow and painful. However, it is hard to see how the former Library Services department, based upon traditional library roles, could readily have adjusted to the agenda of integrating IT support, providing off-campus services, and the need to significantly develop electronic services. The new Learning Support Services department has not only achieved these things but also, for example, integrated the development of web-based study and key skills materials (through Skills for Learning) and has now taken the lead role in putting in place a student information portal. Its staff are now well placed to integrate learning resources into a managed learning environment.

• There is a strong partnership approach with the faculties. The Division is centrally involved in major teaching and learning developments. This includes the implementation of Web-CT as a virtual learning environment, supporting off-campus learning and skills development both of students and academic staff. However, this partnership approach drills down deeper, through for example, the liaison groups and the Learning Advisers to faculty staff at a variety of levels. There is a considerable emphasis upon ensuring that services continue to meet academic needs and the Division remains informed about major academic developments. Evidence for the success of this approach is highlighted through reports of subject assessments of the Quality Assurance Agency and the institutional continuation audit (http://www.qaa.ac.uk/revreps/reviewreports.htm). It is also recognized within the University through the success of Learning and Information Services in having won three of the eight University's Chancellor's Awards for innovation in teaching, learning, and assessment in the last two years.

• The new Division, and particularly Learning Support Services, has a strong customer focus. In 2002 Learning Support Services was awarded the prestigious Charter Mark for excellence in public service (http://www.chatermark.gov.uk/). Organizational convergence has enabled it to seek to provide the facilities of the learning centres and the support for these facilities, in a seamless way to its clientele. However, there have been customer focus issues to be addressed where Divisional staff do not have a direct interface with users, as there is a tendency amongst some staff to place a greater emphasis upon the relationship with technology than the relationship with customers. Work has been needed to develop close working relationships across the Division to ensure that technical and user support come together to provide a quality service; however, this is considerably easier in a converged organization even if colleagues may be working in different departments.

- And, most importantly, users of the learning centres have benefited. The learning centres bring together the library, computing, and media facilities that are needed to support students' learning and make those facilities available over longer hours. Within the learning centres themselves, staff have sought to provide help and guidance in a seamless way to support the integration of facilities. This arguably could only have been achieved through multi-skilling and the redefinition of staffing roles.

UNIVERSITY OF LINCOLN

The University of Lincoln model has evidenced the following benefits:

- a more responsive culture of customer service, which puts the student first;
- increased capacity to monitor service quality through the introduction of service standards and a range of more effective feedback mechanisms;
- the ability of Learning Support to respond more effectively to strategic changes in learning and teaching in the University;
- a new partnership approach with academic staff through the establishment of Learning Advisers, which has increased the support of learning and curriculum development initiatives within the Faculties;
- a more focused approach to central initiatives through work with the Learning Development unit;
- greater diversity of skills within multi-functional staff teams; and
- commonality of approach from previously disparate staffing groups which all now focus on the customer and the service rather than the product and the process.

Less positively, there were a number of issues that took some time to work through and resolve. These were mainly centred on responses to strategic and operational change. Whilst the new staffing structure and its career progression opportunities were widely welcomed at the Lincoln campus, they met with some resistance at the older-established campuses in Hull and Grimsby. This in part was a difference in culture between new teams (at Lincoln) and staff who had been in the Department for some time. The major changes in conditions of service for established staff, together with the changes in roles and responsibilities, required protracted negotiation with trades unions. Implementation of the new structure began in the summer of 1997 and some staff felt displaced and confused as they struggled to undertake new duties in unfamiliar surroundings alongside unfamiliar new colleagues at the start of the academic year. Staff development and training programmes were put in place to support new working practices and over time staff came to value the new opportunities provided by the competency framework and the expansion of the new Service Adviser and Learning Adviser roles. The change to functional management responsibilities for the senior management team was perceived by some staff as diluting the autonomy of campus-based supervisors and tensions in consistency of service delivery between the campuses began to emerge. A new Customer Services Policy group became the forum for developing a consistent approach and identifying areas of work that were different for coherent reasons.

Overall, the benefits outweigh the operational difficulties and over time the restructuring and its rationale have been widely accepted throughout the University. Valuable lessons were learnt through the implementation process and there is a general view that this major restructuring will become part of a new capacity within the Department to respond to constant modification as the University changes and develops in the future.

SHEFFIELD HALLAM UNIVERSITY

At the time of the re-organization of academic services in 1996, the benefits of the chosen model were seen to be as follows:

- to enable the University's teaching and learning agenda, and indeed its technological agenda, to be taken forward in a focused way, each being championed by senior level specialists;
- to underpin technical infrastructure, service delivery, and research and development services, with appropriate organizational structures;
- to enable the separate cultural values appropriate to technology support, proactive client-driven development and service excellence to be separately developed;
- to give coherence at University senior management level (at least until the services established themselves);
- to facilitate change and development without requiring major upheaval;
- to offer integrated, professional service arrangements alongside a strengthened infrastructure for service development; and
- to provide the potential to accommodate highly targeted user services.

These have been confirmed after the six years of operation.

Within this bigger picture, the strength of the Learning Centre model has proved to be its focused mission and internal coherence. At a strategic level, it has been able to concentrate on taking forward the University's teaching and learning agenda, without being distracted by the increasingly complex and mission-critical technical C&IT

agenda. The mix of staff expertise enables it to draw together the multi-skilled teams needed to provide a comprehensive learning development service. Cross-department working has also encouraged skills to be shared. Internally, this focused mission, together with an underlying common learning- and user-centred culture has meant that it is easier to engage the commitment of all staff to Departmental strategic priorities. The inclusion of the University's Learning and Teaching Institute in the Department has enabled the whole Department to be regarded more as a partner in teaching and learning rather than just a support service, and has thus facilitated the integration of information service provision into academic programmes.

In practice, ownership of the University's C&IT strategy has rested with the Corporate Information Systems department, which has meant that the Learning Centre has had to exert influence from outside. A further complication has been the separation of the reporting lines for the two departments, to reflect the business and infrastructure focus of Corporate Information Systems. However, this difficulty has been alleviated by the development of the University's virtual learning environment, which has strengthened the interest of Corporate Information Systems in the teaching and learning agenda and facilitated a true partnership with the Learning Centre. This arrangement enables the Learning Centre to engage fully with the area of C&IT strategy that is, after all, its principal interest.

Operationally, the greatest success has undoubtedly been the contribution of learning centres to student learning, in terms of the range of resources, facilities and learning activities they support and the integrated nature of staff support. The unitary management of these facilities has facilitated seamless delivery and smooth development of service. However, the division of IT user support between the Learning Centre and Corporate Information Systems, while pragmatic, is untidy and requires extra effort to provide students with a good quality and consistent experience.

REFERENCES

Higher Education Funding Council for England et al. (1993), *Joint Funding Councils' Libraries Review Group: Report* (Follett Report). Bristol: HEFCE.

Joint Information Systems Committee (1995), *Guidelines for Developing an Information Strategy*. Bristol: JISC.

The changing staff experience

3

Edited by Jo Norry

Contributors:

University of Aberdeen	Sheona Farquhar
Leeds Metropolitan University	Marie Scopes and
	Liz Waller
University of Lincoln	Philippa Dyson
Sheffield Hallam University	Jo Norry

INTRODUCTION

OVERVIEW

This chapter will examine the experience of staff who have been involved in the organizational processes outlined in Chapter 2, and whose working lives have been changed by the external and internal drivers outlined in Chapter 1. Just as organizational arrangements have been adapted to meet the new demands of their institutions and the learning and teaching environment, so staff roles and skills specifications have also been transformed, with consequent effects on culture, motivation and professionalism. The case studies will demonstrate a learning centre response to these issues, illustrating what is similar and different in the staff experience at the four case study organizations which have undergone changes: the Universities of Aberdeen, Leeds Metropolitan, Lincoln and Sheffield Hallam. It will argue that much of this change and activity has been in furtherance of placing learning, and the needs of learners, at the centre of their work, and have made them both more aware and better equipped to respond to the new learning agenda.

Four areas will be explored in detail, identifying both the 'hard' facts in terms of the activities of organizations, and the 'soft' aspects of the effect on staff and their changing experience of their work:

- *staff roles*: the ways in which staff roles have changed and continue to change, the factors influencing these developments, and the impact upon staff
- *developing staff skills*: trends in new skill and competency requirements to fulfil these roles, and the responses organizations have made in terms of staff development and training
- *culture and the change process*: cultural and psychological issues for staff involved in the management of change, and in the resulting new organizations
- *recruitment and selection*: changes which have been necessary in recruitment and selection processes to ensure organizations can procure the kind of people they need, and the success or failure they have had.

DRIVERS FOR CHANGE

Many of the key changes identified in Chapter 1 have impacted directly on the experience of staff. As with the majority of those working in higher education, the dramatic increase in student numbers, without a proportional increase in staffing, has meant a greater burden of work for most staff, especially those in service roles. At the same time, students as customers of an institution have become more demanding, seeking a return on their own financial investment in their education, and developing high expectations of the services and facilities provided. New methods of managing such large-scale services have had to be found, whilst commercial-style customer focus and service skills approaches have been developed to meet the needs of an exacting user population. Reduced funding per student has put pressure on both schools of study and central services to reduce costs and increase efficiency. Teaching and learning strategies have had to meet both new pedagogical trends and the economic realities of more students on fewer resources – to which the most frequent solution has been the growth in independent, student-centred learning. The growing diversity of the student population and the widening participation agenda have been met by increasingly flexible teaching, learning and support methods, and by targeting of services to meet specialized needs.

For academic support services, in particular, developments in information and communication technologies have caused some of the greatest transformations – from the rapid growth in digital information, through the use of IT to search, acquire, manage and present information, to the move to computer-based learning and virtual learning environments. The much-heralded hybrid print/electronic library is now arriving, with a consequent requirement for a new breed of hybrid staff, no longer fitting the traditional professional templates. Some organizations have met these challenges through organizational convergence within academic support services, with varying levels of operational and structural mergers. However, for the whole sector there has been a consistent need for staff in information, IT and academic fields to work more closely together, to gain an understanding of each other's potential contribution, and to collaborate to meet the demands of the modern higher education institution.

OTHER STUDIES

A number of significant studies over the past few years have investigated the changing staff experience in higher education libraries, notably the 1993 Report produced by the John Fielden Consultancy as part of the Joint Funding Councils' Libraries Review (Follett Review). The Fielden Report examined human resource issues within learning and research support services, and attempted to identify future models of service and staff roles. As mentioned in Chapter 1, considerable role change was foreseen in the next ten years:

> The principal area where we expect major new change relates to learner support ... LIS staff have managed to handle the acquisition of many new skills in recent years; those required by the learner support tasks could be of a new order. (John Fielden Consultancy 1993, p. 45)

The report identified senior managers, subject librarians and library assistants as the groups facing the major burden of this change. The required skills and competencies to meet these new challenges were predicted as facilitation and mediation of learning, face-to-face teaching, navigation of electronic information sources and general IT skills, customer care, team working, and management skills.

The Electronic Libraries Programme (eLib), established in response to the Follett Report, gave rise to a number of projects which explored staff roles, skills and staff development in the new hybrid library environments. The IMPEL2 Project (Monitoring organizational and cultural change: the impact on people of electronic libraries) investigated the organizational, social and cultural impacts of educational and technological change on staff and users (Edwards et al., 1998). It found that restructuring and convergence was widespread, and on occasions gave rise to 'culture clash' and communication problems, as well as uncertainty and resistance to change. Changes in roles, caused by technology and a closer involvement in teaching, were blurring professional boundaries and putting a strain on career and pay structures. Increased staff development provision was required to meet the demand for IT, customer care, teamwork and change management skills.

Also within the eLib Programme, the 1996/97 SKIP Project, Skills for new Information Professionals (Garrod and Sidgreaves, 1998), aimed to identify and evaluate the impact of IT on the skill requirements of library staff in higher education. They found considerable variation in staff roles and in the type and level of IT skills required, largely dependent on the extent to which IT had been integrated into the learning environment and the organizational model providing information and IT services. There was evidence of cultural change in organizations where convergence

59

had taken place, but also of problems in working relationships, and of separate distinctive 'computing' and 'library' cultures. Success factors were clearly-defined roles and responsibilities, and an emphasis on staff development. SKIP predicted that professional qualifications would become less important in recruiting staff, whilst the key requirements would be the appropriate skills, knowledge, and expertise required for a specific job, along with the right personal qualities and attitudes for a service environment.

It will be useful to reflect to what extent the trends and predictions in these studies have been borne out by the case studies.

STAFF ROLES

This section will explore the changing roles of staff, the factors driving these changes, and the impact on staff. It is in this area that some of the most significant developments have taken place, and with the most profound effects. In the case studies it is evident that roles have been redrawn to meet the new organizational arrangements and demands for service delivery. Along with new structures and management arrangements, roles and responsibilities of staff have made a fundamental shift towards learning to meet the needs of new types of learner and changes in teaching and learning strategies. New staff roles no longer necessarily fit within traditional professional boundaries, and a context of flexible management structures and working practices is required to make them effective. Four dimensions can be identified in this shift:

- *Hybridization*: integrating roles from different professions, generally IT and information/library support, but sometimes extending to media support. This results in broader roles, encompassing several job types which were previously undertaken by separate individuals or teams, consequently involving multi-skilling. This is the clearest manifestation of the convergence process, where departments and service points moving closer together has the same effect on staff roles.
- *Learner support*: increased focus on learners' needs as the driver for support roles, matching the shift in the student experience from teaching to independent, resource-based learning. Roles are no longer about supporting solely information or IT needs, but concern the whole picture of students' independent learning.
- *Integration and partnership*: strengthened partnership and liaison with academic staff and schools of study in the educational process, integrating information and IT capability into the pedagogic agenda of teaching delivery and learning models.
- *Development*: developmental and proactive roles, acting as agents of change in educational development and innovation in teaching and learning techniques,

placing these academic services at the centre of learning rather than solely a support function.

Of these dimensions, the last three are directly related to the changing landscape of learning, and the shifting balance from teaching to independent resource-based learning.

SHEFFIELD HALLAM UNIVERSITY

Most library staff roles were redesigned as part of the restructuring process in the 1996 review of academic services. The major catalyst for the review and restructuring was the opening of the new Adsetts Centre learning centre building at the City Campus. The changes were therefore principally related to how services would be provided and staffed in the new building. Physically co-located services and facilities meant that integrated service desks were a logical solution to avoid overlap and user confusion, leading to an operational convergence for information desk services. What follows in this section focuses on the implementation of restructuring in 1996, when the Learning Centre department was formed, and subsequent developments over the past six years.

Hybrid learner support roles

The most significant role change was that of Assistant Librarian to Information Adviser, demonstrating the deliberate move towards learner-centred support and hybridization. This new role is at the sharp end of student support, with a significant element of information desk service work, facilitating student information skills workshops, along with subject team responsibilities in collection management, creating support materials, and developing new services. Information Advisers carry out user support in both information (ex-library) and IT (ex-computing) fields and are drawn from the former Assistant Librarian and computer services Analyst/Adviser staff groups. Information desks have become integrated services offering advice on both IT and information resources, and also on the growing number of computer-based learning packages available in learning centres. IT laboratories outside the centres also have their own helpdesks provided by computer services staff, and act as referral points for the more complex IT that the Learning Centre information desks are unable to deal with. Before restructuring, where information searching, handling, presentation, and access to Internet resources were provided in different locations, librarians on information desks and analyst/advisers on IT helpdesks increasingly needed to refer users to each other. This arrangement clearly did not meet users' needs, and convergence of location and user support for resources and facilities was implemented with the opening of the new Learning Centre. Information Adviser posts, on long career grades allowing for development, are the response to this same shift. The example of computer-based learning packages demonstrates how the reality of user needs accelerates the progression from librarian or IT adviser to learner support. Demand from users for support for computer-based learning, in the absence of lecturers, falls upon the information desk, transcending basic queries about access and printing, towards advice about the actual learning process.

Post titles and job descriptions

The importance of post titles in symbolizing the significance of a role should not be underestimated. The term *adviser* was deliberately chosen to reflect an active and contributory function with positive associations, rather than the more nondescript *officer* or *assistant*, or the use of the more passive word *support*. The job description for the Information Adviser role is contained in one integrated job description, covering all user support staff in the Department through four levels and seven pay grades, from assistant to team manager level (see Appendix A). It unites all with one generic function statement which is developed in the four roles at different levels, and focuses them on *providing and supporting information services*. It is intentionally indicative and generalized in places to ensure flexibility and some element of futureproofing. It is possibly more appropriately seen as a role description than the traditional list of tasks and responsibilities which make up many job descriptions.

Alongside this, new person specifications were developed for each role, outlining the skills, aptitudes, experience and qualifications required for each level, ensuring that people from information/library, IT support or generic learner support were equally placed to apply or to gain promotion. There were challenges in translating some of these requirements from the former librarians' career grade scheme, which involved qualified librarian status for entry and Library Association (now Chartered Institute of Library and Information Professionals – CILIP) Chartership for progression through the first bar, as there is no directly equivalent set of professional qualifications in IT.

Teaching support

In developing new roles, the area of teaching support has been problematic, creating tensions between the changing demands of the teaching and learning process, and the boundaries around roles prescribed by specific grades and conditions of service. Increasing demand for teaching sessions, more participative delivery methods, and greater student numbers have meant that on occasions the demand for teaching could not be met by the Information Specialists, the academic-grade staff in the Learning Centre with responsibility for information skills teaching. One solution has been to involve Information Advisers by delegating more routine teaching, such as inductions, or to deliver a double-handed session with an Information Adviser as facilitator. For those who are able and willing it is a short step to taking on more teaching and delivering classes independently. Nevertheless, there is concern about protecting the academic status of those on teaching grades, and in this respect it is not helpful to blur the boundaries between academic and support work. Involving 'non-teaching' staff – that is, those on administrative, professional, technical and clerical (APT&C) grades – may appear to mitigate against the need for academic staff in the Department, and there is a keen awareness that in some institutions library and IT teaching posts have been abolished or converted to hybrid teaching/professional posts. One solution has been the occasional use of short-term hourly-paid lecturer contracts for APT&C staff, but this also has been problematic. This area provides clear evidence of institutional and sectoral pressures in preserving distinctions between what are becoming seamless and complementary activities.

Integration and partnership

Role changes towards integration and partnership with schools of study were already evident in the Subject Librarian role prior to the 1996 restructuring. These were staff on academic grades who delivered teaching in information skills, were responsible for the acquisition and exploitation of resources in a subject area, and liaised with a specific school of study on information services and curriculum design and delivery. Their roles were already undergoing a process of change following an earlier staffing review in 1992, when their focus was redirected externally towards the schools, and elements of their internal management and mediated user support roles were delegated to other staff. Team managers in the form of Senior Assistant Librarians were given responsibility for the day-to-day management of service and campus matters, freeing up Subject Librarians' time for increasing their visibility in schools and pushing the resource-based learning agenda with academic staff. The restructuring change process of 1996 consolidated this, retitling Subject Librarians as Information Specialists with a strong message about retaining their information emphasis. The role of the Information Specialist is covered in more depth in Chapter 5 (pp. 138–41).

Development roles

The merger of the Library and Learning Resources department with the Learning and Teaching Institute (LTI) to form the Learning Centre was expected to create a new synergy in proactive educational development. The collaboration of developers (LTI academic staff and courseware developers) and practitioners (Information Specialists and Advisers) working together on educational innovation and resource-based learning projects in partnership with schools was an innovative development, with each group enhancing and promoting the other's role. In practice, only a small number of projects benefited from this collaboration initially, as each group focused on its own immediate concerns. More recently, however, there have been further opportunities to reap the benefits of the merger, such as the launch of the virtual learning environment, uniting pedagogic development, technological capability and resource-based learning practice.

Management roles

Managers' roles were seen as vital to successful implementation of the change process and to making the new services work in practice. The growing importance of the management function was evident in targeted development for the line manager role, and in the use of professional managers for specific specialized areas, such as finance, administration and marketing. Sound and consistent team leadership is regarded as essential in a structure and departmental style which aims to empower staff at all levels to take decisions as close as possible to the operational activity, and to develop themselves to meet the changing demands of the organization. Line managers need competence in staff-management skills, such as coaching, motivating, managing staff development, appraisal, managing change, and providing leadership and direction for staff in new roles and working relationships. The University was engaged in a number of initiatives in human resource management and management development throughout the 1990s, consolidating the vital role of effective staff management in achieving the University's objectives. For example, the Investors in People standard set a template for the responsibilities of line managers, which was underpinned by a series of management development activities.

Future developments

The Learning Centre expects the shifts toward learning in its Information Adviser roles to be continued eventually into a more holistic learner support role. The novelty of hybridizing IT with information support is now well past; current demands are less about technological innovation and electronic information and more about how diverse and demanding independent learners can get help and advice at the times and in the ways they need it. However, in a climate of increasing numbers and declining resources, there are limitations on the amount of personal support available to each user, and the commitment of service staff to this approach may need to be tempered in time. For example, the Learning Centre has a relatively expensive model of information desk staffing, using only 'professional'-level staff, which may need to be reviewed. Recently, for the first time, learning centres have been open, without staff support, on an overnight basis, and the viability of this type of self-service can now be evaluated.

LEEDS METROPOLITAN UNIVERSITY

Here, changes in roles took two forms. Chiefly, staff experienced a broadening of their role to cater for the new functions within the Learning Support Services department of the Learning and Information Services division and the learning centres, particularly in the provision of support to users, especially IT support. This involved some element of hybridization in former information and IT support jobs. At a later stage, some specialization in roles and skills was required to deliver on new areas, such as programming, web design and cataloguing of electronic materials. Learning centre teams comprised support and liaison staff, and targeted services, such as off-campus support. Changes in roles have been mostly at the level of professionally qualified staff, with little effect on learning centre assistants at the time of convergence, although there is now a shift to deploy them in IT support roles on the information desk.

Major changes

The most radical role change was that of *Senior Information Officer*, drawn from the former role of Assistant Librarian, and hybridized with computing support functions (see Appendix B for job description and employee specification). A substantial part of their role is the support of learning centre users, particularly via the Information/Help Desks, where they bring together an integrated support function for learners' needs. They had previously combined information desk work and cataloguing with a support role for Tutor Librarians within subject teams.

Under restructuring, responsibility for user support on the IT helpdesks was passed to Learning Support Services. This transfer proved to be quite a challenge and new and existing staff put in a great deal of work to create a flexible and user-centred service. Along with the Help Desk itself, Help Desk Assistants were inherited from the former Computing Services Department. These full-time staff were deployed more flexibly than before, and part-time assistant posts which were vacant allowed the introduction of the new role of *Information Officer*.

Senior Information Officers and Information Officers focus on supporting users face-to-face in the full range of facilities and resources of the centres, including IT and information; while Learning Advisers specialize in the teaching and learning field, although they also contribute to desk rotas. Some Information Officer posts are deployed in other specialist functions of the Department, such as in the traditional bibliographic tasks in the Bibliographic Services Unit, and with electronic information projects in the Online Learning Centre team. (The job description and employee specification for Information Officers is given in Appendix C.)

In addition to the IT support provided by the Information Officers, specialist IT support is now provided at the Information Desk by *IT Help Assistants*, the retitled

Help Desk Assistants, who also 'rove' in learning centre IT areas, providing distributed support to users. It was at first thought that the need for these posts would be temporary because increased self-service plus multi-skilling of Learning Centre Assistants (formerly Library Assistants), would lead to a shift from staffing of counter services towards learner support. However, self-service has taken longer than anticipated to implement, anticipated falls in activity at the issue counters as a result of increased use of electronic services have not yet materialized, and there is a better understanding of what is required in terms of IT support. Although specifically for IT support, there is now a move to broaden the IT Help Assistant role to other service points, such as the issues counter, and to provide generic information desk help, including basic information enquiries. On an integrated helpdesk, it makes increasingly better sense to have integrated hybrid roles with capability in information and IT, rather than to preserve the specialist distinctions which were necessary at restructuring.

Another major change within staffing was the creation of the Online Learning Centre (OLC) team. At the time of restructuring the service had only a Systems Librarian and an Electronic Services Coordinator, who combined this role with that of a Tutor Librarian. Under restructuring, a larger team was developed, led by the Electronic Services Development Manager; its responsibilities included Departmental systems, electronic services development and delivery, a copyright clearance service, and the new Bibliographic Services Unit, which centralized the acquisition and processing of materials. The OLC has expanded considerably through project funding in such areas as the provision of a student information portal and the Skills for Learning web site.

Liaison

Learning Advisers were drawn from previous posts of Tutor Librarian, on which they were largely based, and from computing advisers. Their role is to stimulate effective communication and encourage partnership with academic staff, to ensure exploitation of the Learning and Information Services provision in schools and faculties, and to increase awareness of how its facilities and services can support academic provision and innovation in teaching and learning. They provide support to the academic programme of the University through the identification and acquisition of appropriate learning resources, provision of high-quality information and advice services, preparation of documentation and learning materials, and design and delivery of courses and workshops on information literacy skills. (A job description and employee specification is given in Appendix D.) Under restructuring, job roles were renamed to reflect the move to supporting learning in the new learning centres, and to signal the new organization. Along with libraries becoming learning centres, learning was also placed at the crux of the Learning Adviser role. In addition, Assistant Librarians became Senior Information Officers, removing the 'L-word' and focusing them on information. Other moves towards user services saw Counter Supervisors retitled Customer Services Managers.

New management tier

Restructuring also allowed for a thorough review of the roles required to deliver the Department's new agenda, and the role of *Senior Learning Adviser* was created with the aim of coordinating the work of Learning Advisers and adding a specialist level of management and expertise. These posts liaise with a specific faculty and lead the team of Learning Advisers supporting each of the faculty's schools in a Faculty Academic Support Team (FAST). Senior Learning Advisers also take responsibility for a specialist function and policy area – planning and evaluation, information literacy, and electronic services – while two posts act as Deputy Learning Centre Managers, with line management responsibility for campus teams of Learning Advisers. For example, the role of Planning and Evaluation Manager gives a senior-level focus on setting service standards, monitoring performance and evaluating services. All Senior Learning Advisers contribute to the strategic planning and policy-making process of Learning Support Services and are part of its management team.

There was a conscious decision to opt for a campus approach to management through Learning Centre Managers and Deputies, rather than focusing on functions at senior level, although Learning Centre Managers did also take on service-wide roles such as staff development and quality development. There have been some tensions between service-wide and campus-specific roles on occasions. For example, the team of Learning Advisers is managed by the Deputy Learning Centre Manager on each campus, but in the Learning Advisers' role within their FAST, they are led by one of the Senior Learning Advisers; which, in two of the four faculties, involves cross-campus working. It has taken time to iron out such difficulties, but after some tinkering the problems have been overcome.

UNIVERSITY OF LINCOLN

At Lincoln, the Learning Support department was restructured in 1997 to enable it to fulfil a strategically critical role within the University – the establishment of what was then called an Intensely Supported Learning Environment. Learning Support required a staffing structure that was flexible and responsive enough to deal with the cultures and orientation of individual campuses, schools and subjects, as well as future change as a consequence of the movement towards a 'New Learning Environment'. The strategic imperatives strongly influenced the development of the new Departmental structure.

The restructuring in 1997 involved the establishment of new staff roles based on a set of 'job families', as job groupings were called, each with a specific functional focus, such as service, learning or technical. These were underpinned by the concept of multi-skilling and the establishment of a competency framework, with requirements for each job family and level. Helpdesks were staffed by multi-skilled staff with the aim of achieving a one-stop-shop approach to learner support, whereby 80 per cent of all frontline enquiries, library and information, IT and media support, could be answered at the point of contact. The competency framework is explained more fully in Allan (1998). (See Appendices E and F for samples of job descriptions.)

One of the key features and major successes of the review was the establishment of the Learning Adviser job family, the chief objective of which was to work more closely with academic staff in subject teams to support the University's teaching and learning activity. The development of this role implemented the requirement for closer partnership and integration between Learning Support and the academic community, with active support for the curriculum through course development and delivery, and provision of workshops to support generic learner-support skills in the areas of information retrieval and the effective use of communications and information technology, and media technology. Learning Advisers were required to develop skills in facilitating learning, curriculum development, and product development; further, in addition to a subject specialism, each had a Learning Support specialism, commonly information handling, information technology or media. Some who were appointed initially to Learning Adviser posts had no specific subject background, though they have since demonstrated their adaptability and made a success of this role.

With the exception of shelvers, all other Support Department staff acquired new job roles and titles in the restructuring. The two largest groupings were Learning Advisers and Service Advisers. The former job title resonated within the University environment, while the latter was a generic title that could also be found in any service-oriented sector such as retailing. However, on a pragmatic note, although there were no other Service Advisers elsewhere in the University, there were some staff in faculties who were also called Learning Advisers, so some confusion has arisen.

The review also redefined the roles of managers, creating departmental manager posts which combined managing staff with a functional cross-departmental role. The original intention was to have four managers with responsibility for academic services (including Learning Advisers and Technical Advisers), customer services (including Service Advisers and Shelvers), resources (with no line management responsibility) and IT. However, this last post was deleted.

UNIVERSITY OF ABERDEEN

Library and computing services are provided by a single organization: the *Directorate of Information Systems and Services*, formed in September 1996 by a merger of the

University Library, Computing Centre and Administrative Computing (see Chapter 2). At that time, the creation of the Directorate reflected the longer-term view that the University would benefit from integration of the management of all information systems, printed or electronic, academic or administrative. A focused strategy spanning all information services and modes of delivery would allow much wider scope for development of innovative delivery of teaching, learning and research. Staff in the Directorate were reorganized into a new divisional structure, with core library services being provided by the Library Division and IT services through Infrastructure Systems, Applications Support and Corporate Systems Divisions.

Job titles changed for all library staff to reflect the name of the new converged Directorate: Library Assistants became Information or Resource Assistants or Officers, while Assistant Librarians became Site Service Managers. However, the main change of role was for the former faculty subject librarians (sub-librarian/Academic Related 3/4) who became Faculty Information Consultants. The increased availability of information in both electronic and print format required promotion, explanation and organization. It was perceived that in their new role the Faculty Information Consultants would coordinate and plan for all the information needs of faculties, regardless of the medium in which they are delivered; although based in the library they are part of the Consultancy and Client Liaison Division of the Directorate, rather than the Library Division. They had previously held responsibility for all areas of library service within a subject section or site. Now, many of these duties, including line management responsibility for Information Assistants, were transferred to Site Service Manager posts (previously Assistant Librarian (AR2/3) in a subject area).

This has allowed the four Faculty Information Consultants for the Faculties of Arts and Divinity, Medicine and Medical Sciences, Science and Engineering, and Social Sciences and Law to concentrate on the following areas:

Liaison role

Assessment and monitoring of client needs and client feedback is achieved through regular discussions and meetings with departmental representatives and other staff, attendance at faculty and departmental meetings, client surveys and service evaluations. Data gathered is used to inform and shape Directorate financial and organizational planning processes. Feedback and comment from clients is encouraged.

Providing information and advice on the use of information systems and services. The library budget is devolved to academic departments. The Faculty Information Consultants provide information and advice on the use of departmental library budgets, interlibrary loan allocations and ordering procedures.

Teaching role

Instruction in library and information retrieval skills Faculty Information Consultants (FICs) provide appropriate information skills instruction for academic and research staff and undergraduate and postgraduate students to ensure that staff and students are familiar with library services and have a good working knowledge of subject-specific information resources. For research postgraduate students and academic staff, the majority of instructional sessions are arranged in advance on a one-to-one basis. For undergraduates, the majority of instructional sessions are pre-booked by lecturing staff for specific student groups and link into course work. Undergraduate and taught postgraduate instructional sessions include:

- Provision of information skills presentations, tours, workshops and assignments meeting identified student or course needs. Information skills for first-year courses are delivered via a virtual learning environment program using WebCT software, which is subject course-specific. It includes information on using the library catalogue, location and organization of relevant resources, advice on reference works and web sites, and a short exercise.

- Development of course materials including handouts and assignments.

- Setting and marking of assignments and exercises as agreed with departmental course contact.

- Provision of feedback to departmental course contact for future review, modification or development of information skills element.

While the removal of staff or site management responsibilities from FICs has allowed them to concentrate on their liaison, teaching and consultancy roles, there is potential for problems when they need clerical assistance or other support from library division staff. In the previous subject team staff structure this assistance would have been part of the information assistants' role in the team, but can now depend on the goodwill and cooperation of the Site Services Manager.

The other major change was in the creation of the posts of *Help Desk Services Manager* and three *Help Desk Officer* posts following the development of an integrated Help Desk Service. Prior to integration, there were five different types of help provided to users:

- an *academic advisory service*, based in the Computing Centre, for academic staff and research students;
- two *part-time undergraduate helpdesks* at different sites, staffed by postgraduate students, and open at lunch times and evenings only;
- an *administrative helpdesk* which provided assistance to administrative and secretarial staff;

- an *Information Desk* in the main library building (Queen Mother Library) providing assistance to library users; and
- additional *ad hoc advice and assistance* was being given to library and computing users who asked for help at the Library Issue Desks and at Computing Centre Reception.

By combining the separate services, the new service had sufficient critical mass to enable the employment of new, dedicated, helpdesk staff. The aim of the single, integrated helpdesk service is to eliminate user confusion and to deliver a uniform service.

The Help Desk Officers provide first-line support to users contacting the Help Desk service (see Appendices G and H). They are part of a larger team providing both first-line and back-up support to users of information systems and services. The Help Desk Officers are based at the IT Help Desk in the Computing Centre but also spend part of their time working on the University Library helpdesks on a rota and shift basis. Prior to the introduction of helpdesks, two of the three library sites did not have any separate information or enquiry point so that enquiries had to be dealt with by staff at the main library service counter, in addition to their main role. The integrated helpdesks have allowed an improved level of service; they are staffed for part of the day by Help Desk Officers and for part of the day by Information Assistants or the Site Services Manager. Library staff have been trained in using the helpdesk software system to log and refer calls and to answer first-level IT queries. All staff working at any helpdesk are expected to be able to provide information and advice, at a basic to intermediate level, on the use of the whole range of Directorate systems and services:

- computer systems and the University network;
- commonly used applications software (word processing, spreadsheets, e-mail, Web);
- administrative applications (for example, student records, finance system);
- library on-line catalogue, subject searches;
- library resources and services;
- electronic information resources available over the network; and
- training courses and documentation available to staff and students.

Similarly, Help Desk Officers have been trained in delivering library services and using resources. Much of this has been on-the-job training, initially spending time at library issue desks, and by self-training and guided training (completing prepared exercises) in using electronic and print resources in different subject areas.

DEVELOPING STAFF SKILLS

Clearly, new and strengthened skills and skill development programmes are needed to underpin changing staff roles. This section examines the new skills which are desirable for learner support and hybrid roles, and how they have been developed. The issues are not just about information and IT skills, but concern the personal skills, awareness, and understanding necessary to make a success of a learner-centred organization. As part of the change process, each organization needed to define the skills it required, audit the skills capacity it already had, plan how to bridge any gap through either staff development or recruitment, and establish a staff development process which could continue to support ongoing change and new demands. Libraries and librarians have typically had a good reputation for staff development initiatives and innovation, and there is considerable evidence here of that proactivity.

From a look at the changes in skills requirements, it can be seen that developments have taken shape in the following areas:

- *Multi-skilling*: hybrid roles with a mix of skills from several disciplines, broadening the skill base of staff – for example, IT, information/library, media, teaching.

- *Cross-skilling*: a form of multi-skilling, but more specific to converged structures, where two specific skill sets – IT and information – are partnered together. In most restructurings, information and IT staff were required to develop additional skills in each other's area.

- *New professional/technical skills*: to support the new demands of information organizations, staff needed to develop a capacity in growing areas, such as Web development, project management, pedagogy, and management skills. In some functions, the professional background of a manager is less important than generic management and leadership skills.

- *Personal skills*: to meet the changing ways of working and service environment, for example to facilitate the greater degree of collaborative working on which the success of converged or integrated services depends, staff need to develop enhanced team-working and collaboration skills; to cope within the accelerated change environment, staff need to learn to manage their own staff and career development; and, for working in a user-focused service with increased customer expectations, customer service skills and strategies to deal with pressure.

In planning staff development, organizations have had to contend with a number of issues:

- What skills are required to support learners? Are these existing skills which can be interchanged, or new skills to be developed afresh?

- What degree of multi-skilling is achievable in the first instance? There needs to be a balance between the amalgamation of skills to achieve integrated support and efficiency, and the need to retain effective depth and quality in the skills of staff. Staff may be concerned that multi-skilling means deskilling, or becoming a 'jack-of-all-trades and master of none'. The importance of retaining strengths and expertise, while extending knowledge and developing new skills, cannot be overstated.

- Professional identity can be compromised by hybridization and staff may feel protective towards skills related to their original professional specialisms. Are they still a 'librarian', an 'IT professional', or some new kind of professional? Are professional bodies, standards and qualifications still relevant and important?

- Extended skills will take time to achieve, and the level of expertise and competence required may not be achieved by the time of implementation. The initial period may therefore be uncomfortable, with a feeling of being thrown in at the deep end. Some of the development needs and skills required may not necessarily be clear at the planning stage.

- Demonstrable prioritization of staff development during implementation is essential, recognizing the difficulty in finding time for training with many other pressures of a new service. Priorities must be given to shortage skills, although possibly at the risk of the needs of some staff being lower priority and their feeling less valued.

- There are issues of availability for some areas of development, for example there is ready availability of IT skills off the shelf, but difficulty in sourcing information skills training of the appropriate type and level.

SHEFFIELD HALLAM UNIVERSITY

As part of the restructuring process, a systematic and strategic review of staff development needs for the new SHU Learning Centre department was undertaken in collaboration with the Organization and Staff Development Unit in the Human Resources Department. This involved a training needs analysis exercise and associated training for managers to enable them to identify the needs of their own teams and potential strategies to address them. A prioritized programme for implementation was devised, identifying the new skills required, the timetable for achieving them, target groups, and the methodology.

For example, once the role of Information Adviser had been designed, the next stage was to identify clearly, through a person specification, what skills it required (see Appendix I). It was important to ensure that staff who were transferring into the role felt it accommodated them, whatever their background, and that promotion routes were equitable for both library and IT staff. Staff were clearly concerned about retaining and continuing the importance of their particular professional skills and expertise, and did not want to become too generalist. The approach was to aim towards multi-skilled individuals, by first creating multi-skilled teams: a pragmatic view of how much skill development could be achieved in the first year. This meant that a member of the former computer services team had to staff the information desk throughout opening hours for the first semester, until information staff had developed sufficient IT support competence to take on the dual support role. Although this may have felt inequitable to the ex-IT staff, both in terms of their share of direct service time and their own development, the timescale was adhered to, and their needs could become priority in the latter part of the year.

Cross-skilling

The most urgent skill development issue was to support the integrated helpdesk and the Information Advisers. There was a relatively short period of time before the new Adsetts Centre opened, so a prioritized timetable of training was devised in collaboration with experienced helpdesk staff in the Corporate Information Systems department. This defined a level of IT and software competence which would enable a high proportion of queries to be answered by ex-librarians; with phasing of more specialist training in the coming two semesters, assisted by a part-time secondment from Corporate Information Systems to take responsibility for development of the programme. It was felt that most of the librarians already had a high level of IT skills and familiarity with the relevant software through their current work, but might need reassurance that these were an adequate basis to take on IT-user support for students. Indeed this was one of the drivers for the rapid change, plus their proficiency in handling learner enquiries using reference interview-based skills, and their closeness to the teaching and learning process through support and subject team roles. The picture was quite different for the small number of computer services staff transferred to the Information Adviser role. They had little awareness of information resources and a different style of handling technical enquiries, but already possessed the vital IT skills and experience required in the new learning centre. Since information skills were in plentiful supply with a full complement of librarians, a pragmatic decision had to be taken to prioritize the development of IT skills to deal with the skill shortage, and to deal with information skills for ex-computer services staff in a later phase of the plan.

An 18-hour programme of IT and Microsoft Office training was commissioned from a local external provider to allow all librarians to reach a common platform of skills prior to the opening of the learning centre. Post-implementation, a variety of methods were used to deliver the remaining training, primarily in a work-based mode, accommodating different learning styles, and also offering educational consistency with university-level teaching and learning strategies – independent, self-paced, resource-based learning. Of the different methods – drop-in workshops, problem-solving exercises, and shadowing of experienced staff – the last was the most successful, although also the most difficult to achieve on a busy information desk. It was a constant struggle for staff to prioritize the urgent demands of the new service and their own development needs. Looking ahead to the next stage of implementation, staff due to adopt the new role at other campuses the following year were involved in shadowing and job exchange in the new learning centre to assist their transition.

Information skills for ex-computer services staff were delivered chiefly in-house with on-the-job training in subject teams. This training involved shadowing and coaching, combined with more light-hearted methods, such as subject team quiz events to test knowledge of print information sources. It was particularly difficult to identify external or accredited training which both fulfilled this information-skill training need and was manageable to implement. For example, the NVQ in information and library skills was felt to be too onerous on the organization to administer.

Teaching skills

Support for teaching skills is provided to new academic staff in the University by the compulsory New Teachers' Course, a part of the Postgraduate Certificate in Higher Education. The development needs of learning support staff have been recognized and addressed by a subset of modules of this course aimed at those such as Information Advisers, and Student Services Centre staff. This area of training is increasingly being seen by Learning Centre staff as the most relevant form of staff development for their roles, rather than purely librarianship or IT courses and qualifications. The incorporation of the Learning and Teaching Institute within the Learning Centre has opened up opportunities for training and development, bringing together pedagogy and practical learner support – such as a seminar on best practice in running workshops, or sharing the results of research projects on current educational developments in the University.

Developing managers

The increasing profile of managers' roles was underpinned at both University and Departmental level by management development initiatives. University management programmes spanned the range of management levels – from the First Line Manager course, offering NVQ Management Level 4, to support for MBAs provided by the Sheffield Business School. The Government's Investors in People standard was adopted as a template for the University, and departments and schools of study devised action plans towards achieving it. Investors in People offers a framework of good practice in staff development, including organizational commitment, planning, implementation and evaluation. It lays particular emphasis on staff understanding of the objectives of their organization and their own role in fulfilling them. A new appraisal scheme was introduced for all staff, involving personal objectives and staff development plans, aligned with the objectives of their team, their Department and, ultimately, the University itself.

For the Learning Centre, this scheme was a valuable tool in helping staff to understand the context and the changes they were working in, and to develop their awareness of what the Department and their role contribute to the learning process. Alongside the University's requirement for a Departmental annual plan, each team was encouraged to develop its own plan, to which team members made contributions. This was supported by a monthly team-briefing process, which communicated Departmental, institutional and sectoral issues and developments to staff, enabling them to appreciate the context of their own work and to anticipate changes. To improve the relevance and impact of these initiatives, the Learning Centre integrated a range of management workshops into its own programme, the Management Development Forum, with the assistance of the Organization and Staff Development Unit. This allowed the training to be designed and delivered in the Department's own style, context and culture, and assisted in team building amongst managers, and in sharing good practice locally. The Department achieved the Investors in People standard in 2000.

A reminder of the importance of staff development having its appropriate place in a change programme was offered by a less successful initiative. As part of the new learning centre development, there was an outline plan to provide frontline support to learners for media services, such as design, TV and so on, in an open access area. In anticipation of this, a customer-service skills training course was commissioned and delivered by an external provider. However, this was in advance of a detailed implementation plan being developed and, more importantly, of the new service and change in role being agreed with the relevant staff. Without the recognition of the need for the training, and the commitment to new skills, the programme could not achieve its objective.

LEEDS METROPOLITAN UNIVERSITY

The University context

Staff development in the Learning Support Services department at Leeds needs to be set within the broader context of the institution as a whole, which has held Investors in People status since 1998 and underwent a successful review in January 2001. The Staff Development Manager for the Department reports the development needs of its staff to the University's Staff Development Unit, and this informs the University's staff development programme as published in the regular 'Looking Ahead' brochure.

Courses and training offered in this way are heavily used by learning centre staff and contribute greatly to their development. The Staff Development Manager also networks with individuals in similar roles within other institutions, allowing for the useful exchange of good practice and joint training initiatives.

The new roles in a converged division meant a similar pattern of skills development was required as at Sheffield Hallam University, especially the hybridization of the Assistant Librarian role. However, it was clear that, with a more extensive convergence, all staff had to broaden their skills portfolio, particularly in terms of IT competence. Assistant Librarians needed to develop a level of IT skills appropriate for working on an IT helpdesk, while some ex-computing advisory staff transferring into Learning Adviser roles had extensive development needs in information skills and knowledge, and less need of the former professional IT skills. The Department has been concerned to gauge a level of multi-skilling that is adequate to meet the needs of learners while also allowing sufficient depth of skills to be developed. In addition to the area of IT skills, new areas such as project management, team leadership, supervisory skills and budget management have been identified for development.

Development for staff from IT backgrounds has recently benefited from a collaboration with the School of Information Management within the University. Staff have been able to undertake and gain credit for individual modules on the masters programme (initially the Information Sources module), in order to develop their knowledge and understanding in information skills for direct application to information desk and teaching roles. There are plans to extend this collaboration to continuing professional development opportunities for other staff. Another area of emphasis for University staff is that of customer care training, with all staff expected to undertake a one-day course run by an external trainer. This has proved to be most effective, with both staff and service benefiting.

Organization and delivery of staff development

Staff development is managed by the Staff Development Manager, chiefly through a staff development working group, with sub-groups contributing to specific areas such as the planning and running of the 'training hour' programme, visits and job shadowing. Needs are discussed at an annual staff development interview between staff and their line manager, and their development plans contribute to the Department's staff development strategy for the next year. Specialist working groups are set up from time to time to deal with current issues, such as training to support the joint information/IT desk. Development and training is delivered through a range of methods:

- *Training hours*: themed one-hour sessions to develop knowledge or awareness of services or projects, usually for all staff.
- *Group training*: directed at a group with a specific training need, for example, the library management system.
- *Individual training*: taking up opportunities to attend courses, conferences, workshops and seminars offered internally and externally. For example, an external training agency has been used for the past three years for IT training in Office software.
- *Accredited training*: staff are keen to gain a recognized qualification for their training. The European Computer Driving Licence, for example, is a popular choice, even for those already possessing advanced IT skills.
- *Job shadowing*: this has proved an effective and popular means of staff development, allowing staff to experience the roles of others within the service. Information officers or graduate trainees, for instance, have shadowed Learning Advisers.

Particular emphasis is placed on the need to practise new skills immediately after training in order to consolidate the development. Time is always at a premium, but this is seen as an essential element of the staff development process. The training of part-time, evening and weekend staff can be problematic, as they are not always available for organized training sessions.

IT skills

IT skills permeate the work of the whole Department and are now required for all posts. Individuals are assessed on appointment, via an IT skills questionnaire as part of the induction process, so that necessary training needs can be identified as soon as possible. Learning Advisers, for example, require IT skills to carry out their liaison role with schools, which extends beyond information matters to the full work of the Division, including IT and media, as well as for their input to information desk duties and to perform their day-to-day work using office software. This breadth of liaison is especially demanding, and it has sometimes proved difficult for Learning Advisers to be fully briefed on the IT situation, particularly if there are IT problems to communicate to schools of study.

Under convergence, the role of *IT Skills Developer* was created, with a remit to manage IT skills development for the Department's staff. IT skills audits have been conducted twice to identify broad issues regarding IT skills development. The first audit outcome indicated wide-ranging needs, with some priority for Microsoft Office software. In response, tailored sessions were run by external trainers on PowerPoint and Word to meet the needs of Learning Advisers and Information Officers. The Word module of the European Computer Driving Licence course was attended by

Learning Centre Assistants, along with hour-long drop-in sessions for staff on various applications. The second audit was adapted from the questionnaire developed by the JISC-funded SCAITS (Staff Communication and Information Technology Skills) project. (A project which aimed to create a strategic planning tool for use within higher education to develop a C&IT-capable workforce.) This second audit showed a marked shift away from software skills to Internet skills, especially amongst support staff, and also more diverse and specialized needs to support the specialist applications and projects then underway. It was useful to see the shift indicating some success in the training initiatives following the original audit.

After this initial drive to boost IT skills capability, it may now be more appropriate to integrate IT skills development into the overall staff development process by transferring responsibility for IT skills development to line managers and the annual staff development interview, although still supported by the IT Skills Developer. The IT Skills Developer will concentrate on anticipating and planning for future training, as new software and initiatives arise – for example, Word 2000 and Windows XP.

Supporting learning

Learning Advisers required continuing development in their established roles of teaching and learning, and in liaison. The expansion in student numbers, widening participation initiatives and the increase in independent learning have placed extra pressure on them to innovate in their teaching and to develop learning materials for new formats such as the Web. This is one of the staff development priorities for the immediate future. Some have embraced the opportunity to apply for fast-track membership of the Institute for Learning and Teaching, which is seen as particularly relevant to their roles. The University has provided practical and financial support, by means of seminars and payment of registration fees and the first two years' subscription. Learning Advisers' involvement with school and University quality assurance processes, such as Quality Assurance Agency subject reviews, has helped develop their understanding of teaching and learning issues. Learning Advisers take the opportunity to attend and contribute to the University's annual Learning, Teaching and Assessment Conference, and in 2000 won a Chancellor's Award for the flexible delivery model of 'Know-it-Alls', information skills learning/teaching packages. It is clear that the profile of Learning Advisers has risen within the University since restructuring, and this has been assisted by the further shift of emphasis from teaching to learning, and the advocacy of their role at University level.

UNIVERSITY OF LINCOLN

The University of Lincoln's competency model was the framework underpinning the development of staff roles, skills and staff development (see Appendix J). The framework is generalist and cumulative, with the logical outcome that the more senior the staff, the more multi-skilled in the three areas of information handling, IT and media they would be required to be. This was arguably taking the multi-skilling ethos beyond the needs of the service. Competencies in behaviour, skills and knowledge are articulated at up to four levels for each job family. The framework was mapped across to staff levels and grades and used to underpin both staff development, and recruitment and selection. Staff were required to demonstrate the competencies associated with their new role within a three-year period after restructuring, and this was linked to salary progression. Every member of staff was expected to submit a portfolio on an annual basis to demonstrate the level at which they were working in order to gain progression. The positive aspect of this is that some staff have gained accelerated progression through demonstration of appropriate competency levels and there is no other department in the University where that could have been achieved as a matter of course. On the other hand, vast amounts of staff time were devoted to the completion of portfolios in early summer at the busiest time of year, causing much stress and anxiety. Nor did this method allow for those staff whose lesser proficiency in producing portfolios did not necessarily correlate with their effectiveness as members of staff. Requirements have been relaxed over time in order to simplify the process.

As part of the calculation of staffing levels required, and as part of the attempt to ensure that multi-skilling would be achieved, each member of staff in 1997 was assigned a notional four hours a week to use for self-managed staff development. In practice, this did not always work as intended, since at times of pressured workloads staff felt that they should be focusing on more immediate tasks. However, the four hours were always intended to be used flexibly and could go towards attendance at external events which might require an absence of one or several days. The Department had, and continues to have, a very respectable record in supporting staff, both through time allowance in this way and also financial support for those wishing to undertake long courses, or attend other events. The University's Staff Development Unit was a heavily used and free source of provision. Informal staff development also took place, for example, through work shadowing. The skills that staff were most interested in developing tended to be in the areas of IT and media. There was less interest from staff without information-handling skills seeking to acquire them – IT and media being seen as more useful and interesting, and information handling perhaps as somewhat duller.

The Department was committed to NVQs as another strategy for developing and accrediting the skills it required. It had its own NVQ centre offering qualifications in Information and Library Service, Customer Service, and Administration. Starting with an in-house Centre Co-ordinator and one Assessor in 1997, assessor and internal verifier awards have since been achieved by other staff. All that the centre has lacked is a healthy throughput of candidates, since in times of uncertainty about

Departmental direction, NVQs tend to become sidelined. Another casualty of institutional uncertainty is an accredited programme of units which formed part of the University's suite of programmes for work-based learning. These covered teaching and learning, working and supervising in Learning Support, but, although validated, they have not been implemented.

Professional accreditation membership of the Institute of Learning and Teaching has been encouraged throughout the University, and the Department has continued to operate a Library Association (now CILIP)-approved staff development programme as preparation for Chartership.

UNIVERSITY OF ABERDEEN

Here the creation of the Directorate of Information Systems and Services, new roles for Directorate staff and the increasing everyday use of IT for all levels of staff, regardless of location or post, required a review of how existing skills should be developed and new skills acquired.

A Staff Development and Training Strategy Group, managed by the Management Services Division of the Directorate, was formed to include staff representatives of all Divisions of the Directorate, to advise on development and training needs. This group's declared aims are:

> To develop a strategy for meeting future skills requirements and the personal development needs of Directorate staff and to create a culture which embraces training combined with continuing support for development.

These aims are achieved by:

- development of an induction programme that includes an introduction to all areas of Directorate activities and promotes an awareness of the range of functions carried out by the Directorate and its place in support of the work of the University;
- development of a core 'good working practice' programme;
- ensuring staff awareness of technological innovations and techniques and developments in the areas of information resources, systems and services;
- encouraging all staff to take advantage of training and development opportunities and to take a personal responsibility for planning and managing their own development and progression;
- encouraging line managers to ensure that their staff have and continue to develop the necessary skills to provide an effective and efficient service; and
- keeping the training and development process under constant review.

The main mechanism for delivering training, developed by the Staff Development and Training Strategy Group, is through a programme of development and training activities for an hour each week during summer vacation. The programme, which is open to all Directorate staff, consists of information sessions and practical sessions; some are led by external trainers, some are 'in-house' sessions. This has been successful and inclusive for library staff, with all site libraries closed between 9am and 10am on Wednesday mornings throughout the vacation. Staff are expected to attend these sessions, or to use the time for self-training or for a section training or development activity. The programme has been less successful for other divisions where services are not closed and some sessions are perceived as not being relevant, particularly for technical staff. For all staff, follow-up activities and having sufficient time to embed training received continues to be an area that needs to be addressed.

The Staff Development and Training Strategy Group has also been active in the following areas:

- making an initial examination of the skills and competencies needs of each division within the Directorate;
- developing skills checklists for use in the induction and probationary periods and, as skills requirements change, ensuring that staff have the necessary skills to provide a high-level service as effectively and efficiently as possible;
- examining the timing of internal training courses and evaluating their effectiveness for future programmes;
- developing a Training Needs Assessment to include input from appraisal;
- introducing a framework for Personal Development Plans; and
- promoting in-house tailored development activity to meet staff needs.

CULTURAL ISSUES AND THE CHANGE PROCESS

This section explores the cultural and psychological issues related to the change management process in the case studies. Some of the phenomena are common to any period of change, but there are also distinctive issues related to IT and information services, and convergences in particular. In all change processes people need time to readjust to a new environment, to be clear about their own and others' roles. They will be concerned about any threat to their job, to their status or professional identity. Moreover, they will need to feel valued in the new organization and that the work and skills they contributed in the old structure are recognized. Some may soon enjoy their new roles and relish new opportunities, while others may resent the changes, feel loss of status, or find it difficult to perform their new role. New appointments will be made and these 'incomers' will not share in the 'history' of the old order. Negative factors can, to some extent, be mitigated by good change-management strategies: for example, frequent and meaningful communication about the change process; taking time to explain the benefits of the change and the ultimate goal; participation in decision-making; involvement of staff in determining their new roles and job titles; addressing promptly concerns about job security; recognition of cultural issues; and exploring differences and areas of conflict. In the context of this type of organization, it is important that staff can see the direct impact of changes in organizational and staffing arrangements, both on learners and on the work of schools of study, and understand how their own new roles will contribute to the business of the institution. Change is not complete with the implementation of the new organizational arrangements, although the severest impact is generally felt during this period. All the case study organizations are continuing to change and readjust, both to embed their new roles and to address consequent implications, continuing to respond to the discontinuous change environment in which they now operate.

In the context of change the word culture frequently appears, which might be defined as 'the way we do things around here' – in other words, the values shared by staff, the customs and traditions that surround working practices and relationships. Achieving the right culture for the new organization and avoiding conflicts of different cultures is critical to embedding new staffing arrangements. These cultural forces can be seen to derive from two directions: from the management of the organization trying to create a new style to achieve its new objectives; and from the staff groups themselves bringing their professional, team and individual cultures into the melting pot. In the first case, there may be organizationally-driven efforts to articulate and move towards new cultural values and style – learner-centred or service-driven culture, for example. In the second context, issues are less predictable, and depend upon the existence of different traditions, loyalties, working methods or professional identity between groups, and to some extent on personalities and past history. These issues are particularly acute where one group may feel there has been a takeover, rather than a restructuring, and that they are now in a minority, perhaps feeling their skills and contributions are not understood or valued. These two elements, being organizationally- and staff-driven, can mitigate against each other: for example, the new organization encourages collaborative working, while individual differences in approach mean collaboration is avoided, or previous methods of working are retained.

UNIVERSITY OF LINCOLN

As regards the positive side of the psychological impact of changes in the staff experience after 1997, all staff here were on a wide salary scale and in theory progression was possible from the bottom to the top. Indeed, accelerated progression was available to those who could demonstrate that they warranted it and some staff who grasped the opportunities offered undoubtedly benefited considerably. In particular, some Service Advisers progressed further than would have been possible previously when there was a bar at the top of clerical grade 2 and few opportunities to progress above it. On the negative side, some staff exhibited the classic symptoms of change management – such as lack of control, no enthusiasm and little motivation, and grieving for their previous role. In particular, there was some misinterpretation of attempts to improve the year-on-year staff progress review process, which some staff saw as little more than moving the goalposts.

Some aspects of the culture of the Department have been permeated by the implications of the 1997 collective agreement. This was a document, agreed and signed by the University senior management and the relevant union, Unison, which represented a complete change in the conditions of service. Its avowed intent was to make working practices more flexible; however, its implementation has had the opposite effect in some areas – for example, its failure to accommodate extended opening hours and weekend working. Another feature of the agreement was a flexible working allowance, whereby service staff were paid an enhancement of 4.25 per cent as part of their normal salary, on the understanding that they would work additional hours. In fact, this has resulted in somewhat unbalanced working practices, with some staff eager to work additional hours while others were not, thereby depriving the University of value for money. Objective-setting at Departmental, team and personal levels was also introduced as part of the 1997 agreement.

It is worth pointing out that the Department has maintained a high quality of service provided to users, and that the commitment and dedication of staff generally to this high standard of service has never been in doubt. What has been debated at length within the Department is how this could be achieved most effectively.

SHEFFIELD HALLAM UNIVERSITY

As will have been apparent in Chapter 2 (pp. 42–3), the restructuring of the SHU Learning Centre, unlike many in the academic services field, was not so much a full convergence as an integration of user-support activities, initially in a single location, plus the merger of Library and Learning Resources with the Learning and Teaching Institute. Nevertheless, many of the elements of staff response to change and cultural issues were still evident, even if not to such a strong degree as elsewhere. There was a restructuring process to be designed and implemented, involving new roles for some, new job titles for most, and an extensive skill development programme. However, there were a number of factors which allowed the reorganization to be achieved swiftly and relatively smoothly. The timetable for the change process necessitated a speedy pace, as it all needed to be achieved over the summer vacation. In some respects this was a disadvantage, as staff felt there was little time to consider the proposals, and thoroughness might be compromised. On the other hand, negative factors of protracted decision-making and prolonged periods of staff anxiety and uncertainty were largely avoided, and issues could be resolved quickly. There were no issues of job security for permanent staff and concerns of staff on temporary contracts were allayed early on, by contract renewal or transfer to the permanent staff. Only a very small number of staff were transferred between the Learning Centre and Corporate Information Services departments, so the amount of readjustment and potential cultural conflict was minimized. The areas of role change were confined to specific staff groups, while some other staff remained relatively unaffected. The approach was deliberately incremental, with implementation at only one of five campuses in the first year.

Participation and involvement

Planning for the restructuring was as participative as the timetable would allow, and wherever possible involved staff in the changes which would affect them. There was clearly a need to ensure that staff felt ownership of their new roles and they were therefore consulted as to what level of change they felt could be achieved; for example, to what extent information and IT skills could be successfully combined in Information Advisers' roles. A balance needed to be struck between encouraging staff to recognize the relevant skills they already had and acknowledging the significance of the role change and the staff development programme needed to achieve it. The University's formal processes of negotiation with the recognized trade unions were also followed, while maintaining direct management communication and consultation with all staff affected, including non-union members. Job titles were a particular concern, with staff challenging the proposal to include the term 'learning centre', for example, Learning Centre Assistant or Adviser. It was felt that this term had no currency outside the University at that time, and that job titles should represent a role with universal meaning and retain their identity with the information profession. This related to some other concerns that these developments were exclusive to the University, and might represent a transient fashion, rather than a trend in the sector. On the whole, there was a ready acceptance of the need for change, the benefits for learners and the proposed roles. The planning for integration of services within one building was already well established, so the logic of integrating support roles, although proposed at a later stage, was not difficult to grasp. Information Advisers, who experienced the greatest change, had a high level of commitment to user support through their previous posts, and readily saw the advantages to learners. A majority of the Assistant Librarians, perhaps because relatively recent entrants to the profession, were comfortable with the inevitability of change and enthusiastic about developing new skills and opportunities for career progression. Once they could see how it would enable them to support users and reduce overlap with other services, they welcomed it, although some with trepidation. However, the very small number of staff who transferred between departments may have felt especially isolated by their minority status, and that their views and feelings were not as valued as those of the larger groups.

Culture and values

Managers were conscious of the cultural issues involved, and to some extent the organizational structure sought to avoid the more problematic elements of integrating professionals with different cultural values. As part of the change process, there was a deliberate attempt to articulate the kind of style, or culture, to which the new Department was aiming. Rather than just a series of objectives and strategies, the new mission statement identified the values of the department as follows:

- maintaining a clear focus on meeting the needs of users;
- delivering high-quality provision through well-trained staff;
- maintaining open and friendly working arrangements;
- using resources efficiently and adopting an entrepreneurial approach to the generation of income; and
- reflecting the University's mission as a national professional university through the reputation of the Learning Centre.

The strong message was that user, or learner, needs were paramount, a value to which it was expected all staff would subscribe. These values recognize that staff issues are at the centre of the Department's success – in terms of staff development and working relationships – and also encourage a sense of pride in the reputation of the Department. These are essentially the values of the former Library and Learning Resources (LLR) department, however, and, with ex-LLR staff predominating, it is not surprising that their culture remained largely the same, or perhaps became stronger, within the new environment. Areas less involved with direct learner support, such as media production, tended to develop cultures of their own, while the Learning and Teaching Institute, with a completely different staff group of academics, researchers and courseware developers, largely retained its own culture within the merger.

Areas of conflict

Areas of cultural conflict were and still are evident between the frontline service and technical support roles, relating to differing views of priorities, working methods and expectations. Learner support staff are impatient of factors that interfere with the smooth delivery of services to users, while the technical support team are concerned to preserve the necessary integrity of essential procedures and professional standards. So much of the success of the service relies on the technical infrastructure, that service staff can feel frustrated at their lack of control, and uncomfortable with their dependence on another department. This is all the more problematic at times of technical failure, when they have the responsibility for responding to users, but only limited opportunity to influence the solution. These situations have been the most stressful for information desk staff and those who manage them – the classic problem of responsibility without authority. The concept of second-line support is another symptom of cultural difference. From the frontline IT support in the learning centres, information desk staff are required to refer more complex enquiries to an IT helpdesk run by Corporate Information Systems in another building. Although this referral process is designed to provide a better solution to technical queries, staff feel that it compromises their ownership of learners' enquiries; their expectation of being able to provide a solution to a question makes referring it on feel like failure, while not finding out the eventual answer exacerbates the situation. Although they will occasionally have to call on the expertise of others in information enquiries, this does not have the formality of the second-line support procedure.

Positive results

Staff experience of their new roles is mainly positive, despite the occasional frustrations. They are now much more aware of how their roles and services contribute to the academic experience of the student, and consequently to the University's teaching and learning strategy. Their job satisfaction has increased in the sense that they can offer more support to students in their learning – information in a range of formats, facilities, access, study environment, skills development and personal support – and are fully aware of the value of their work to the learner and the University. For themselves, they have gained more marketable job skills, both in the higher education sector and outside it. The hybrid role has been seen as a success, but information and IT professionals still retain their original specialism, and perhaps librarians have been seen as preferred in terms of potential and promotion, although this is beginning to change. Some clearly now identify themselves with a new species of hybrid learner-support professional, rather than a librarian or IT professional, so, for example, they see more relevance in achieving membership of the ILT than chartership of CILIP.

LEEDS METROPOLITAN UNIVERSITY

Here also, change was variable according to staff groups, and the greatest change was felt by those in hybrid roles on support desks, those responsible for managing them, and those whose role changed entirely from computing to information support. Initially, the restructuring process was very protracted and took over a year to sort out, but thereafter changes took place very rapidly. There was inevitably some concern for the safety of jobs and salary levels, but the University's Management of Change process was applied for those staff who did experience very radical changes in their roles, or who transferred to other University divisions. In the event, no one within the former Library Services department suffered compulsory redundancy or a reduced salary.

Consultation process

The restructuring process was prompted by the Ford report, an external consultancy report (see Chapter 2 p. 24), which criticized Learning Support Services (the predecessor of Learning and Information Services) for its lack of strategic planning and called for the production of an Information Strategy. The Vice-Chancellor circulated the report to all Learning Support Services staff for comment. Before establishing a structure for the new division, the Head of Learning Support Services initiated an extensive consultation process, comprising open meetings with all staff, individual meetings with senior managers, written submissions by individuals, and meetings with Deans and Faculty Management Teams. It was generally agreed that there was a need to improve the information services currently delivered and to play a more proactive role in learning development. There were a small number of reservations expressed, but the majority was in favour of adopting the proposed structure. A cascade approach was taken to the filling of posts, so that staff within the various units and departments were not appointed until the Heads and other managers had been appointed. This slowed down the process, but meant that managers in new departments were involved in the design of staffing structures, design of posts, and appointments. All posts were job-sized by Human Resources as part of the process of implementation of the new structure. Consultation with staff took place at each stage of the process, and, when more detailed proposals had been prepared, with the trade unions Unison and NATFHE. However, the slow progress made some staff anxious and, despite the consultative process, some complained they had not really been listened to, and that the proposed changes were out of their control.

Psychological impact of changing roles

In fact, the long hiatus before the restructuring plans were agreed and implemented caused some stress and anxiety for many staff. Furthermore, the new job descriptions were not all as anticipated and some felt they had not been given enough information about their proposed new roles. Senior Information Officers were offered a choice between working in the Bibliographic Services Unit or the learning centres, but some felt it was difficult to make an informed decision. Those who opted for work in the learning centres felt they were thrown in at the deep end on the IT helpdesk, as very few of the former Computing Services support staff transferred to the learning centres. They had little knowledge of the IT framework, software, IT lab booking processes, the faculties or the people involved, and to many it felt like starting a new job. There were inevitably pressures for everyone in developing into a new role while trying to deliver a service to meet the high demands of staff and students. There was also a feeling of isolation at first, as only the Senior Information Officers and the Learning

Centre Managers were involved in the management of the IT Help Desks. On the positive side, those staff who already had well-developed IT skills welcomed the expansion of their role and experienced much less anxiety.

The establishment of the Bibliographic Services Unit at the time of restructuring created tensions, as both Senior Information Officers and Learning Centre Assistants had to choose between working in the learning centres or the Unit. Job descriptions were written in such a way as to allow flexibility so that individuals could choose to work between the two areas. Many did not opt for the Unit because of location, the learning curve associated with taking on a new role, or because they preferred the customer interaction. There is now a movement away from generic job descriptions to allow for more specific roles to be properly defined.

Senior Information Officers have adapted to their new role and are proud of their achievement of successfully combining technical knowledge with traditional information skills, and their job satisfaction and motivation have probably increased, although it may have been a stressful experience at the time. They feel that they have got to know a new clientele and have forged new relationships with academic and administrative staff in the faculties. Some Senior Information Officers may no longer use some professional skills, such as cataloguing, but they are aware of the development of other valuable skills. The roles of Senior Information Officer and Information Officer are still quite fluid, responding to the different demands of learner support at the information desks, while other roles, such as Learning Adviser or Learning Centre Assistant, remain more structured and stable. On the whole, Learning Centre Assistants were not opposed to the restructuring, although some felt initially that they would not benefit. They were encouraged by the creation of more Senior Learning Centre Assistant posts, offering them more opportunity for promotion. However, it is probable that the role of Assistants will change more radically in the future when loan activity falls through increased use of self-service or electronic information services.

The 'new' role of Learning Adviser was, in effect, largely unchanged from the previous role of Tutor Librarian. However, some former Computing Advisers were reassigned as Learning Advisers, and on the whole they were much less happy about the change in their role. They had previously acted as intermediaries between the technology and the users, providing substantial IT software support to students and academic staff. After restructuring, this role was largely delegated to the new lower-level posts of Senior Information Officers and Information Officers, and subsequently IT Help Assistants, although many of them did not at first have the technical skills required. Some Computing Advisers felt that the new role of Learning Adviser was in effect a de-skilling process for them, as their computing skills, although still needed, were not being used, while they had to acquire new skills as 'librarians'.

The addition of the Senior Learning Adviser tier to the structure, with responsibility for coordinating teaching and learning work and partnerships with faculties as well as the work of Learning Advisers, was not welcomed by all Learning Advisers. Some perceived the addition of this new level, coupled with the revision of the Advisers' grade to Lecturer, as downgrading their own role, although existing post-holders did have protected salaries. Nevertheless, the new role did offer a welcome promotion opportunity for those who chose to apply for the posts, and allowed staff to develop managerial roles and specialist expertise in areas such as information literacy, and planning and evaluation.

New working practices

Some staff felt initially that the vision of the new structure was imposed without an understanding of the effect on the service to users. In practice, most staff had a library background and struggled to offer support for software; for example in the context of the integrated information/IT helpdesk, originally envisaged as being staffed by Learning Advisers, Senior Information Officers, Information Officers and IT Help Assistants, all able to offer support for both technical and library services. At first, not all these staff had the requisite technical skills, although many have since acquired them, and there were insufficient numbers of IT Help Assistants as the new Learning Support Services inherited vacancies for the former posts of Help Desk Assistants. More IT Help Assistants have been recruited, and at City Campus they now staff the integrated information desk, together with Senior Information Officers, Information Officers or Learning Advisers. All staff involved agree that the new integrated service is a success, both for users and for the staff themselves, who have gained considerable expertise from each other as a result of sharing the joint information desk. At the Beckett Park campus, where the geography of the building makes physical integration difficult, the Information and IT Help Desks remain separate, although some Information Officers work on both desks.

Cultural issues

Convergence has strengthened the customer-driven service model of Learning Support Services, giving them responsibility for all direct student support through the learning centres. However, the relationship with the department of Computing Services did encounter some difficulties and, to begin with, there was tension arising from the separation of the technical service (provided by Computing Services) from the support to users (now provided by Learning Support Services). For example, shortly after restructuring there was a period of serious network failure when Learning Support Services staff experienced the problem of being perceived as responsible for services, yet lacking the power to easily put things right. Staff working on the Information and IT helpdesks had to deal with unhappy customers and complaints, while division-wide liaison responsibilities of Learning Advisers and Senior Learning Advisers also meant they had to represent Computing Services at faculty and school committees, which included managing the general dissatisfaction about the network failures and the degradation of service. There were problems in that some staff were inadequately briefed about such Computing Services matters, and lacked confidence in understanding the complexity of some of the issues. Inevitably they found this stressful and frustrating at times. Progress in developing the customer service focus was recognized in 2002 by the award of the Government's Charter Mark to Learning Support Services for excellence in public service.

There are now much better mechanisms for collaboration and liaison which have considerably improved the working relationship between the two units. The networking difficulties have been resolved and Computing Services provides much enhanced C&IT facilities for its students. Computing Services has learnt a great deal from this unforeseen emergency and as a result is addressing issues in respect of prioritization and project management. There does, however, continue to be an issue around inadequate computer technician support for hardware and networking issues in the learning centres at weekends and evenings when services are open, but computing staff are not available except in emergencies.

Convergence may have brought some distributed roles together to streamline the Department's contribution to the learning process, but in other respects new structures have created divisions. Staff in the Online Learning Centre and Bibliographic Services Unit are perceived to some extent as separate from learning centre learner-support and service-delivery staff. Having previously worked together in subject teams, the roles of Senior Information Officers/Information Officer and Learning Adviser have diverged markedly, creating a widening gap in their working relationships. Senior Information Officers/Information Officers can feel undervalued, as Learning Advisers are still perceived as decision makers and have greater autonomy. Many Learning Advisers also feel they now have little input into decision-making, and that their academic role is not recognized or valued by Senior Information Officers/Information Officers. However, all agree that the increasing role that information and IT usage plays in the teaching and learning process and the associated importance of students' information skills, have enhanced the role of all Learning Centre staff.

Career prospects and progression

Career prospects have improved for some, although increased specialization has made some routes more restrictive. For Information Officers, promotion to Senior Information Officer is the route upwards, and currently a further level of Principal Information Officer for each campus is being developed, to manage the Information Desk service. The path to more senior posts would appear to be via Learning Adviser to Senior Learning Adviser, making the division between staff groups more stark.

However, the new expanded role of Senior Information Officers/Information Officers has undoubtedly improved their future career prospects by opening up external opportunities in IT-based jobs, although this could also lead to higher turnover of staff for the Department. For staff without professional qualifications, a number of new promotion opportunities opened up their internal career prospects: Customer Services Manager, Service Supervisors, Copyright Clearance Officer, BSU Supervisor, and Evening Service Supervisors. The creation of the Online Learning Centre team also offered new opportunities for staff to specialize in the development and delivery of electronic services, and to work in multidisciplinary teams with technical specialists, such as programmers.

RECRUITMENT AND SELECTION

Having defined the roles and skills for the new learning support environment, organizations need to consider how and from where they can recruit appropriate staff for these roles. How is the job market placed to provide candidates with the required skills and aptitudes, and the motivation to work in these kinds of contexts? Will managers need to change the way they recruit, how they attract applicants, where they advertise, what information they provide, and how they select the best candidate? What place would professional librarianship qualifications have in the new structure – essential, desirable, irrelevant?

UNIVERSITY OF LINCOLN

Here, where the staff roles in the department of Learning Support were generally more radically defined than most, it was clear from applications received in the early days that what the Department did was not understood. This was addressed by comprehensive documentation sent to potential applicants. Recruitment and selection is undertaken using the competency framework as a reference point. There has been little difficulty in recruiting to junior levels of staff; however, it has been harder to recruit to more senior posts, especially if a particular skill set is required to fill the gap in a team, or, in the case of Learning Advisers, fulfil the requirements of the Faculty concerned – for example a librarianship qualification or equivalent. There is little potential to weight competencies to fit particular circumstances, such as the supervisory skills required when recruiting a team leader. The competency framework was reviewed in early 2000 with the intention of making adjustments after an existence of three years. Revisions have been used to inform the person specifications which mark the next restructuring of the Department in early 2002.

SHEFFIELD HALLAM UNIVERSITY

The recruitment and selection process for information services posts was re-engineered, both to take account of the complex needs of the new roles, and to improve overall success in recruiting to all the Department's posts. As all of these require personal and customer service skills, the shortcomings of the traditional interview in delivering reliable evidence for decision-making were recognized. Candidates were now asked to demonstrate actively the attributes and aptitudes required through an assessment centre-style selection event, comprising practical exercises related to the job tasks, such as IT user support, teamwork exercises and written communication, as well as an interview. For the new hybrid learner-support roles, such as Information Adviser, qualifications and previous experience, although still important, were no longer predictors of the ability to carry out the new role. For example, it could not be assumed that recent graduates of information courses would have the requisite IT skills, or be confident enough in their IT knowledge to support users. It is clear that some measure of success has been achieved. Candidates appointed in the first few months since restructuring were drawn from a range of backgrounds – libraries, IT support in the private sector, work-based NVQ IT qualifications, self-employed IT support, learner support in student services. As at Lincoln, applicants did not always fully understand the role from the written information, and the selection event gave them a taste of the duties involved, and of the Department's style and culture, enabling them to decide whether the post suited them.

Throughout the six years since restructuring, recruitment of hybrid skills to the information adviser roles has been relatively easy, although the longstanding problem of filling non-standard hours posts with appropriately skilled and experienced staff, such as weekend only and weekend/weekday, has not improved. This issue continues to grow in significance, as the demands for extending opening hours increase, and the commitment to support learners at times and in ways which meet their needs becomes more pressing. Professionally qualified librarians still dominate the Information Adviser role, but there has clearly been a shift towards employing IT professionals with the capacity to develop the hybrid role.

LEEDS METROPOLITAN UNIVERSITY

The emphasis in recruitment to the Learning and Information Services is on individuals who are multi-skilled to support the customers in the learning centres. Substantial changes have been made to job descriptions to incorporate IT skills, so that these skills are now present in all job descriptions from a scale 2 Learning Centre Assistant and beyond. A graduate trainee scheme is in place offering a year's traineeship followed by a guaranteed place for the one-year Master's course at the

University's School of Information Management. Staff recruited to these posts are a valuable acquisition and the relationship with the school is a fruitful one.

Leeds is a competitive employment market for multi-skilled people, and the University is one of many higher and further education institutions in the Yorkshire area competing for such staff. This seems to have led to a reduction in numbers of applicants for Learning Adviser appointments and, as usual, posts that involve non-standard hours continue to be difficult to fill. IT help assistants were initially mainly part-time and student appointments, who found the technical and customer service experience valuable in gaining other employment after graduation. More recent appointments to these posts have been full-time permanent appointments and these have proved to be most successful.

CONCLUSION

This chapter has explored changing staff roles, their impact on staff skills and development, implications for staff culture, and the new challenges for recruitment and selection. A picture of considerable transformation within the case study organizations has emerged, with new organizational models redefining jobs, focusing on integration, partnership, learning and teaching development, and hybridization of jobs, blurring traditional boundaries. An increasing emphasis on IT-related roles and skills is not surprising, given the growing diversity of electronic forms of information, but it is in support for teaching and learning that some of the most profound changes have occurred. Reflecting back on the Fielden Report and eLib project predictions for the future outlined in the introductory section of this chapter, it can be seen that learner support has indeed been the greatest area of role change. The trends for new skills have continued: teaching, facilitating learning, IT skills, competence in navigating electronic information, team working, innovative management skills, change management, and customer care.

Rather than supporting purely such 'things' as books, journals and PC use, staff now can be seen to be supporting learners and the whole teaching and learning process. There is clearly enthusiasm amongst staff for broadened roles and increased opportunities to contribute, despite the inevitable cultural problems caused by major change. They have a greater awareness and understanding of their role in the work of the University, and of their value to it. Their work with learners is central to the University's success and their roles are 'centred on learning'.

REFERENCES

Allan, B. (1998), From library assistant to service adviser: the role of competences in staff development at the University of Lincolnshire and Humberside. *SCONUL Newsletter*, 14, Summer/Autumn, pp 27–9.

Edwards, C., Day, J.M. and Walton, G. (1998), *Monitoring organizational and cultural change: the impact on people of electronic libraries – the IMPEL2 project*. London: Library Information Technology Centre.

Garrod, P. and Sidgreaves, I. (1998), *Skills for new Information Professionals: the SKIP Project*. [Internet] Bath, UKOLN. Available from: <http://www.ukoln.ac.uk/services/elib/papers/other/skip/> [Accessed 8 January 2002]

John Fielden Consultancy (1993), *Supporting expansion: a report on human resource management in academic libraries, for the Joint Funding Councils' Libraries Review Group*. Bristol: HEFCE.

4   The student experience

Edited by Alison Ward

Contributors:

Leeds Metropolitan University	Katherine Everest and Philip Payne
University of Lincoln	Dilys Young
Sheffield Hallam University	Alison Ward

INTRODUCTION

Academic libraries have always been central to the student experience and continually review and update their service provision to anticipate and respond to its changing needs. This chapter examines the student learning experience and its impact on library services.

The experiences of Sheffield Hallam University, Leeds Metropolitan University and the University of Lincoln are used here to illustrate a learning centre response to these issues. All three enjoy the benefit of modern new buildings and share many similarities in vision and concept; all are strongly user-centred. The contributors to this chapter examine the ways in which services and staff interact with students to support their learning and how students work within the environments created by the new learning centres. They identify what students need from a learning centre and how the learning centres at the three universities have responded to those needs. Separate case studies are included to illustrate in detail some of the services developed to facilitate student learning for particular student groups – distance learners, disabled students, and researchers – and also in extending access to facilities through 24-hour opening.

CONTEXT

THE CHANGING STUDENT PROFILE

The developments and changes in higher education described in Chapter 1 have had a huge impact on the student experience. Government policy on student funding, the phasing out of maintenance grants and the introduction of course fees have all affected student finance, and also perhaps altered the relationship between student and institution. The profile of the student population has changed considerably since the early 1990s, not only in terms of increased numbers but also in the diversity of students. The number of students on part-time courses has increased at a greater rate than for full-time courses. From 1995/96 to 1999/2000 the number of students in higher education increased by 136,236 of which 48 per cent were part time (HESA). Chapter 1 examined the increase in mature (over 21) students and postgraduates. Such students have different needs to full-time undergraduates in library or learning centre terms.

Even full-time students may not be as full-time as they used to be. A study of full-time undergraduates at the University of Northumbria found that 37 per cent of students had term-time jobs and 45 per cent had worked during the academic year (Barke et al., 2000). This study reflects trends towards greater debt and term-time working. Students in focus groups held at Sheffield Hallam University spoke of having to fit their studies around their job rather than the other way round.

The motivation to enter higher education is increasingly about future job prospects and financial rewards. The investment made by students in their course of study and the debts they are likely to incur by the end of their course – currently between £12 000 and £15 000 on average – make students more demanding consumers with high expectations of resources and services.

Other non-traditional groups include disabled students whose numbers have risen considerably in the last few years. Between 1994/95 and 1999/2000 the number of first-year students known to have a disability rose from 15 699 to 26 720, taking the percentage from 2.6 per cent of all first years to 4 per cent. Changes in the patterns of study with distance learning courses and block-mode delivery have increased further the diversity among the student population.

CHANGING LEARNING AND TEACHING METHODS

The underlying shift of emphasis from teaching to learning has significant implications for the way students study and the skills they need to succeed. They must adopt more varied learning styles, such as group work, grasp the potential of e-learning and generally become more independent learners, capable of self-management.

Technological developments have altered the way in which students experience their learning, with e-mail, the Internet and electronic resources necessitating the acquisition of new skills and making access to a PC an essential element. The development and implementation of learning, teaching and assessment strategies by higher education institutions has also focused attention on new ways of interacting with students.

The quality agenda within higher education has put the student experience at the centre of institutional quality procedures and this must be reflected in the adoption of a student-centred approach by academic libraries. To reflect on how far things have changed, it is worth considering the following scenarios:

A typical scenario, 1991:

Student looks at watch, 8.45 am. Joins the queue outside library for 9.00 am opening, dashes in, drops off short-loan item at issue counter just in time. Dashes off to lecture and hopes to be able to come back later in day to pick up more texts between tutorials and lectures. Plans to come back this evening to do a few hours' study before going home to start writing assignment.

Fast forward to 2002:

Student looks at watch, 8.45 am. Wonders if there is time for a visit to refreshment area on the ground floor before lecture; after all, has been working in the learning centre since 5 am this morning to finish this assignment – thank heavens for 24-hour opening. Decides against it, as must e-mail finished assignment to lecturer. Remembers need to book group-study room in learning centre for later today: group project requiring presentation and peer assessment, so will need to spend a good few hours on this later. Plans to come back after lecture to check out the computer-based learning programme on oral presentations to help plan for this afternoon's work ...

THE LEARNING CENTRE RESPONSE

The learning centre approach is one such student-centred response. Its starting point is to look at provision from a student, rather than organizational or service, perspective. The outcome is that learning centres have attempted to adopt the approach of providing a one-stop-shop, where resources, information, IT facilities and support mechanisms are integrated within one building that also provides learning and teaching space for groups as well as individuals. Longer opening hours have been a priority for many institutions; access has also been extended by developing ways to use resources from off-campus. With less time available to spend visiting a learning centre, a student with work or family commitments needs other ways to retrieve material for their course, and students who may study wholly abroad and never visit their home institution need support services in place for their benefit.

Services for a diverse user population have been examined and specific services have been developed for groups of students such as disabled students and distance learners. One effect of widening participation is that students come to higher education with different skills and experience, and learning centres have had to reassess their role in skills teaching and support. They aim to integrate their services and resources into the academic process.

The learning centres at Leeds Metropolitan University, the University of Lincoln and Sheffield Hallam University have moved into new buildings or refurbished old ones and this has given them the opportunity to review services. The organizational frameworks adopted have been discussed in detail in Chapter 2 and the building designs will be examined in Chapter 6, but all have used the students and their needs as the basis for their planning.

The underlying customer-focus of the learning centre model can be illustrated by the approach taken at the University of Lincoln. Here the establishment of a Learning Support centre provided Learning Support (the converged central service department), with the opportunity to focus more closely on the diversity of the student learning experience, as all services were now provided from one building. In addition to Learning Support services, the centre also houses specialist support for disabled students, including an adviser from the central disability unit who is available to meet students referred from any of the helpdesks in the centre. A dedicated distance learner service has also been developed to meet the needs of the growing number of distance learner students in the University. In addition, support has been expanded for research students and research activity undertaken within the faculties.

Intrinsic to the changes in service provision delivered in the new centre is a new staffing structure that focuses staff more closely on the student experience and defines students as 'customers' in order to refocus the relationship. While the usual customer service model associated with areas such as retail work did not completely match that of service provision within an educational establishment, it was a useful metaphor with which staff and students could identify. It also aligned with an increased awareness of students as consumers, especially since the introduction of tuition fees. In addition, every member of Learning Support staff had experiences of what it felt like to be a customer and were able to bring these to discussions about realigning services to be more customer-focused.

Behind this new focus was the intention to provide a one-stop-shop to information within the centre, while at the same time setting up a range of quality assurance mechanisms to ensure that the service was responsive to student learning needs. An increased number of feedback mechanisms were introduced to monitor the delivery of the service, including service standards and sector comparisons to chart progress and continuous improvement.

To successfully implement this change of focus, a structured staff development programme was established (see Chapter 3, pp. 79–81). This enabled staff from previously separate arms of the department (IT, library, media and modern languages support) to work together to develop a common approach to enquiry work and effective communication with students. It involved exploring how to support the 'customer as learner' and promote student independence through individualizing the response to enquiries and understanding more widely a range of learning styles that might affect student take-up of the range of available learning opportunities.

A large new Learning Support centre brings its own problems as customer expectations rise and staff struggle to develop new working practices in a changed environment. However, increased customer feedback has encouraged the development of new services that align more closely with changing student needs, and the move into the new centre has provided staff with the opportunity to change procedures and become more customer-focused and supportive of the increasingly diverse student population.

WHAT DO STUDENTS NEED?

Academic support services must deliver on a number of fronts if they are to satisfy the needs of the student learning experience:

- access to the full range of information and learning resources appropriate to individual programmes of study
- access to the IT resources that now underpin almost every aspect of students' learning experience
- the skills to use these resources effectively
- a study environment to accommodate the different modes of learning, including interaction with other students or teaching staff
- staff support to resolve individual problems and offer more general guidance to enable students to use the resources effectively
- an awareness on the part of students of the facilities, resources and services available and the means to influence provision
- access to these facilities, resources and services at the times of day and days of the week compatible with students' study, family and work commitments.

There are many issues arising from these needs. Learning centres need to acquire relevant information resources and make them accessible for as long a time as possible on or off campus, support students in their use and teach students to use them effectively. They need to provide the right sort of working environments to facilitate learning and group work, and they need to anticipate future developments in learning needs. Each of these issues is now examined, together with a learning centre response.

INFORMATION RESOURCES

The range of resources available to students is now vast and encompasses, videos, broadcasts and computer-based learning packages, databases, and Internet sites, as well as the traditional media of books and journals. An indication of relative use is provided from the Sheffield Hallam Learning Centre annual survey, which asks students what they had done or used on a particular visit: 57.5 per cent had searched the catalogue; 48.1 per cent had borrowed or returned books; 23.4 per cent had used electronic information databases and 16.1 per cent the Learning Centre web pages; 6.6 per cent had used computer-based learning software, and 5.4 per cent had watched videos.

Books

Students still want books: 'more copies of books; more up-to-date books; more rapid reshelving of books; more liaison with lecturers to ensure that reading list books are in the libraries' (Horrocks, 1998, p. 22). Academic libraries have well-developed strategies to manage the circulation of book stock, although no entirely satisfactory way has been found to meet heavy student demand for core texts. The financial situation of many students has made it more difficult for them to buy their own copies of textbooks and access to books remains a difficult problem which has been exacerbated by the shorter time periods of modules delivered in semesterized systems. The delivery of this material electronically is the obvious answer, with electronic reserve collections and projects such as HERON having a growing impact, although they do raise a number of issues, including the transfer of costs to students, through printing (Kingston, 1998).

Electronic journals

These have proved to be a very useful addition to the range of resources and have extended the journal literature considerably for libraries and learning centres that have not traditionally supported research collections. Services such as Emerald from MCB University Press and IDEAL from Academic Press, as well as the access offered via Ingenta, Swetsnet and Science Direct, have greatly extended access for both multiple concurrent users and also off-campus users, in addition to widening the information base of students, researchers and staff.

Databases

Now accessible to the end user without the mediation of staff, the resources provided by databases can greatly enhance the student's learning experience. Full-text journal databases are now used extensively in some subject areas and students are coming to expect this type of delivery – indeed they can be very disappointed when a recommended database produces bibliographical details and abstracts only. Some databases can be integrated into a course programme and provide raw data for analysis or as a simulation of a real-life situation. For example, databases such as Mintel or Datastream can provide students with experience of information like that used by commercial organizations; and projects to produce business or market plans are thus made more realistic and applicable to the environment in which they may work in future.

The most significant developments for electronic resources are integrative: aggregation by commercial suppliers, their presentation on the desktop, their inclusion in the broader information landscape, common search interfaces, linkages between bibliographic records, full-text and document delivery. The Distributed National Electronic Resource, a major element of the new Joint Information Systems Committee strategy (2001), represents a significant development in this respect, with its aim of providing a resource which appears seamless to the user. The Elib Hybrid libraries programme has also taken forward this agenda.

Many libraries and learning centres have made significant local progress in helping students and academic staff navigate around the various systems on offer. Lists of e-journals organized by subject or title, with links to the relevant web site guide the user. E-journals are often catalogued in the same way as print journals and hypertext links are added to catalogue records to take users as directly as possible to the journal title.

Leeds Metropolitan University have developed 'Learning Centre Online' to provide access to information resources, help and support, and (through 'Skills Online') access to materials to support the development of key skills. One of the sections within this system contains subject guides for novices or experts, which describe and provide links to relevant databases. The Learning Centre at Sheffield Hallam University has developed a database of databases which also contains a search skills element. ERIS (Electronic Resources/Information Skills) lists databases by several criteria – title, subject, off-campus, and new – and provides further information on the contents, coverage and password requirements of each one. Databases are assigned relevancy indicators so that, within a subject grouping, students can sort the list by relevancy to their subject area thus avoiding long lists in alphabetical order.

INFORMATION TECHNOLOGY

The student experience in accessing the information resources of learning centres may be little different than that of any academic library. However, use of information technology, and indeed its integration with those information resources, is more distinctive. As Chapter 1 made clear, IT is now well-integrated in higher education and is one of the core competencies a student must acquire. Furthermore, the introduction of virtual learning environments, e-mail and computer conferencing, and the web delivery of materials have made access to computers a core requirement for students.

Learning centres are well placed to support this rapid increase in the use of communications and information technology (C&IT) through the location within their buildings of PCs and support staff. Extended opening hours and the availability of staff help for long periods, together with the opportunity to combine PC use with other learning tasks, provide the integrated and supportive environment many students need. The Student Experience Survey conducted at Sheffield Hallam University in 2000 showed that students used PCs mainly within the learning centres even though computer suites were provided in other buildings.

Student use of IT within learning centres is varied, but e-mail and the Internet figure prominently. The annual user survey for 2001 at Sheffield Hallam University's Learning Centre showed that, on visits to learning centres in the survey period, 78 per cent of respondents replied that they had used e-mail, 72.2 per cent the Internet, and 51.9 per cent Office software including Word, Excel and PowerPoint.

The use of learning technologies in higher education is already changing the student learning experience and increasing pressure on IT resources. Physical access to the technology is one of the most frequent issues to emerge from student feedback, very often as a complaint about the availability of PCs during the busiest parts of the day. Increasing the number of PCs in learning centres is the obvious option, but initial and replacement costs can be prohibitive and the benefits in terms of students' perception are doubtful. Extended opening of learning centre buildings does increase seat hours – and some students are prepared to work at 3.00 am – however, it cannot provide a completely satisfactory solution. And, although booking systems are also used to control access, their management and policing can add considerably to staff workloads and stress levels. The rise in personal ownership of computers can create different demands, whether for better off-campus access or different on-campus facilities. Demand for plug-in facilities, with associated technical complexities, is increasing; wireless access is already here.

Student use of IT facilities can itself be a topic of concern. Use of e-mail and the Internet has shown a substantial increase over the last few years and in addition to academic use, its recreational use can cause resentment to other students trying to find a computer, particularly at busy times. In practice, however, the increasingly pervasive use of e-mail as a learning tool makes it very difficult to prevent its social use.

A research investigation into computer-mediated conferencing observed and interviewed students working in the Adsetts Centre at Sheffield Hallam University. Monteith and Smith (2001, p.126) discuss the issue of the students' use of e-mail and suggest that, it 'now has become a vital part of students' experience'. E-mail was used to communicate with lecturers, for peer group communication on projects, and also for social purposes, with family and friends (this was especially important for international students). Monteith and Smith found that students were multi-tasking and going into their e-mail as a break from work. The researchers found that this evolving use of e-mail contrasted with the opinion of staff in learning centres and computer rooms that e-mail activity should be work related.

The social use of learning centre buildings is discussed in more detail in Chapter 6.

IT SKILLS

Many students now arrive in higher education with good IT skills and surveys at both Sheffield Hallam University and Leeds Metropolitan University indicate that around 78 per cent of students have access to a PC outside their university and, of these, around 55 per cent have Internet access. Levels of IT literacy are varied in new students and this seems to vary from course to course. However, even where students have previous experience of IT, this may be from a leisure perspective and does not necessarily mean they can use the technologies for the purpose of learning. For instance, students using what is a favourite search engine for non-academic purposes can have problems when it fails to retrieve material for an assignment. Nor does students' experience of recreational e-mailing appear to automatically bestow confidence in computer conferences.

For those student groups who have been out of the educational system for some years the changes in learning and teaching methods can cause problems. Strategies to help students learn to use IT include providing detailed guides to various software applications and common procedures, such as saving work and transferring files, and holding drop-in sessions regularly throughout semester for individual help.

The converged services used in many learning centres enable students to find IT help and support within the building, and information desks tend to deal with as many computer-related enquiries as information-related ones.

At Leeds Metropolitan University, Learning and Information Services, the converged central service, of which Learning Support Services is a part, is responsible for IT training of academic staff; the University's schools have responsibility for teaching IT skills to students. As many courses have compulsory IT modules, some students receive an excellent introduction to IT. Others, however, receive little or no training; which has significant implications for their studies, as they will be routinely required to use IT for word processing, spreadsheets and presentations. Furthermore, when students do not have basic IT skills it places a considerable burden on the help and support available in the learning centres.

Within Learning and Information Services, the Learning Support Services department is working on a pilot with two schools of study – Health Sciences, and Tourism and Hospitality Management – to establish a University scheme to address these issues. It has been agreed that a range of generic IT competencies that equate to those of the European Computing Driving Licence (ECDL) is required. These competencies will later be applied within the context of an individual student's course of study. The IT skills project involves diagnostic testing of all new students on Web-CT, the University's virtual learning environment. Students then have a choice between self-instructional materials with support clinics, or attendance at a class. Staff from Harrogate College (the further education faculty of the University) deliver the classes in the learning centre. Successful completion of the course leads to the ECDL. Health Science students who choose the self-instruction route use learning materials on Web-CT, while Tourism and Hospitality Management use a web-based package called 'Learn ECDL'. All students are required to log onto Web-CT regularly and undertake module tests so that progress can be tracked. Special provision is made for those who are new to computers or have limited confidence in using IT. Harrogate College offers six-hour primers to get students started. The pilot is at an early stage, but it represents a major example of effective partnership between Learning Support Services, Harrogate College, and the University's schools.

STUDENT INFORMATION SKILLS

Information literacy is regarded as a key skill nationally and the concept of lifelong learning and transferable skills has moved the acquisition of skills high on the agenda in higher education. As described in Chapter 1, in an information-driven, increasingly global society it is not feasible for students to graduate with just a core of knowledge in one subject area; that will not sustain them throughout their chosen career. Employers are seeking to recruit graduates skilled in manipulating and utilizing information to support their work, rather than someone with a static knowledge of facts and processes.

Information skills are therefore an essential element of student learning. They encompass the identification of information needs, the identification and selection of relevant sources, the ability to construct search strategies, sound judgement about information retrieved and the organization, presentation and referencing of the information. These skills have always been important but the need for students to operate effectively in the electronic environment makes them even more crucial. The SCONUL (2000) discussion paper on supporting the E-University identifies how the move to Internet-based information sources removes the usual safety barriers found in libraries – where everything was carefully selected, evaluated and catalogued. Today, students need to be equipped with the skills to deal with largely unfiltered information and to be able to use retrieval tools that can be hopelessly inaccurate in the hands of the unskilled user. The vast amount of information available electronically, especially in the Internet environment, can overwhelm many students, whose searching strategies may have been limited to a single search engine. The ability to evaluate the information is also an essential element, given the nature and quality of some web sites. The move towards student-centredness in learning, therefore, necessitates a fairly sophisticated level of familiarity with, and confidence in using, learning resources. It is unlikely that many students will arrive in higher education with these skills.

How do students learn to use the resources and facilities available to them? Many academic libraries have seen it as their role to provide training and guidance to students to enable them to find their way around the information resources effectively and become more confident as independent learners. As can be seen below, this extends from basic orientation to information literacy, and employs various modes of delivery, including taught sessions and workshops, interactive learning packages and written guides. The aim of enabling students to be competent and confident users of information is central to the learning centre approach.

Induction and orientation

The first, immediate priority is one of familiarization: to make students aware of systems and services so that they can begin to use them at the very beginning of their course. Induction also provides the opportunity for students to meet the member of staff responsible for their subject area. Students need enough information to start using the system but too much will leave them confused. This introduction is equally important for postgraduates, as some may have been away from formal education for some time, may have done a first degree at a different institution with a different type of library, or may not have a first degree.

These induction sessions have been provided for many years by libraries but have had to change in a number of ways. The increase in student numbers and the large size of some courses have meant that tours of the building have largely been dropped. Student feedback may indicate that this is one aspect they would like to be included in their orientation but in practice it is no longer feasible, both in terms of staff time and in the disruption it would create within the building. Lecture-style talks are the norm in many institutions and the use of IT – for example, Powerpoint demonstrations, video tours and online demonstrations of the campus network – can to some degree make up for the lack of a tour. The location of teaching rooms within learning centres has meant that a visit to the building has at least been part of the process.

Induction sessions are not just about processing large numbers of students. Specific groups such as distance learners or disabled students need sessions tailored to their own particular requirements.

Information skills

It can be more difficult to meet student needs for more in-depth knowledge of using the resources at the time they need it. Ideally, given the varying levels of information literacy of new students, this needs to be flexible, self-paced, and with the opportunity to return to it when needed. Students need to be able to see the relevance in this training and to gain skills that can be transferred to all areas of their course and beyond. These skills also need to develop progressively throughout their course. Libraries and learning centres have used various methods to provide this training, some of which are given below.

Taught sessions Many students get instruction as a timetabled activity, integrated into the curriculum, sometimes as a section of a first-year IT or wider skills unit. The indications are, however, that many students do not use electronic resources much and may reach dissertation stage having not used databases in the intervening time. Information skills training, in common with other skills training, is more and more being integrated into subject-based units, rather than separated out as part of a general skills course. It can then be related to a specific assignment, with collection of data as one of the learning outcomes. The relevance of the information sources is more obvious, and motivation to learn about them greater, if their use is assessed.

The workshop mode of delivery allows students the opportunity to work at their own pace or as part of a group, and allows different learning styles to be used. It also allows hands-on experience of using electronic sources and is preferable to a lecture style of teaching. It is, however, very intensive in staff time.

Drop-in sessions At Leeds Metropolitan University a programme of 'Know-it-All' classes is delivered covering key areas of information skills, where students can drop in to learn about areas they may have missed or about which they feel less confident. Know-it-Alls are now available on video and on the web; print and web-based documentation supports most areas and self-instructional materials, such as an audio tour, have been developed to enable students to learn when and how they prefer. At the University of Lincoln a Skills Zone has been developed to bring together a range of study guides, including software manuals, user guides, quick reference material and generic study skills materials, along with a staffed helpdesk. Sessions on IT skills (Confident Computing), and information skills are held. These allow students an opportunity to revisit skills training at a time when they need them.

Guides Every academic library will have a range of help sheets, handouts and printed guides to inform users about resources and their use. The advent of web page guides now means that guidance is available more readily. In the case of electronic resources, consultation can be integrated more with the use of the databases themselves. Leeds Metropolitan University has developed a range of electronic services, notably 'Learning Centre Online', the philosophy of which is to replicate in an electronic environment the support and services available from the physical learning centres. The intention is that 'Learning Centre On-line' will allow those with access to the web to find information, gain assistance, and tap into a range of learning support facilities when and where they wish. Additional support is built in to take account of the fact that students may not have the competencies and confidence to use them effectively. So, for example, not only is access to electronic abstracts and indexes provided, but also a support page for 'novice' users which explains what these resources are and how they can be used.

Interactive learning packages Interactive packages are now being developed to allow students to work at their own pace through a system that integrates exercises and provides feedback. One such resource developed at Sheffield Hallam University is InfoQuest, which is discussed in more detail in Chapter 5 (pp. 141–4). This is an interactive learning package consisting of five modules: the Catalogue, Literature Searching, Information Databases, the Internet and the Finished Product, which covers issues such as plagiarism, bibliographies and copyright. InfoQuest allows students to work at their own pace and in their own time and also to revisit sections when they need to refresh their knowledge. Feedback from the initial trial was positive and unit leaders reported that student work had shown an increased level of awareness of information skills.

Learning Support Services at Leeds Metropolitan University has also developed learning systems to allow students to develop a range of skills for their course and beyond. Skills for Learning is a web-based package covering eight major themes: study skills, information and research, using IT, teaching and learning, group skills, assessment, personal development and employability skills. Academic staff working collaboratively with Learning Support Services have developed the Skills for Learning resources (Anderson and Douglas, 1998). This partnership approach has encouraged a high degree of ownership of the system, integration of its use into students' everyday work, and appropriate content. The package offers support through accompanying videos, guides and workpacks, books and IT packages; again, allowing students flexibility of learning. A web-based package devised by Queensland University of Technology for the development of information literacy skills has also been adapted for use by the University students. The Pilot module helps students acquire the skills necessary to conduct research for tutorials, assignments and dissertations.

Additionally, systems like the Resource Discovery Network Virtual Training Suite and the Internet Detective on SOSIG, the Social Sciences portal, are freely available and have been used extensively in many universities.

Integration into teaching

The support systems described above have been designed with flexibility in mind, but they will often not be used unless students perceive them to be central to their course of study; information handling and research skills need to be integrated into the curriculum at a time when students need to use them. For example, at Leeds, where the second year BA Business Studies students are taught about the current European Motor Industry in the early stages of their Business Simulation module, timely input from a Learning Support Services' Learning Adviser makes the students aware of the resources available to them from an early stage of the module. This early intervention enhances their achievement of the learning outcomes. The School of Information Management has taken a slightly different approach, whereby all first-year students are introduced to the skills and resources they need in the first-year Professional Skills and Personal Development module. The skills learnt are then incorporated into all the other modules that they study concurrently. Both approaches develop skills that students need for the duration of their course and enable them to use individual resources necessary to their research in the short term. However, more importantly, the aim is that students develop the ability to transfer these skills.

Given the huge amount of information available to students via the Internet, the development of critical faculties is a necessary and useful skill. Ottewill and Macfarlane (2001, p. 48) discuss the necessity for students to 'develop their critical faculties with respect to the purpose, as well as the substance, of the material to which they are exposed and the sources they are required to tap as an integral part of their learning experience', and goes on to emphasize the importance of collaboration between teaching staff and information specialists.

Students need the freedom to explore the wealth of information so easily accessible via the Internet, but may need help and guidance to achieve a balance in this. Information literacy training that aims to guide students towards quality-controlled web resources and gateways such as the RDN subject portals should also include the Ask Jeeves or Google approach to information gathering. Guides to web resources in different subject areas, inclusion of links to valuable web sites in the catalogue, on reading lists and in guided e-learning sites such as Blackboard and Web-CT resources sections are also used to encourage good practice in using the Internet as an information source. The acquisition of information skills should perhaps be regarded in the same way as that of other skills – as something which develops over a period of time – and the input into a student's course needs to be at an appropriate pace: more targeted guidance for first-year students, especially for their first assignment, with further opportunities for exploration as their course progresses.

WORKING ENVIRONMENT

Students need a variety of physical spaces and facilities to accommodate a wide range of learning activities, both individual and group-based. For example, responses to the 2001 SHU Learning Centre User Survey indicated that on the day that they completed the questionnaire, 56.5 per cent of students had used learning centres for silent or private study, and 28.1 per cent for group study. The needs that fit least comfortably in academic libraries are probably those associated with group work. Students need to meet together to discuss group projects, to practise presentations and to have group access to other facilities such as video playback, live satellite programmes and IT resources. At the same time, they want to be able to work comfortably on their own. Many are happy with some background noise; others need a quiet or silent environment.

One consequence of introducing group areas is that the noise created can spill into the quiet areas. This is discussed in more detail in Chapter 6 with regard to overall building design, but student perception of the issue of noise in the working environment is the concern of this chapter. At Sheffield Hallam University's Adsetts Centre, the response of students has been mixed and hard to interpret. Staff–student committees and other school-based feedback mechanisms have been critical, especially, as can be expected, from final-year student groups, but responses to the larger student surveys give a somewhat different picture. The 2001 Learning Centre survey showed that 31.9 per cent of students thought that noise was a problem, yet 39.7 per cent did not. Another issue relating to the question of noise has been the use of mobile phones – a problem not restricted to learning centres and libraries in higher education. Again, student opinion on this is split, with the Learning Centre User Survey showing a growing tolerance of them – 53.9 per cent of respondents finding mobile phones distracting in 2001 compared to 64.7 per cent in 2000. However, the opinion of the majority continues to find them a nuisance.

Student perceptions of noise levels are also affected by factors such as age and level of student. Surveys of postgraduates and researchers show a much higher level of dissatisfaction with noise and mobile phones. The University's Postgraduate Experience Surveys for both taught and research postgraduates highlighted noise levels as an area of considerable dissatisfaction.

The learning centres at Leeds Metropolitan University have had similar experiences to those of Sheffield Hallam. In 1996, Beckett Park Learning Centre was designed to include 15 group study rooms, reflecting the emerging emphasis on group study work. However, demand for these was great, with an overspill moving into quiet and silent study space and disrupting students wishing to study quietly. The University learnt from that experience and included eight group study rooms on every floor (total 24) of the new City Campus learning centre, together with separate print/photocopy rooms to distance the noise from the equipment and from queuing students. The success of this approach was reflected to some extent in the 2001 Libra survey, where 28 per cent of users thought Beckett Park learning centre to be too noisy, in comparison with only 19 per cent at City Campus. Although this shows that the design of the building can help, noise is still perceived by many students to be a problem. There are many benefits to bringing together under one roof different forms of learning support, but one significant disadvantage is that users who used to have a shared understanding of acceptable behaviour in a library, no longer have a common understanding of acceptable behaviour within a learning centre.

STAFF SUPPORT

Academic libraries have a strong tradition of providing direct support for student information needs at enquiry or information desks and in developing student information skills. Students nowadays have many more support needs, some of which, like remote support via e-mail, just extend this basic model, others which may be beyond the accepted skill base and role of Library and Information Services (LIS) staff. Where general purpose IT facilities are available, students will require guidance on using applications software, on basic operational functions and on the diagnosis of problems, both hardware and software related. The extent to which LIS staff can support student learning is a much bigger issue, as it could be seen to encroach on the responsibilities of teaching staff. And yet there is undoubtedly a need for this support in libraries and learning centres. The reduction in contact time with teaching staff and the growth in resource-based and independent learning shift the focus of student learning even more into libraries and learning centres. This trend is likely to accelerate as learning materials are delivered through virtual learning environments.

The learning centre approach, with its emphasis on holistic and integrated provision of integrated resources, forces these issues to the forefront. Its focus on different staff models and a greater integration of support within teaching programmes provides a distinctive way of addressing them.

Direct support (one-to-one)

The staffing models described in Chapter 3 are based on the principle that students want one place to visit for help with their questions and problems. They do not pretend to be able to satisfy all of these on the spot, but they do provide students with a first contact point for help and management of their queries through referral on to other specialized services within and beyond learning centres.

Electronic and distant access

Academic libraries have developed various models to provide support for off-campus users, or students studying outside opening hours. The electronic enquiry desk has been one response. A study at Sheffield Hallam University identified various models in operation. These include e-mail links either to a given address, a mail-to link from a web page or an electronic form; frequently asked questions databases or lists; chat facilities; and video conferencing. There are also collaborative ventures like the 'Ask-

A-Librarian' scheme of EARL (Electronic Access to Resources in Libraries), or the 'follow the sun' approach piloted by the Library of Congress.

At Leeds Metropolitan University, Learning Support Services delivers support to students who rarely or never come on to campus in a variety of ways. The 'Offsite' service provides a tailored package of services to support the course-related learning; these include an enquiry service, postal book loans, journal article supply, help in accessing other libraries, and database searches. Off-campus users can also access academic information sources, help and support, and materials for the development of key skills through 'Learning Centre Online'. A dedicated telephone and e-mail enquiry service has improved the response to enquiries from off-campus users.

These initiatives have been complemented by the growth of reciprocal arrangements, which have delivered substantially enhanced access to library facilities. The most significant example of this is UK Libraries Plus, a reciprocal borrowing scheme for part-time and distance learning students, which counts over a hundred higher education libraries as members, and continues to grow. There are now moves to develop a similar scheme for access to IT facilities, as students increasingly depend upon virtual learning environments.

Support for learning

For those students who are campus-based, learning centre buildings increase the scope for learning support by bringing together all forms of curriculum-related support into one environment. This, in turn, facilitates collaborative approaches to support with other providers; for example, all three universities featured in this chapter provide services for disabled students within their learning centres. Specialized hardware and software resources are supported jointly by learning centre staff and university student services staff.

The Adsetts Centre at Sheffield Hallam University houses a Learning Help area, which is staffed by lecturers and support staff at regular times for any student to receive individual advice and help, for example with maths and writing. The University's Student Services Centre also holds weekly 'Skills for Learning' sessions in the building that are supported by providing targeted resources in forms such as related books, audiocassettes and videos available via a broadband network as part of an 'LCTV' channel. Workshops are provided on reading and taking notes, managing workloads, writing assignments, motivation, presentation skills and preparing for exams.

At Leeds Metropolitan University, the faculties of Information and Engineering Systems, and Health and Environment have their own facilities within learning centres. A bookshop, operated by John Smith Retail, is located in the Beckett Park learning centre and the bookshop at City Campus is located adjacent to the learning centre in the Leslie Silver Building. Students now perceive that there is a single source of support for independent learning, bringing all the vast majority of the facilities together in one place.

Support within the curriculum

LIS staff increasingly support learning within the curriculum through teaching on units such as research methods or dissertations units, literature searching and referencing, and also on individual units which require particular types of resources. One such unit at Sheffield Hallam University is a second-level unit on a Finance programme called Principles of Investment. The assessment for this unit is a report to the manager of a unit trust advising on investment strategies for which students need to research the Stock Market and monitor the performance of companies before choosing an investment portfolio. Learning Centre staff teach students how to use Datastream, an online investment tool, and how to analyse and present data using the Datastream system. The teaching sessions are run jointly with lecturing staff who can help provide expert financial analysis of the data. The assessment criteria include the use made of this resource and how the data was presented. Staff in learning centres continue to help students with this work after the initial training has been given and advise on its use.

The inclusion of the Information Specialist on course planning committees and programme review committees gives the opportunity for learning centre staff to be involved with the design or re-evaluation of a course and facilitates the integration of resources and information literacy skills into the curriculum.

The increasing use of virtual learning environments such as Blackboard and Web-CT (see above) provides an opportunity for learning centres to give support through the medium used daily by the students. Guidance on resources and the integration of information literacy programmes are one way forward in providing students with the support and guidance they need.

COMMUNICATION BETWEEN THE LEARNING CENTRE AND THE STUDENT BODY

The explicit customer focus associated with learning centre provision brings communication and consultation with the student body at or near the top of the agenda. It is not just that students need to be made aware of facilities and resources; they need to have the means of influencing provision.

Communication with and through academic staff is crucial. They define much of the student learning experience and have a strong influence on student expectations and perceptions. This informal and formal liaison is at the heart of the role of the Information Specialist described in Chapter 5 (pp. 138–41).

Attendance of learning centre staff at school or faculty boards and committees is particularly important, whether to provide the opportunity to contribute to developments at the planning stage, or to become a part of the feedback process. After all, it is here that student concerns are raised and formally minuted.

Many libraries undertake annual surveys of customer satisfaction, which can confirm staff perceptions or identify issues needing investigation. They are usually influential with institutional decision-makers. Software such as Libra, which is used by Leeds Metropolitan University, the University of Lincoln and Sheffield Hallam University, provides sophisticated indications of student perceptions and also enables trends to emerge. University-wide student surveys tend to include library and learning centre facilities and services as part of their questionnaires and these too can provide interesting, though usually not detailed, data which are broken down by undergraduate, postgraduate and researcher.

Quality indicators feature in many annual reviews of services and some services produce student charters and service level agreements to formalize some of their activities. It is important to use the communication channels and formats that students will use for other aspects of their experience. While there is a continuing role for service-owned publications such as web pages, integration into school of study communication tools, student e-mail conferences and the virtual learning environment are likely to be more effective.

Informal and direct means of interaction with users are particularly effective, providing action is carried through and communicated. Student panels, staff–student consultative meetings and both paper and electronic comments forms are common. These give students the opportunity to raise issues with service staff directly and for staff to respond or seek more information – a useful mechanism that enables them to delve deeper and investigate issues that often surface in a general way in a wider survey, such as 'not enough books for my course'. Comments forms provide a valuable form of communication with students, as well as providing information and feedback to the learning centre. For example, at Sheffield Hallam University a large percentage of responses concerning extended opening hours helped to inform decisions on which weeks to focus limited resources for 24-hour opening.

The challenge is to interpret this feedback and, in consultation with academic staff in schools and departments, translate it into action plans. Limited resources require a balanced approach to ensure that vocal and articulate groups do not give misleading pictures of demand. Below is an account of how Learning Support Services at Leeds Metropolitan University approach the issue of communication with their users.

Communication and integration at Leeds Metropolitan University

Academic staff play a crucial role in ensuring that the facilities, resources, and expertise available through the learning centres are integrated into the students' learning experience. The staff of Learning Support Services at Leeds Metropolitan University work very closely with the staff and managers of the faculties and schools to achieve this. One of the primary roles of the Learning Advisers within Learning Support Services, for example, is to work together with academic staff to ensure that awareness of learning support is promoted and that the use of learning resources is integrated throughout the academic curriculum.

Liaison and communication is evolving along a spectrum from academic liaison, through partnership with the academic community, to achieving effective integration of learning support in the design and delivery of learning. The current focus is predominantly upon partnership, with a number of initiatives being pursued to achieve closer partnership arrangements and to enable better management of expectations. This partnership approach can be seen in formal agreements such as the Collection Development and Information Access Policy statements, the aim of which is to facilitate agreement between academic staff and Learning Advisers on priorities for information access and collection development. It facilitates management of expectations by outlining a picture of current spending, profiling the range of resources to which students require access, identifying priorities for improvement, and noting other issues relating to information access. Once agreement has been reached, the Learning Adviser and head of school sign off the document. It is then used to guide decision-making about expenditure of the school's allocation for information access.

Learning Support Services has also entered a dialogue with its users through the development and implementation of services standards. In 1996, Library Services, Computing Services, and Media and Education Services worked together with academic staff to reach a Service Level Agreement – the first between the converged academic support service unit and its clients. Since then, the division has been restructured and responsibilities reallocated. As a result, Learning Support Services drew up its own completely new set of service standards for its learning centres in summer 2001. Again, these were drawn up in partnership with users; but this time, greater emphasis was placed on student input. The issues to be included in the new service standards were drawn from evaluation work undertaken directly with users: focus interviews, customer comments and the results of Libra-user satisfaction surveys. This ensured the inclusion of those areas that are important to service users. Functional teams of staff then set their own standards and established their targets, which had to be realistic in terms of being achievable, yet challenging enough to be part of the culture of continuous improvement. This engaged staff in the routine process of reviewing and developing their work. The process benefited staff, who no longer perceived the standards as being an end in themselves but as being of use in their work; and benefited users, who now feel that they have a say in the running of one of their support services.

As well as formal partnership agreements, Learning Support Services assesses user needs through a number of different surveys. As at Sheffield Hallam, a Priority Search Libra Survey is carried out with students, allowing them to identify and prioritize their own service improvement agenda. In addition, approximately a quarter of the University's Annual Student Satisfaction Survey is taken up with learning support issues, which presents a university-wide perspective on key issues of interest. Learning Support Services is also part of a benchmarking consortium with three other new universities, which allows comparisons of levels of service and satisfaction across the sector. These are regular surveys that allow Learning Support Services to track progress in addressing issues and to make use of existing mechanisms for comparison. Additionally, customer comments cards are always available for users to feed in any comments that they may have. It is, of course, necessary to complete the feedback loop by communicating to participants the results of these surveys, and any action taken as a result. This is done through posters, displays, web pages, and dissemination through University and faculty committees.

Other investigative studies and surveys take place on specific issues. It is from one of these that Learning Support Services has discovered that there are significant issues around the awareness and take-up of electronic information services (Hewitson, 2000). As a result, steps have been taken for better promotion and integration of electronic services. The University's School of Information Management has been commissioned to undertake further investigative work into the impact on students' learning of e-services provided by Learning Support Services.

All Learning Advisers are members of course committees and Senior Learning Advisers are members of faculty committees. This enables them to fulfil the dual role of listening to users and feeding back information from Learning Support Services. As such, they provide a vital interface between the two. However, Learning Support Services is just part of the wider converged Learning and Information Services division, and often its public face. Learning Advisers consequently have to promote and discuss developments in the sister units for which they are not directly responsible, or may not have full information. This has led to the recognition of the need for excellent lateral communication within the whole division, an issue that is still being addressed.

EXTENDING AND ADAPTING ACCESS TO BETTER MEET USER NEEDS

In Chapter 1 the changing profile of the student body was discussed and the changes identified indicated an increasing flexibility in learning, with more part-time and distance learning students coming into higher education. Family and work commitments were also identified as factors that led to an increased need for more flexible access to resources. Academic libraries have worked towards extending access in a number of ways, including off-campus and web delivery of resources and by extending opening hours; however, full 24-hour opening of libraries is unusual, as the perception has been that demand is largely for IT resources. Opening IT rooms overnight has been an option employed by some institutions, but this is really only a minimalist approach to meeting student learning needs. It is here that the learning centre concept, in terms of providing integrated access to information, IT and learning materials comes into its own. As can be seen from the experience of the Learning Centre at Sheffield Hallam University (described below), it is possible to provide round-the-clock access to all of these resources.

Responses to the SHU Learning Centre annual user survey had consistently identified demand for longer opening hours as a way to extend access to resources. Of particular interest and significance was the priority given to information resources, not just to IT facilities. Funding was obtained to introduce continuous opening (except for Friday and Saturday nights) at two of the three learning centres for a trial period during the core teaching weeks in the 2000/01 academic year. Planning involved consultation and visits to other institutions, including retailing organizations such as Tesco, which already had experience of 24-hour opening. An external security specialist company was employed. This arrangement allowed reference use to paper resources and unsupported access to networked IT facilities and resources. Access was limited to staff and students of the University.

Entry figures showed a steady increase in usage from 657 in the first week of operation to a peak of 4068 by the beginning of December. The total number of entries in the first semester to mid-December was 29 802 across both campuses. The time of signing in showed a peak in the hours between 21.00 and midnight, with numbers dropping off significantly between midnight and 6.00, before increasing again.

Evaluation of the project included a user survey conducted during the first semester. Analysis by mode of attendance showed that of those returning a completed questionnaire only 1.9 per cent were part-time and 0.4 per cent were on distance learning courses. This was an unexpected result as these groups were expected to make up a higher proportion of users.

Not surprisingly, students' reasons for visiting the learning centres were predominantly study-related, with 48.9 per cent reporting that their reason for visiting was to work on an assignment, especially word processing it. Other work included 19.2 per cent using print resources – reading, researching, and using journals or key texts; 13.4 per cent visited to use e-mail or the Internet. When asked where they would have usually done this work, 68 per cent responded that they could not have done it elsewhere and that they needed to use University facilities.

Students also gave the following reasons for using the learning centres at night:

- availability of computers – 62.2 per cent reported that machines were not available at other times or that network speed was better at night;
- better working environment – 58 per cent of respondents expressed this opinion (night times were less noisy, there was a more conducive working atmosphere, and fewer distractions);

- other commitments during the day including family and employment, but also timetabling issues including the lack of continuous working time between lectures; and
- some students simply felt that they worked better at night.

Where students reported that they had access to a computer at home, reasons for using learning centre facilities included that the University had better resources, the working environment was better, and that they wanted to use the Internet.

Evening and weekend opening had always been based on the principle that the level of staff support should be as near as possible to that provided during weekday, daytime. The impact of having only a security presence overnight was therefore of concern. The majority of students answering questions on support had not needed help, although a sizeable minority had. Their difficulties ranged from log-in problems to system crashes, not being able to borrow books and lack of guidance in using resources. The issue of not being able to borrow books was addressed by the installation of a self-issue machine at one of the campuses; another one is planned for the other campus during 2001/02. Staff support is, however, more intractable.

Other issues raised by students included concerns over security and safety in getting to and from learning centres. Requests for better lighting in proximity to the buildings, security cameras, car parking and public transport issues were mentioned as problems and this also affected which learning centre some students chose to use at night. In the light of this, some students raised the possibility of providing key texts to support subjects not taught at that campus. The provision of refreshments was also mentioned; although both the learning centres housed drinks and snacks machines, students requested that machines be kept well stocked and provide food and hot drinks too.

The trial of 24-hour opening was judged to be extremely successful from the students' perspective. Unsurprisingly, however, it was not long before requests were being made to include Friday and Saturday nights in the scheme. All of the students in the focus groups held to investigate perceptions of the learning centre for this chapter valued 24-hour opening and one, part-time with a job, said: 'The 24-hour opening was a godsend. It should be extended to all week and particularly open all year.'

From 2001/02, 24-hour opening has been consolidated into the pattern of learning centre opening hours – on the same basis as in 2000/01, with some minor alterations to the weeks during which it operates.

CASE STUDIES: SERVICES FOR SPECIFIC NEEDS

The learning centre response has also been to examine the needs of specific groups of students, with a view to integrating their learning experience within a whole provision. Such groups include distance learners, disabled students, and researchers. All three learning centres discussed in this chapter have made provision for these groups but the following case studies examine in detail work done at Sheffield Hallam University and the University of Lincoln.

THE DISTANCE LEARNING SUPPORT SERVICE AT SHEFFIELD HALLAM UNIVERSITY

Different learning modes have huge impacts on the provision of learning resources – distance learning both UK-based and abroad, and block mode where students may visit their institution for study blocks. Many academic libraries and learning centres have attempted to support the needs of these student groups within the wider learning context. The arrangements at Sheffield Hallam University illustrate how these services have developed.

The Distance Learner Support Service (DLSS) at Sheffield Hallam University was formally established in 1994 with the appointment of an Information Adviser (librarian) and an Information Assistant (library assistant). However, the origins of the service go back to 1987/88 when library support was offered to off-campus MBA students in Sheffield Business School (then part of Sheffield City Polytechnic).

The Learning Centre service ethos, which informs its work with distance learners, is that all Sheffield Hallam University students should have supported access to library and information services. The first services offered from 1987 were mediated searches of databases, and the supply of journal articles. The postal loan of books was introduced in 1993. In the early days of the DLSS no databases were available off-campus; with rapid changes in information delivery many distance learners can now access databases remotely and retrieve full-text articles from some of these.

There are now more than 2000 students registered with the DLSS, although only around 40 per cent of these actually make use of its services. It is hard to obtain an accurate figure of the number of distance learning students at the University, because many students are studying more flexibly now. For example, on some courses students have the option to study particular units by distance learning.

The number of requests for database searches has fallen, but there are still some databases which are not available off-campus. Requests for book loans and for copies of journal articles continue to increase, as do requests for help with joining local libraries. The services which are offered via the DLSS are:

- postal loan of books (within the United Kingdom only);
- supply of articles, from journals or books, on receipt of a signed request form;
- database searches on behalf of students – usually for students who don't have adequate access to the Internet, or if students need information from databases which are not available off-campus;

- advice and help with information queries, including questions relating to using electronic information databases which are available off-campus; and
- help with accessing other libraries or information services.

Students may contact the DLSS staff by e-mail, phone or fax. There are no charges for these services. Students are, however, expected to meet the cost of posting books back.

The effectiveness of the service is monitored by a biennial questionnaire to students registered with the DLSS. Feedback is regularly received from students, including praise for the service as well as suggestions for improvements.

The changing patterns of study for many students mean that the difference between distance learning students and on-campus students is no longer clear-cut; many on-campus students only attend on an occasional basis. The Learning Centre is reviewing its services to all postgraduate students, with a view to offering an enhanced service to these students using the DLSS service as a model.

SUPPORT FOR DISABLED STUDENTS AT SHEFFIELD HALLAM UNIVERSITY

As numbers of disabled students have increased, particularly the number of dyslexic students and students with mental health difficulties, the Learning Centre at Sheffield Hallam University has re-examined its support for this group of students.

The University adopts the social model of disability, accepting that disability is socially created. The Disabled Student Support Team, which is part of the SHU Student Services Centre, works with students, academic and support staff to identify barriers and obstacles and then to provide support services, equipment and physical adaptations to remove them.

All disabled students receiving a firm offer of a place at Sheffield Hallam University are invited to attend for an Assessment of Need. This identifies the individual requirements of students and makes detailed recommendations regarding support needs, specialist equipment and technology, and study strategies. The resulting Profile and Learning Contract is agreed between the University and the student and may include recommendations for the format and delivery of course materials, examination and assessment arrangements, personal assistance as well as specialist equipment and software, and Learning Centre provision.

In the Learning Centre, where services are delivered across several campuses operating on an open access basis and with extended opening hours, the Departmental Disability Coordinator works closely with a number of colleagues, designated Disability Contacts, to ensure that the needs of users are met. They provide support for individual students who find it helpful to have a regular Learning Centre contact, in accordance with the recommendations made in Learning Contracts. As a group, the Learning Centre Disability Contacts advise departmental managers of legislative and institutional issues, requirements and practices; they contribute to service planning and development, coordinate staff awareness and training activities, and ensure that Learning Centre practices and procedures comply with legislative, sector and institutional requirements and guidelines.

The Disabled Student Support Team organizes an induction programme for undergraduate students, which takes place each year in the week preceding University enrolment. The Learning Centre contributes orientation tours for individuals as well as introductions to services and facilities for deaf and hearing-impaired students and for students with dyslexia. The Disabled Student Support Team produces guidelines for teaching staff working with deaf and hearing-impaired and dyslexic students. Learning Centre Information Specialists, responsible for teaching information skills, work to incorporate principles of good practice in their teaching. Courseware developers, and systems and web designers, similarly take account of guidelines in the design and delivery of printed, electronic and web-based publicity, teaching and support materials. The Learning Centre receives positive feedback from students and works closely with the Disabled Student Support Team to develop and improve support for disabled students.

Disabled students are allowed extended loans and are assigned a special borrower category that alerts service staff to the fact that a user may have other support needs, which may or may not be visible. All members of staff help students by carrying books, locating materials on the shelves, photocopying, and assisting with database and catalogue searches. This support, along with a dedicated telephone renewals service, e-mail enquiries and developments in the electronic information desk and off-campus support, constitutes good Learning Centre practice for all users.

Specialized software packages are networked throughout the University and complement two Assistive Technology Resource areas that have been established at two of the three Learning Centres. These are made available for use only by recommended students and provide networked PCs with some stand-alone software, as well as some specialist equipment including a CCTV unit, adjustable work station, ergonomic keyboards, scanners and TFT flat-screen monitors. The Resource areas form an integral part of the Learning Centre and as such are available on a 24-hour basis for open access use and for individual and group training purposes. Support is provided by Learning Centre staff along with staff from other departments.

RESEARCH SUPPORT AT THE UNIVERSITY OF LINCOLN

Researchers as a group have varying needs from academic libraries and these are sometimes hard to define given the range of working patterns. The obvious need is access to specialized resources to support their research, which may not necessarily be available within their institution's library. Awareness of other research collections and access to them is also an important part of these students' learning experience. They may also require IT facilities and working space if these are not available from within their department, but they do not have the same requirement as other students to work as groups and tend to prefer quiet space. Researchers also require support and induction into the library's or learning centre's facilities. Learning Support at the University of Lincoln has examined the needs of researchers and an examination of their support model follows.

The Research Support Libraries Programme (RSLP), was introduced in 1999 to support, develop and extend access to research collections. Funding allocations were made for the three academic years commencing 1999/00 with up to £30 million being distributed over the three-year duration of the programme.

The RSLP was derived from the deliberations and conclusions of the Follett Report (1993) and the Anderson Report (1996) and brought together existing and new forms of access to library resources, making particular reference to support for research. The programme was intended to stimulate collaboration and resource sharing and to enable better arrangements for research support in the use of the research infrastructure. This would be achieved by taking steps to:

- sustain and enhance personal access to research resources;
- extend collaborative arrangements for collection management;
- increase availability of information about the location of the UK's rich information resources;
- improve ability to navigate around important collections; and
- provide new technological and organizational arrangements to support the strategy.

The University of Lincoln was successful in receiving £26 000 under one strand of the Programme, to support access to major holdings libraries, for each of the three years of the programme. Having established that the funding could not be used to purchase additional resources which could be targeted at researchers – for example, back copies of research journals or strengthening the research reports collection – the University decided to consider developing a new staffing post to focus on supporting researchers and research students.

As the Learning Support Department was still settling into the staffing restructure undertaken in 1997, it was decided that, instead of developing a completely new post, it would be more appropriate to use the existing job description of the Learning Adviser role and realign it with a focus on research rather than an existing academic subject/department focus. The post therefore became one which crossed existing faculty teams and could support other learning advisers in their work with subject-based postgraduate researchers and research staff. It had three main foci:

- to develop new services to support researchers by the provision of a range of facilities including an embryonic distance learners service;

- to develop information about existing services to promote increased access to the collections for all users, most notably researchers from other institutions; and
- to provide a focus for the support of research activity within the University by liaison and collaboration.

A distance learners' service, begun the year before, had failed to make an impact, owing to the competing time demands made by existing services. The appointment of the Learning Adviser for Research provided the impetus to develop the service and focus it on identifiable groups of research students. A frequently asked questions (FAQ) database was constructed and a dedicated telephone and e-mail address used to centralize the service from all campuses.

To develop information about existing services and promote increased usage of the collections, the Learning Adviser for Research revamped the Learning Support web pages, restructuring the navigation paths and adding useful links to research collections within other higher education institutions. She also administered the department's membership of the UK Libraries Plus scheme and other reciprocal access and borrowing schemes, and was able to advise on the most appropriate collections to support researchers.

The post also allowed close liaison with each Faculty Research Director to prioritize Learning Support services. In each case the needs for these were different. For example, in one faculty the Learning Adviser developed a researchers' guide to information retrieval, in another she worked with academic colleagues on a bid for the development of a newly acquired research archive and in a third she worked on delivering research skills workshops to PhD students. At a University level, she assisted in the returns for the Research Assessment Exercise and throughout her time in post made a positive contribution to academic subject reviews, most notably in the area of student support and guidance.

The postholder was able to take a departmental role in the development of support, some of which crossed boundaries between academic and customer services, and worked at a policy level within the University as a member of the Research Committee and Faculty Research groups.

CONCLUSION

Earlier in this chapter two suggested scenarios sought to illustrate how the student experience of learning has changed in the past ten years. The differences are considerable. Learning centres have sought ways to respond to the circumstances of students at a time of great change in higher education, and to develop innovative solutions to support issues. Students still need resources for their study and space in which to study but they also now need different skills to work within a flexible, virtual learning environment. Support is crucial and the role of LIS staff in supporting students looks likely to grow as different roles emerge for staff as learning advisers and information skills trainers, and as contact time with tutors decreases. The communication links must keep the dialogue open to help ensure that students receive the service they want and need. The new buildings have proved to be popular and efforts to make them welcoming places conducive for learning activities seem to have worked. Longer opening hours have extended access to resources and helped to maximize investment in facilities. Off-campus access to resources and staff support has helped students use the systems at times conducive to their changing learning patterns and study modes. The changing emphasis from teaching to learning is putting the learning centre at the centre of the student's experience in higher education and this trend seems set to continue.

REFERENCES

Anderson, V. and Douglas, J. (1998), Skills for Learning: the System!, in C. Rust (ed.), *5th Improving Student Learning Symposium*, held in Glasgow. Oxford: Oxford Centre for Staff and Learning Development, pp. 534–8.

Barke, M. et al. (2000), *Students in the Labour Market – Nature, Extent and Implications of Term-Time Employment Among University of Northumbria Undergraduates*. DfEE Research Brief 215. Nottingham: Department for Education and Employment.

EARL (Electronic Access to Resources in Libraries). http://www.earl.org.uk

HESA (Higher Education Statistics Agency). http://www.hesa.ac.uk

Hewitson, A. (2000), Awareness and Use of Electronic Information Services by Academic Staff at Leeds Metropolitan University. *Library and Information Research News*, **24**(78), pp. 17–22.

Horrocks, A. (1998), What do Students Want? Using 'Priority Search' Surveys to Determine User Satisfaction with Library Services. *SCONUL Newsletter*, 15, pp. 21–4.

The Internet Detective. http://www.sosig.ac.uk/desire/internet-detective.html

Joint Funding Councils' Libraries Review Group (1993), *Report* (Follett Report). Bristol: Higher Education Funding Council for England.

Joint Funding Councils' Library Review (1996), *Report of the Group on a National/Regional Strategy for Library Provision for Researchers* (Anderson Report). Bristol: Higher Education Funding Council for England.

Joint Information Systems Committee (2001), *JISC Five-Year Strategy 2001–05*, http://www.jisc.ac.uk/pub01/strat_01_05/exec.html

Kingston, P. (1998), Managing Electronic Reserve Collections, in T. Hanson and J. Day (eds), *Managing the Electronic Library: a Practical Guide for Information Professionals*. London: Bowker Saur.

Learning Centre (2000), 24 Hour Opening Semester 1 Report September–December 2000. Unpublished report, Sheffield Hallam University Learning Centre.

Monteith, M. and Smith, J. (2001), Learning in a Virtual Campus: the Pedagogical Implications of Students' Experiences. *Innovations in Education and Teaching International*, **38**(2), pp. 119–32.

Ottewill, R. and Macfarlane, B. (2001), Learning, Teaching and Assessment Activities, in B. Macfarlane and R. Ottewill (eds), *Effective Learning and Teaching in Business and Management*. London: Kogan Page, pp. 46–58.

Resource Discovery Network. *Virtual Training Suite*. http://www.vts.rdn.ac.uk/

SCONUL (Society of College, National and University Libraries) (2000), *Information Support Issues for the e-University: a Discussion Paper*, London: SCONUL.

Building new partnerships: changing institutional relations

5

Edited by Kay Moore

Contributors:

University of Aberdeen	Sheona Farquhar
University of Lincoln	Philippa Dyson
Sheffield Hallam University	Kay Moore,
	Linda Purdy and
	Stephen Wan

INTRODUCTION

We have seen how the vision of the learning centre concept has emerged. Resources were secured, organizational structures adjusted, staff regrouped and trained, and state of the art buildings created. This infrastructure may be well planned but ultimately the success of the learning centre approach depends on its ability to integrate all of this capability into the academic process. It is, more than ever, a client-driven service; its staff need to understand fully the needs of their clients and equally they must realize and capitalize on the potential that new learning centre buildings offer.

To achieve this state, it is not sufficient just to maintain the existing good – though usually patchy – relationships with academic staff; reliance on a few academic champions is no longer adequate. The successful development of service provision depends on the involvement of staff in the academic and decision-making processes of the institution. Furthermore, the investment in new learning centre buildings has to be justified in terms of making a difference to teaching and learning. It is vital to demonstrate the worth of academic services to the institution and to embed them firmly at the centre of the academic process within academic departments and programmes of study.

In doing this it is also necessary to recognize that academic liaison staff are no longer independent operators. Chapter 2 outlined the operational and structural changes that have taken place in recent years, leading to the organizational convergence of academic services. The most significant of these organizational changes in terms of relationships are likely to be the collaboration between libraries and educational development services and the forging of much closer, more integrated working arrangements with IT services. This chapter looks at how these changes are now embedded into the working lives of higher education institutions and examines the opportunities that have arisen to create more dynamic support for the academic process.

The context is provided by the key influences that have driven or facilitated changed relationships with the academic community. The experience of the Learning Centre department at Sheffield Hallam University (SHU) is used to illustrate the nature of these changing relationships. The University of Lincoln has faced similar challenges and the approach adopted there is compared to the SHU approach. The importance of developing relationships with colleagues in educational development services is drawn out and there are practical illustrations of how the day-to-day operations with IT services are impacting on the academic support process.

Separate case studies are also included to illustrate how these changing institutional relationships are reaping benefits in practice and how other institutions have taken a different path to achieve the same aims. They include:

- the changing role of the Information Specialist at SHU;
- cross-team collaboration to support information skills development at SHU – the InfoQuest project;
- learning centre–computer services collaboration – the Computer-Based Learning project at SHU;
- the new relationship mix to support IT at the University of Aberdeen; and
- changing roles and relationships at the University of Lincoln.

KEY INFLUENCES ON RELATIONSHIPS WITH ACADEMICS

Most staff working in learning centre environments today, particularly those who have had experience of working in an academic library for some time, would agree that the relationship between themselves and other staff across the institution has changed dramatically in recent years. Learning centre buildings have moved to centre stage in many institutions. They are high profile, high investment resources that are important contributors to institutional strategy. Witness the steady stream of prospective students and their parents touring the latest showcase learning centre on open days to see how central they are to the recruitment drive; ten years ago it was unusual for the library to even get a mention at these events.

So what has brought about this change and how are learning centre staff working with others to capitalize on the advantages that this creates?

CHANGES IN TEACHING AND LEARNING

The last five years have seen sustained changes in teaching and learning in higher education. The reasons are well documented, and reviewed in Chapter 1. One result of such changes is increased emphasis on learning rather than teaching. Academics are increasingly seen as facilitators of learning rather than just transmitters of knowledge. New learning environments are being mapped out to take account of the drive for independent and lifelong learning and the opportunities presented by Communications and Information Technology (C&IT) developments. The rise of the learning centre concept is a direct response to these changes.

This change of approach cannot happen in a vacuum. As student learning becomes more autonomous and more self-directed, the role of staff who manage the physical and virtual learning environments becomes more critical to the whole process. The emphasis on partnership in the delivery of teaching and learning is increasing. This was highlighted in 1993 in the Follett Report, where it was argued that 'the library as a resource base for independent learning should be a partner in course delivery, and its management co-ordinated with the general planning of teaching and learning within the institution'. This, in a nutshell, is a paradigm shift for the role of the library in an academic institution. For example, many academics at SHU now view the Learning Centre as an extension of the classroom and see its staff as an important part of their core team. The presence of Learning Centre Information Services staff, who have frontline responsibility for information and IT services and support, on key planning groups in schools of study reflects this shift. This is illustrated below in the case study outlining the changing role of the Information Specialist (see pp. 138–41).

The prevailing drivers for efficiency in the higher education sector have resulted in dramatically reduced tutor contact time, with a consequent clear shift of learning activity. Learning centres are becoming the hubs of student learning. The case study on the development of Computer Based Learning provision at SHU (see pp. 144–5) illustrates a response to this shift and describes how academics, and information and IT professionals are working together to resource student learning. The rise of virtual learning environments in higher education shows early signs of mirroring this pattern. Library and Information Services (LIS) staff are working with academics, IT specialists and courseware developers to provide teaching material, embed resources and give frontline user support for them.

Students are becoming increasingly engaged in active learning outside class contact time. Much of that time is being spent using the resources of libraries and learning centres, whether physical or virtual. It has been acknowledged (Breen et al., 2001) that this will mean that 'Universities know less about the way students' learning time is spent', as they rely increasingly upon software packages, computer-based learning materials and electronic information resources to guide their learning. Or, as one academic at SHU described it, Learning Centre staff are the bridge between the student experience inside the classroom and the knowledge and skills gained outside.

THE SKILLS AGENDA AND INFORMATION LITERACY

One of the most obvious changes in the relationship between LIS staff and academics since the mid-1990s has been that forged by the increasing importance of information skills to the academic curricula. The impact of skills development on students is discussed in the preceding chapter, but it is also clearly affecting the teaching role of LIS staff and their relationship with other teaching staff. It is this interface that is now explored. As we have seen in Chapter 4, during the last decade, the old library tour scenario has been left a long way behind. For some time now, LIS staff have been actively involved in teaching information skills in lecture or workshop situations. Along with the higher profile that learning centres enjoy comes a greater understanding on the part of academics of the potential of LIS staff to support their students' learning and development. This has led to even greater demand, both for face-to-face skills teaching and for provision of support for information skills development in the virtual learning environment. (See below the case study on InfoQuest, pp. 141–4.)

The table below illustrates the growth in demand for post-induction skills sessions for students at SHU in the last five years. Although the Learning Centre is in the early stages of supporting information skills development through its virtual learning environment, Blackboard, at the time of writing there were over a thousand students enrolled on its information skills unit, InfoQuest.

	1997/98	2001/02
Number of LIS hours teaching	583	1,170
Number of students attending sessions	7,465	14,897

It is not just the volume of teaching undertaken by LIS staff that is changing their role, but also what they are teaching. An emphasis on skills and competencies rather than accumulation of knowledge is becoming apparent in the redefined curricula. The University of Lincoln, for example, typifies this in defining its curriculum in terms of:

- helping students to acquire basic concepts and operations;
- developing transferable skills of formulating questions to which answers are needed;
- identifying resources that might provide the answers;
- searching data; and
- presenting it cogently.

The focus is on empowering students to acquire knowledge and skills – something that the information professional has been doing for a long time. Their role in supporting this shift to student-centred learning is being carved out and it is recognized that LIS staff are moving away from being keepers of knowledge, towards a much more integral role in the educational process. This can been seen more fully in the case studies below.

The context for this increase in demand for skills teaching has to be seen as part of institutional learning and teaching strategies. The SHU learning and teaching strategy aims to create a learning experience that provides amongst other things:

- student-centred learning within a supportive tutor-led environment;
- a variety of learning, teaching and assessment methods and approaches, supported through the appropriate use of technology and other resources;
- integration of key skills at all levels of study;
- preparation for employment incorporating relevant skills; and
- progressive growth in learner autonomy, knowledge and skills.

The SHU key skills agenda now clearly separates information skills from IT skills and positions them within the communication skills area; this encompasses writing, oral communication, visual communication and information skills. Many academics acknowledge that they are not good at teaching information literacy – as one academic put it: 'after all, if academics were really so good at developing information literacy skills with students, all students would move effortlessly through the management of information they need. Clearly they do not.'

SHU academics are valuing the new partnerships being created between the Information Specialists and Courseware Designers, based in the Learning Centre's Learning and Teaching Institute, who bring with them the skills to create stimulating and appealing learning packages. There is a current proliferation of online packages for Information Skills – for example, Inhale (based at Huddersfield), Tonic (based at Newcastle) and, at SHU, InfoQuest. The best examples of institutional-based resources are being developed in partnership with academics. LIS staff have fully taken on board the lessons learnt from years of standing up and teaching information skills in a vacuum – poor attendance, poor motivation and divorced from the main business of teaching and learning.

Research conducted at SHU on the use of key skills resources clearly showed that the most effective programmes were those that were fully integrated into course delivery, rather than provided as an optional extra. The University's guidelines on the integration of key skills (Drew, 2001) underline this experience and strongly support the stance that key skills are 'best developed within the curriculum and contextualised to make their relevance clear to students'. Course teams are required to plan key skills into their curricula and to implement those plans. Information skills are now increasingly subject-based and integrated into the curriculum, developed in partnership with academics and often delivered using a team teaching approach. This approach has now continued in the response to supporting information skills in virtual learning environments as illustrated in the InfoQuest case study.

IMPACT OF COMMUNICATIONS AND INFORMATION TECHNOLOGY

How much has the potential of C&IT to impact on teaching and learning really been embraced by the average academic? Experience indicates that this is still very patchy, despite recent well-funded initiatives such as the Teaching Quality Enhancement Fund (TQEF). Higher education institutions are typically still at the point where there are C&IT 'champions' in most subject areas, but for each champion there are many more who have managed to avoid close involvement and who have fairly limited C&IT skills.

Contrast this with the average LIS professional: over the last five years the vast majority working in learning centre environments have been saturated in C&IT. Ambitious training programmes (as outlined in Chapter 3) have radically changed the C&IT skills, knowledge and outlook of many LIS professionals. The basic tools of their trade now exist mostly in electronic formats, requiring new skills, new visions and new approaches to supporting users. As a profession, LIS staff are noticeably ahead in their development in this area and are also committed to continuous updating of these skills. Furthermore, not only are they mastering these new C&IT-enabled resources and environments, but also equipping themselves with the skills to teach and support others in their use. They have taken part in programmes such as EDULIB (from the Electronic Libraries Programme); they have obtained teaching qualifications and are achieving membership of the Institute for Learning and Teaching.

Whatever the situation in academic libraries, students are coming to learning centres in increasing numbers as their contact time with tutors is further eroded. They are required to maximize their learning time by drawing on the increasingly complex range of resources available to them in these centres. Inevitably, this results in increasing demands for learning centre staff to equip students with the skills to navigate and make sense of rapidly expanding information in their subject areas.

LIS staff have risen well to this challenge, so well, in fact that they are now faced with a situation where students can be more information-literate than their tutors. Unless the same vigour is applied to supporting the development of information skills in teaching staff, then there is a real danger of them being left behind. Research conducted at SHU in 1999 (Moore and Ward) revealed that most academics did not visit learning centres and most did not use electronic information resources on a regular basis. Their students do, however. This puts the academics in a difficult situation, as they become more reliant on the skills and knowledge of learning centre staff. The situation is likely to change in the future as the initiatives in higher education start to impact progressively on a wider number of staff and as new generations of C&IT-literate academics join the workforce. For the immediate future, however, LIS staff are in a strong position to use their skills and knowledge to make a real difference both to the student experience and to supporting the work of the academic. They must now capitalize on this and cement strong working relationships for the future.

ACADEMIC QUALITY

Although the debate about quality in higher education still rages, the rigours of subject review in recent years have undoubtedly had an important impact on the academic/learning centre relationship. Just as learning centres were rising to prominence within institutions, they were also being subject to closer external scrutiny. This examination was not just about the quality of learning resources, but significantly considered the way in which academics and learning centre staff interact with each other to ensure appropriate learning resource provision for students.

For perhaps the first time, learning centre staff were having to justify their relationships – or in some extreme cases to hastily create new relationships – with groups of academics. Directives from senior institutional staff to ensure that appropriate and timely liaison was happening gave added impetus. Learning resources strategies that spelt out explicit relationships were drawn up, with academic and learning centre staff having joint authorship.

The School of Education at SHU defines its Learning Resources strategy in terms of being able to ensure that:

- students can access the resources they require to learn effectively, both on site and at a distance;
- students have access to up-to-date information and facilities reflecting the professional demands placed upon them;
- students acquire appropriate skills to access relevant resources;
- there is good communication between resource providers;
- there is efficient use of limited funds for dedicated specialist facilities;

- there is effective support for staff in fulfilling diverse teaching and learning support roles;
- electronic and paper-based resources are of high quality and students are encouraged to generate learning resources of a similarly high standard; and
- there are effective feedback, monitoring and review processes so that continual improvement of access to resources is achieved.

The revised SCONUL aide-mémoire for assessors (SCONUL, 2001a) recommends that checks are made not just on the effectiveness of the academic–LIS relationship but also on the academic–LIS–IT interface, recognizing the complex partnerships that now exist to support teaching and learning. There is much more emphasis on strategic planning and liaison, including such prompts as 'how do computing and library services become aware of course development and review'. Systems and checks to ensure that these arrangements were working effectively were put in place. However cynical staff may be about subject review and the burden of inspection, from an LIS perspective it has had the effect of shining a spotlight on them and illuminating the need for academic partnership.

External validation of the worth of the SHU Learning Centre has helped to maintain its profile, and work done on subject review planning teams has helped to forge new or stronger relationships. These relationships will be sustained and further developed as revalidation committees, annual quality reports and continuation audits all rely on evidence from the Learning Centre of the quality of its resources and the role its staff play in supporting student learning.

CLIENT EXPECTATIONS

Learning centre services are very much user-focused and as such are strongly influenced by the expectations of their client groups. For example, the whole academic community will be aware of the development of learning centre buildings, as a result of extensive consultation and publicity; in some cases there will be disruption to work and study brought about by the development. All this activity results in raising expectations in client groups and this in turn will affect the way relationships with them develop.

Academic expectations

What were the schools of study expecting from the new learning centres at SHU? Substantial resources were invested into the Learning Centre department to enable learning centre buildings to be created. This happened in a climate of devolved school budgets, which were under increasing pressure year on year. While there was general support for the learning centre concept, there were undoubtedly some expectations that the Department would be playing a more active role in supporting teaching and

134

learning activities within the University. The incorporation of the Learning and Teaching Institute into the Department raised those expectations considerably. During the consultation and publicity process, the learning centres were promoted as an extension of the classroom, as an arena for resource-based learning and integrated IT support. The success of the learning centre concept relies on academics taking ownership of the resource and using it creatively to support their teaching.

Student expectations

How have changing student attitudes impacted on relationships? The impact is twofold. Whether due to changes in student finance or the increasing numbers of students combining study and career, students are treating their time in higher education as an investment. They see themselves as stakeholders in the institution and as such feel able to make demands about how it looks and feels for them. Student support environments have to be geared to their needs. Increasingly, this means adopting an open-all-hours, one-stop-shop approach. Small specialist faculty libraries with limited opening hours might have supported students effectively in the past, but with widening participation and rising numbers the supermarket-style learning centres are providing the response now required for higher education consumers. Pulling together library and information services, IT provision, audio-visual services and even student guidance services into one building provides the sort of instant access learning environment required by many of today's students.

This complexity of services has to be planned and managed by new mixes of staff. Learning centre services have been creating new modes of operation to cope with this complexity and to create as seamless a service as possible for their users. This chapter now explores how these services are working in reality, the sort of issues faced and some of the responses to these.

KEY PARTNERS IN ACADEMIC DELIVERY

EDUCATIONAL DEVELOPMENT SERVICES

The Learning and Teaching Institute (LTI) at SHU was established in 1993 to provide a focus for supporting developments in learning, teaching and assessment within the University through staff development, educational development projects and educational research. In 1996 it was brought into the newly created Learning Centre department and, along with library, media production and user computing, it strengthens the Department's role in providing a wide range of services to support the University's programme of teaching, research and consultancy.

135

The work of the LTI is described in Chapter 7; the aim here is to examine it from the perspective of its relationship to the rest of the Learning Centre, particularly Information Services staff. The impact of including the LTI within the Department has been considerable. It has raised the profile of the Department within the University, created a more academic focus to its work and facilitated the inclusion of Information Services within a wider range of educational and research projects. LTI staff are academics from a range of disciplines who have become specialists in curriculum development, pedagogy and learning technologies. Other areas of the Department's work now have on hand a team of experts who can provide advice and support to staff in the development of academic programmes.

Initially, it felt very much like an arranged marriage between Information Services and LTI staff, with neither group knowing quite what to make of the other. In the last two or three years, however, there has been a gradual shift in the nature of this relationship, moving towards one of mutual understanding and respect. The two key drivers for this have been the SHU response to the TQEF initiative and the rise of the virtual learning environment. TQEF funding at the University is managed by the LTI. The requirements for schools of study to bid for money from this fund and to develop strategic responses to teaching, learning and assessment, led to the rise of Teaching, Learning and Assessment Committees within most schools. These committees normally have a membership mix that includes LTI and Information Services staff, which has created opportunities to establish closer working relationships and has fostered an increased awareness of the contribution that each group can make to support the schools. The LTI acts as a catalyst for bringing together the right mix of skills between LTI, Information Services and school-based staff to drive TQEF-funded projects; InfoQuest is an example of this.

Virtual learning environment developments have been led and coordinated by the LTI but strongly underpinned by Information Services activities. Information Services staff are closely involved in the integration of resources into Blackboard, frontline user support and the development of information skills to support its use. Blackboard academic support units consisting of LTI staff, seconded academics, Information Services and Corporate Information Systems staff have been created. Their function is to provide 'at elbow' support to academics who are preparing to teach in this environment.

LTI staff have also been taking forward the Key Skills agenda in the University. This has been geared around a self-managed learning package called Key Skills On Line. Information Services staff have contributed to the development and updating of this resource and have been involved in the team teaching delivery of key skills using this and other resources. Working alongside LTI staff, they have created Key Skills resource areas in learning centres and have cooperated on initiatives such as the Writers in Residence project, to enable writing workshops to be hosted in learning centres. The importance of the Key Skills agenda in higher education, together with the roles that Information Services and LTI staff play in supporting this, is giving rise to more opportunities for collaboration.

The other notable benefit of having the LTI located within the Learning Centre is that their expertise can be used as a resource to develop other staff. Many Information Services staff have taken the opportunity to attend short courses or seminars run by LTI staff on a range of subjects to build up their knowledge and understanding of current curriculum issues in higher education. Recent seminar and training events have covered such diverse topics as on-line assessment, preparing to teach in virtual learning environments and the impact of Curriculum 2000 on higher education. This has undoubtedly placed Information Services staff in a stronger position to enter into the academic dialogue and to work with academics in schools from a more informed base.

IT SERVICES

The relationship between information services and IT services is an increasingly critical one. The apparently inherent cultural differences described in Chapter 3 can also make it an uncomfortable one that needs careful management.

At Sheffield Hallam University, certainly, the most crucial service relationship for the Learning Centre is that with the Corporate Information Systems department (CIS), which amongst other things manages the networked C&IT environment. The increasing interdependence of the two departments is evident in University Information and Teaching and Learning strategies and integral to the operation and management of Learning Centre physical and virtual environments.

Robust mechanisms have had to be introduced to coordinate strategy, to support collaboration and to facilitate seamless and responsive frontline support to Learning Centre users, between departments with different cultures and sometimes priorities. Two sets of staff, often not speaking the same language, need to work hard at establishing and sustaining a relationship of trust and understanding. In some areas, the relationship is one of customer–supplier, in others something closer to partnership is needed. A service-level definition has been developed to clarify what the Learning Centre can expect from CIS, although in practice it has not been called on to defend a particular position.

At the strategic level, the framework for the relationship is provided by the University's Information and Teaching and Learning strategies and converted into action through the University's business planning processes. An increasingly common agenda in the areas of student support and, more recently, the virtual learning environment makes consistency and mutual support essential. Account meetings between senior staff of the two departments provide a forum to share information on developments of general interest, to consult where developments are likely to be of direct interest and to identify projects requiring joint development. They are also used to address issues of significant concern.

As outlined in Chapter 2, part of the Learning Centre service model is for its staff to provide frontline user support for information and IT enquiries, and for CIS to have responsibility for escalated IT advisory support and technical support.

The most crucial (and sensitive) operational relationship is that between Learning Centre information desks and CIS technical and second-line advisory support. It is here that tensions between user support and IT specialists are likely to be most evident. Learning Centre staff need to understand and maintain ownership of user problems. To do this, they need to be able to identify them accurately, to know how they are being progressed, when they are fixed, or what the user needs to do to resolve them. CIS staff need Learning Centre information desk staff with the competence and confidence to analyse problems, to deal with a high proportion themselves and to communicate referrals accurately. This liaison is approached in several ways: fault-reporting systems track problems; personal relationships are developed – through job shadowing, for example; and training programmes to keep Learning Centre staff up to date with technical developments. Learning Centre information desk managers and CIS helpdesk managers meet regularly to review performance and improve liaison.

A dedicated team of CIS staff based in the City Campus learning centre provides technical support. Maintenance and developmental priorities are negotiated and agreed as part of a formal work-planning process, and day-to-day issues are addressed more informally between the technical support team leader and the Learning Centre Systems Manager.

Another aspect of the evolving relationships between Learning Centre and CIS staff is the increasing necessity for them to work in partnership to support teaching and learning developments in the University. Subject review preparation is a prime example of this, where the CIS representative and an Information Specialist are frequently meeting in the same academic forums and have developed expertise in managing the quality assurance system and providing advice and support to academic colleagues. This helps to create a greater bond between the two service providers, increasing knowledge and understanding of each other's operations to the extent that they now often cover for each other in academic meetings when one or the other cannot be present. Inevitably, the challenge of delivering virtual learning necessitates closer partnership between CIS, LTI and Information Services. The computer-based learning case study below provides a practical illustration of this in action.

CASE STUDIES

THE CHANGING ROLE OF INFORMATION SPECIALIST AT SHU

It is the Information Specialist who is charged with first-line contact between the Learning Centre and the schools of study. There are six Information Specialists, designated as Senior Lecturers, supporting a total of eleven schools, most supporting two schools each. They manage a team of Information Advisers (previously Assistant Librarians).

Although much of the relationship between the information professional and the academic is based on repeated opportunity for informal contact, it is the growth in the means of formal contact between the two parties that really tells the tale of how things have changed in recent years. The change of title from Subject Librarian to Information Specialist with the establishment of the Learning Centre in 1996 heralded much more than a change of name. Information Specialists were empowered with a new vision, a new sense of direction for their role in the University.

The groundwork was already in place. New Senior Information Adviser posts had been created to take over the day-to-day management and administration issues for Information Specialists, to free them up to spend more time working directly with Schools (see Chapter 3, pp. 61–3 and Appendix A, p. 218). There were many examples of Information Specialists already working dynamically with staff in their schools on an ad hoc basis. The general picture, however, was of patchy involvement with schools for anything other than information skills teaching, or ensuring access to resources via library liaison committees or representatives. The Information Specialists had been fortunate in being longstanding members of School Boards, although often in a rather passive role, as they simply did not have enough involvement in other school developments at that time; their contribution was therefore often limited.

Set in the context of the changes documented earlier in this chapter – particularly new approaches to teaching, growth of C&IT and the rise of the skills agenda – the Information Specialists started to realize the potential of their role to make a difference to the academic process throughout the University. They already had extensive experience of electronic resources. Once they developed the additional skills and knowledge necessary to work in the new learning environments, they were ready to take a more proactive role in supporting the academic process. Rather than being asked to respond to changed programmes in schools, they wanted to be there at their conception, influencing their structure and content, and helping academics to harness the potential of Learning Centre resources and expertise.

It is difficult to determine how much the creation of the new Learning Centres influenced this new sense of purpose. Information Services staff were conscious that they had a magnificent resource that could make a real difference to the University, if they could hit the right buttons with academics to spark their interest. In turn, the higher profile that the new learning centres had created for the Department made it easier for Information Specialists to venture into schools, where there were already expectations that something new was happening, and a growing interest in getting involved.

Change has been gradual over the last five years, but in comparing the formal involvement between Subject Librarian and Schools and Information Specialists and Schools, it becomes clear just how much progress has been made:

Subject Librarian

Formal involvement with the school processes typically involved:

- *School Board*: the formal meeting of senior school staff and representatives from each area of the school. The Subject Librarian was a long-standing member of this board. Membership was typically used as a means to keep up-to-date with developments in the school and to identify a suitable library response.

- *Course committees*: the forum for staff and students of individual courses. Subject Librarians were invited, on a regular or ad hoc basis, to hear about library issues, or to raise awareness about new services.

- *Library liaison meetings*: semi-formal meetings with a member of academic staff designated as library liaison representative for their school. Used to highlight resource issues, discuss budgets and so on for their school.

Information Specialist

Formal involvement in school processes now usually involves all of the above, although an Information Adviser sometimes deputizes for the Information Specialist at Course Committee meetings. In addition, Information Specialists will normally be members of a range of other school forums, including the following:

- *Course planning committees*: it is normal for Information Specialists to be invited to attend either all, or at least some, of the course planning committees in their schools. Rather than discover details at the validation stage, or even later, they now have an opportunity to be actively involved in the planning stages of new courses. As a University academic comments 'It is the period between developing the course on paper and actually offering it for the first time that the most productive links take place between Learning Centre staff and academics'. Information Specialists are able to: influence the attention paid to information literacy development; identify opportunities for maximizing the use of Learning Centre services and resources to support the course; provide advice about off-campus support and access to resources; and identify general resource implications for the course. They increasingly provide advice about integrating resources and skills development material into the emerging virtual learning environment.

140

- *Validation sub-committees*: the next step up from course planning is the internal validation of these new or modified courses through a school's own validation processes, before the proposals go to the University Quality Office. The Information Specialist is now often a member of this committee and will be able to pick up on wider issues, such as the suitability of new partner college agreements, or advising on the likely impact of proposed changes to course delivery on access to resources.

- *Teaching learning and assessment committees*: most schools now have a formal TLA committee, initially set up to make recommendations about the investment of monies devolved to the School from the TQEF allocations. It is significant that Information Specialists are now seen to be important members of these forums, meriting their place by virtue of their role in the support of teaching and learning in the new learning landscape.

- *C&IT committees*: it is common for the Information Specialist to be a member of this school forum, whose remit is to coordinate the provision and effective utilization of information technologies for the school. The C&IT committee usually also includes a member of CIS staff, providing a useful forum to discuss Learning Centre/CIS issues of relevance to the school.

Information Specialists are now more fully entwined in the academic life of their schools. In addition to the growth of formal opportunities for Learning Centre–school collaboration, there has been a comparative increase in other areas too. Information Specialists are regularly involved in school staff development events, giving them an opportunity to keep staff up to date with resource developments and, more recently, to help those about to venture into the virtual learning environment to benefit from their experience and knowledge in that area. They are usually invited to strategic planning events in the school and other major events in the school calendar. The Information Specialist is now considered more vital to the work of the school and this is reflected in the closer working relationships, both formal and informal, that they now enjoy.

INFOQUEST AT SHU: WEB-BASED LEARNING FOR INFORMATION SKILLS SUPPORT

This section describes a project that sought to implement and evaluate a web-based learning package, in order meet the diverse information literacy needs for new entrants at Sheffield Hallam University. It demonstrates how a collaborative team approach between staff from central and school-based departments can be highly effective in meeting new challenges in curriculum development and course delivery, and highlights the role of the Learning and Teaching Institute (LTI) in facilitating cross-team activity.

Context

Sheffield Hallam University provides information management skills support through introductory skills workshops to all new students. The workshops are delivered by Learning Centre Information Specialists or Information Advisers and are repeated for all courses in each academic year. The Learning Centre had identified problems in dealing with such issues as catering for an increasingly wide spectrum of student skills on entry to the University, and the common perception that skills sessions were external to the curriculum and thus less important to students. Demand for skills workshops has escalated considerably in recent years as learning centres and the resources within them have become more complex and the necessity of information management skills more apparent. Information Specialists also raised issues over adequate replacement support for students who were unable to attend skills workshops for their subject group in their induction week.

The Learning Centre sought to address these issues by developing an on-line learning package as a substitute for the traditional information skills workshops. The rationale for the initiative derived from a response to changes in the higher education environment which has seen larger student numbers and a more diverse student population. Aligned with the University Learning, Teaching and Assessment strategy, the web-based package would seek to encourage flexible and student-centred learning. An opportunity to trial the proposed initiative arose when the School of Social Science and Law expressed an interest in using such a learning package for a new Level 1 introductory unit entitled Information Management. This interest stemmed from the School's formal LTA strategy document, which stated that the School would place an emphasis on exploiting the 'interactive potential of ICTs' to provide flexible learning opportunities and student support.

Course of action

The development of the InfoQuest package was a collaborative project involving the School of Social Science and Law and several areas of the Learning Centre: Information Services, the LTI and the Centre for Multimedia (CME). It was developed with a view to ensuring subject specificity, to increase relevance and instil a sense of ownership for the student user. Two versions were produced for separate undergraduate cohorts – Applied Social Science and Psychology. Information Specialists and Advisers liaised with the academic School staff and CME to provide pertinent content for InfoQuest.

This kind of working relationship has been advocated by Breivik, who argues that librarians 'need to collaborate more with instructional designers and media producers', so that they are able to 'contribute their information literacy expertise just as faculty members bring their subject expertise to a course or project production team' (Breivik,

1999, p. 274). Indeed, the role of the Learning Centre staff was central to the whole developmental process of the project. While working to meet the immediate objectives to deliver an interactive, user-friendly and student-centred package, the courseware developers also envisaged the potential benefits to allow for a flexible design that could lend itself easily to cross-subject transferability for any future development. Furthermore, the Applied Social Science and Psychology versions were required to support the assessment for the Information Management Level 1 unit. An LTI Research Assistant evaluated the initial roll-out of the learning package and disseminated the findings in the form of a report to all stakeholders.

The design of the Information Management unit directly addresses University requirements to incorporate key skills for learning in all courses. Other external factors – such as employer and professional body expectations, quality reviews and the University's devolved manner of using TQEF monies for LTA strategy development – have also necessitated a shift in the way in which academics approach their curriculum development and course planning activities. Increasing support from central departments has led to a working environment in which academic staff are drawing upon expertise outside their own subject field for effective teaching and learning.

The InfoQuest project is an example of the benefits that can be achieved by the positioning of educational development services within a learning centre department. This has much to do with the ability of educational development academics to facilitate the development of closer academic partnerships between academic services staff and school academics. The harnessing of a plethora of staff skill backgrounds on the InfoQuest project has largely been overseen by the LTI, which has an overall goal 'to enable Schools to successfully achieve their Learning, Teaching Assessment Strategies within the context of the general Sheffield Hallam University strategy' ('Role and Strategic Priorities', p. 1), with an outcome that results in 'changes in learning experiences to impact on large numbers of students through the developments made by large numbers of staff across the university' (ibid., p. 3). At a practical level, this has led to the formation of effective teams and has demonstrated the proactive role in which the Learning Centre is able to influence curriculum development.

Conclusion

The InfoQuest project typifies many developmental initiatives which draw upon the expertise and human resources of a number of specialisms to work collaboratively to benefit student learning. The initiative is also an example in which school learning, teaching and assessment strategies can be aligned with academic services targets to meet the overall University priorities of enabling flexible, student-centred and computer-based learning.

Current proposals are underway to harness the potential of cross-subject transferability of the learning package. Learning Centre staff have drafted a proposed model for the future development of InfoQuest that features a modular approach, whereby subject groups are able to customize 'InfoQuest courses' for their students. The proposal will also consider its integration with the University's new virtual learning environment. Such implications will undoubtedly require the future development of extensive working partnerships between the Learning Centre and school academics to fulfil course planning and delivery needs, as well as planning for learning facilities required by students in the Learning Centre and schools.

COMPUTER-BASED LEARNING IMPLEMENTATION GROUP AT SHU

The vision of the Adsetts Centre, the City Campus learning centre, was to provide an integrated learning environment which would meet the many and differing needs of SHU students. When it opened in 1996, it was already clear that IT developments and the changing patterns of teaching and learning were going to play an important role.

The Learning Centre took a proactive role in encouraging and supporting teaching staff to introduce and integrate computer-based learning materials into the curriculum. The Computer-based Learning Implementation Group was established in 1997 to manage their implementation within learning centres. It draws together the key players from within and outside the Learning Centre: Information Advisers, courseware developers, LTI staff working with teaching staff on curriculum developments, and Corporate Information Systems (CIS) staff with responsibility for the infrastructure. The remit of the Group illustrates the broad range of issues addressed and shows how important it is for a broad cross-section of staff to work together to ensure the successful implementation and smooth running of C&IT. The objectives of the Group are:

- to advise the Learning Centre Executive and thereby contribute to the development of a computer-based learning strategy;
- to plan, assist and monitor the implementation of computer-based learning; and
- to promote computer-based learning with teaching staff.

Computer-based learning materials appropriate for a course of study may be identified by an Information Specialist or Information Adviser. The materials are previewed with the tutors who teach that subject and evaluated in terms of content, flexibility, interface and navigability, and price. Before an order is raised, CIS staff are involved in the process to test the stability of the software for network delivery. If the materials are suitable, a licence agreement is negotiated and the software installed on the network.

Alternatively, a subject need may be identified that cannot be met by commercially available packages; in this case, they may be developed in-house. Such a project would again draw upon the expertise of staff from many areas – Information Specialists and Advisers, academic staff, courseware developers and CIS specialists.

Resourcing suitable materials and making them available on the network is only one aspect of the support available to academic staff. The availability of PCs for group work and on-hand support to deal with practical problems is all part of building the confidence of teaching staff to integrate computer-based learning materials into the curriculum.

Forty-eight PCs in the Adsetts Centre are ring-fenced, with priority being given to their use for computer-based learning work. Teaching staff can book these machines to use a workshop environment to introduce their students to the software. Students are then able to work with the materials with confidence and can access them on any PC on the University network. The Implementation Group manages the total process of identifying, supporting and managing the running of computer-based learning materials across the University network.

Management information regularly informs the Group about usage of the materials. Software no longer used is removed from the network after consultation with the teaching staff concerned; new releases are installed and older versions removed; evaluation studies are regularly undertaken and publicity and promotional materials produced.

C&IT is integral to the working life of the University. The initiative taken by the Computer-based Learning Implementation Group has been a success and the role is still evolving. The University is moving towards a Managed Learning Environment, and integrating use of computer-based learning materials into the courses delivered via the virtual learning environment is a natural step to take. The success of the Group is due to the close working relationship of staff from several areas of the University, sharing their expertise and working towards a common goal.

NEW RELATIONSHIPS TO SUPPORT IT AT ABERDEEN

Background

Within the Directorate of Information Systems and Services, library and computing user services at Aberdeen are the responsibility of the Consultancy and Client Liaison Division. This department manages the relationship of the Directorate with its clients, to ensure the delivery of effective services to support the needs of the University. It is in this area of the Directorate's activities that convergence is a day-to-day reality and where the changing relationships between Directorate staff and also between them and service users are particularly evident.

One area where convergence has brought together staff and services in geographically separated locations and different functional areas is an integrated Help Desk Service, which was created from five different types of help.

Issues prompting change

The distinction between administrative and academic support was becoming increasingly blurred. There was duplication of effort, with both administrative and academic helpdesks supporting word processing, spreadsheets and e-mail; secretaries were supposed to ring one helpdesk and academic staff the other: it was all extremely confusing.

Furthermore, the level of service given to academic and administrative staff was not consistent. In some areas, such as PC installation and configuration, University Office staff got a better service; academics were expected to unpack the boxes and plug in the systems on their own. Yet, in other areas, such as using e-mail and other Internet services, the experience of the academic helpdesk staff was superior to that of the administrative helpdesk.

The level of service available to undergraduates was also inconsistent. While academic libraries have always provided advice and assistance to their student readers, computing services, having evolved more recently from a research emphasis, provided only patchy, part-time help for students – which was becoming increasingly inappropriate for a modern university.

All branches of the Library have clusters of PCs, in increasing numbers, for student use; where there are computers there are inevitably people with problems. Information was increasingly being delivered in electronic format; however, staff on the Library Desks were not trained to give assistance with IT-related queries and were finding this increasingly frustrating. And, in the Taylor and Medical Libraries, where there was no Information Desk, the Issue Desk staff were finding it increasingly difficult to deal with both routine Issue Desk tasks and the more time-consuming subject- and IT-based enquiries.

As the dependence of administration staff on PCs grew, administrative computing staff employed for their Oracle or other MIS (Management Information Systems) technical expertise were having to spend too much of their time providing PC support. This was aggravated by the fact that the Administrative Computing department was located in the University Office building, so administrative staff would keep popping into the office, expecting a 'quick fix'. Similarly, experienced technical staff in the Computing Centre found themselves spending too much time on basic word-processing and e-mail problems. Moreover, there was a lack of adequate communication between the separate organizations. Users could find themselves bounced between Library, Computing Centre and Administrative Computing, as the staff in one didn't understand the activities of the other.

The development of integrated helpdesk services for all Directorate customer services was a response to these problems. The information/enquiry desk and advisory services, formerly run separately in the Computing Centre, University Office and Libraries, were combined into a single, integrated helpdesk service, providing information and advice on all aspects of the Directorate's services. A central helpdesk, specializing in IT-related help, operates within the Computing Centre and satellite helpdesks are located in three of the site libraries (Queen Mother, Taylor and Medical Libraries).

This re-engineering of the frontline services necessitated a review and rationalization of the background support that was provided; which, in turn, necessitated communication between the different groups and teams within the Directorate, as all now supported the same helpdesk service.

Help Desks

The different user help facilities were integrated in four phases between 1997 and 1999. Help Desk Software, Support Magic, is used to log all queries, fault reports, and requests for advice or assistance. First-line calls are answered at the Help Desks, with any queries or problems that cannot be answered or dealt with immediately being assigned to the appropriate technical or subject support group. The software acts as the main communication and monitoring tool that enables staff to track the progress of queries to ensure they are answered and followed up.

Staffing

Staff at the Help Desks provide first-level support for IT- and library-related queries, with access to technical and expert support and advice from other Directorate staff. Those answering queries directly at the Help Desks have varying skills and varying levels of expertise within the range of Directorate systems and services. Staffing at different times is drawn from a team of full-time helpdesk officers, part-time post-graduate students, computer operators, library staff, IT trainers and applications experts. If the staff on duty are unable to provide an immediate solution, they will log the query and try to find the most appropriate way of providing an answer.

Changing working practice

The introduction of the integrated Help Desk has brought about changes in working practices for the technical experts as well as for the staff in the front line. All calls for assistance, be they network connection requests, requests for the installation of an item of teaching software or a request for assistance in searching for legal information on the Internet, are channelled through the Help Desk and then referred on to the appropriate technical support group. This means fewer disruptive phone calls for the technical staff and helps them to plan and schedule their support activities as a group. After the initial, inevitable, resistance to change, the support groups now acknowledge the benefits this has brought them and have developed a good working relationship with the frontline staff. The technical staff play their part in the training and provision of information to frontline staff, recognizing that the more straightforward calls that can be dealt with by first-level support, the more time they have available to deal with the genuinely complex (and more interesting!) problems.

Advantages for the University population

- As more courses and information resources are delivered electronically, staff and students have a single contact point for computing and information resource queries.
- All queries are logged so,
  - users can be sure their query won't get lost in the system;
  - where appropriate, users can contact the Help Desk to query the progress of their call; and
  - Help Desk statistics inform staff and students of the nature and extent of problems dealt with.
- Students have a more comprehensive help service available throughout the working day.

Advantages for Directorate staff

- The software allows statistics about the volume and nature of the queries to be gathered and analysed for areas where services can be improved. These management statistics can also be used to inform resource planning and budgeting.
- Support staff can keep track of calls and refer calls on appropriately and electronically.
- Technical and expert staff can concentrate on the problems and queries that require their expertise.

CHANGING ROLES AND RELATIONSHIPS AT THE UNIVERSITY OF LINCOLN

In 2000 a new Vice-Chancellor arrived at what is now the University of Lincoln and almost immediately put in place preparations for the realization of a new vision. Twelve months later, the University looks and feels different. A strategic review is under way, encompassing a reconfiguration of campuses and a change of name, a restructuring of service departments and faculties, and the incorporation of the Lincolnshire campuses of De Montfort University.

Response to curriculum changes and the emerging skills agenda

Visionary change is not new however. One of the developments that has given the most impetus to the standing of the Learning Support department with the academic community was the establishment in the early 1990s of the Chair of Learning Development, funded by an endowment from British Petroleum. Learning Support staff played a key role in promoting and embedding the Effective Learning Programme within the University curriculum, as the first stage of a University Skills and Capabilities Curriculum. The programme is intended to address the need for students to acquire study and employability skills. These were compulsory elements in the curriculum, to be delivered as prepared by the Learning Development Unit, or an equivalent devised by the subject area. The vehicle of delivery has been the University's Intranet, now called the Virtual Campus. Learning Advisers have also participated in associated project work. Several years later, Learning Support staff participate in the delivery of this programme in various ways, such as delivering units or, for Learning Advisers, being unit coordinators for their subjects.

More generally, the Department aligns itself closely with the University's Learning and Teaching strategy, with staff membership of relevant committees as appropriate. Indeed, the Department does not currently have its own strategic plan, perceiving instead that it is preferable for its strategy to be subsumed within the faculties' learning and teaching plans. Future work in this area at a University level will be the result of a close working relationship with the Best Practice Office established in April 2001.

New roles and relationships for Learning Advisers

Learning Advisers have become the linchpins of the particularly close relationship that exists between the Department and the faculties, spending up to 40 per cent of their time in direct support of their subjects. Their role is that of educator not just facilitator. There has been a drive within Learning Support to upskill staff in the area of teaching and facilitation to support institutional developments in learning and teaching. Several cohorts of staff have been put through an in-house Certificate in Training Practice, which is approved by the Institute of Personnel Development. Other staff have been supported in the completion of teaching qualifications. Membership of the Institute of Learning and Teaching has been encouraged throughout the University.

The new staffing structure was based fundamentally on the response of the Department to the evolving curriculum-delivery processes and activities within the University. The distinction that had often been used in the past between teaching and non-teaching was no longer deemed appropriate. Each member of the Learning Adviser team would bring to the delivery process their own expertise and engage in

149

whatever activities were appropriate for the effective and efficient delivery of the curriculum to the students in a particular subject area; these activities included teaching if that was a requirement of the subject. This marked an end to the previous practice of Learning Support staff whereby teaching was considered as outside normal duties.

Learning Advisers act as an interface between the subjects for which they are responsible and Learning Support. Since there are more subjects than Learning Advisers, subjects with which Learning Advisers are not specifically aligned are supported in a liaison relationship. The original intention of achieving equivalence between numbers of Learning Advisers and numbers of subjects has never been achieved, and Faculty Learning Adviser teams cover residual subjects between them. The subject alignments of new appointees have been identified after consultation with faculties. The spread has sometimes been perceived to be uneven with regard to intensity of usage of facilities, particularly information provision or with regard to student numbers. Subject support has extended beyond the Learning Advisers to Service Advisers, who have worked with designated Learning Advisers in support of designated subjects.

Future strategy will be dictated by University priorities, which are currently focused on the student learning experience and learning and curriculum development. The University perceives the need to develop a coherent strategy for supporting learning in learning resource centres both in the development of teaching and learning materials, and in the construction of a learning environment linked to on-campus self-directed study. Learning Advisers act as faculty coordinators for the Virtual Campus, maintaining web pages and bulletin boards for their subjects.

Learning Resources (the proposed name of the Department) will be grouped organizationally with the Best Practice Office and Teaching and Learning Research. The Department expects to work particularly closely with the former, in its role as coordinator and supporter of faculty learning and teaching strategies, and prime mover in the development of the e-learning on campus and the distance-learning infrastructure in the University.

Conclusion

In summary, institutional relations have evolved and the pace of that evolution has usually depended on the pace set by University senior management. Ten years ago, the BP endowment generated progress in the area of skills support and changes in learning and teaching, and Learning Support staff look to developing in the future a mutually beneficial relationship with the Best Practice Office. A permanent and successful relationship throughout has been the one with the academic community, the cornerstone of which is the work of the Learning Advisers.

CONCLUSION

Creating shiny new buildings may entice more students to come into them but will not necessarily change anything else. Creating partnerships that encourage and enable the resources, facilities and, most importantly, the staff expertise to be used to their maximum potential is the only way to ensure the payback on the investment that learning centres represent.

Sheffield Hallam University and the University of Lincoln have taken different paths but arrived at the same destination. Their learning centres are playing an increasingly important role in the life of their institutions. Dedicated LIS staff are working directly with School teams and other specialists in a way that is predicted as the future for their profession: 'Increasingly librarians will be judged as part of multi-skilled teams, as effective collaborators outside the comfortable box' (Brindley, 2001). The typical working week for these staff bears little resemblance to that of even five years ago. It is now common practice for Information Services staff at Sheffield Hallam University to spend at least 50 per cent of their week in direct collaborative work with schools and other partners in the institution. This gives rise to another issue about new roles. There are some concerns among staff that their remit is being widened beyond their capabilities of time and resources; the fear is that they will end up doing increasingly more, but less well. For the future, it is essential to ensure that technology is harnessed to deal with the routine library management issues so that staff are able to channel their time and energy into those activities where they can add most value.

The SCONUL vision for Information Services in 2005 acknowledges that 'academic liaison will have to ensure strategic alignment and operational attunement and will need to be managed in conjunction with other support functions, such as educational developers and learning technologists' (SCONUL, 2001b). The learning centre approach adopted by Sheffield Hallam and other universities offers a strong framework to enable this type of partnership to flourish and to ensure that academic services staff continue to play a significant role in supporting teaching and learning.

REFERENCES

Association of College and Research Libraries (2000), *Information Literacy Competency Standards for Higher Education*, at: http://www.ala.org/acr/ilintro (accessed 20 Octoer 2001).

Breen, R. et al. (2001), The role of information and communication technologies in a university learning environment. *Studies in Higher Education*, **26**(1), pp 95–114.

Breivik, S. (1999), Take II – information literacy: revolution in education. *References Services Review*, **27**(3), pp. 271–5.

Brindley, L. (2001), What use are librarians (working in libraries)? *Relay: the Journal of the University, College and Research Group*, 51, pp. 5–7.

Drew, S. (2001), 'Integrating key skills: guidance notes for staff'. Sheffield Hallam University Learning and Teaching Institute, internal paper

Higher Education Funding Council for England et al. (1993), *Joint Funding Councils' Libraries Review Group: Report* (Follett Report). Bristol: HEFCE.

Moore, K. and Ward, S. (1999), Information Provision for Academics. Unpublished research paper, Sheffield Hallam University Learning Centre.

'Role and Strategic Priorities of the Learning and Teaching Institute', internal paper presented to Sheffield Hallam University Academic Board on 21 June 2000.

SCONUL (2001a), *Quality Assurance Agency – Aide mémoire for reviewers evaluating learning resources*, at: http://www.sconul.ac.uk/quality_ass/Aide_MemoireJul2001.pdf (accessed December 2001).

SCONUL (2001b), *Vision: Academic information services in the year 2005*, at: http://www.sconul.ac.uk/vision2005.htm#vision (accessed December 2001).

6 Building new environments: the physical space

Edited by Roger Hines

Contributors:

Leeds Metropolitan University

University of Lincoln
Sheffield Hallam University

Meg Message and
Norma Thompson
Dilys Young
Roger Hines

INTRODUCTION

The continuing centrality of an appropriate physical environment to the student learning experience is evident from the list of student needs identified in Chapter 4. However, Chapter 1 suggested that the physical limitations and accepted role of academic libraries constrained their ability to meet the demands of the new learning and environment, in terms of learning styles and technologies.

The aim of this chapter is to present the learning centre model as a response to these developments in teaching and learning, and in communications and information technology. It incorporates the academic library into a new type of building with a distinctive vision and role within the institution. In addition to drawing out what is distinctive about this approach for physical design, facilities and services, it will also investigate how this approach is distinctive in the ways it responds to different student requirements.

The first hurdle faced by any proposal to spend significant amounts of money in refurbishment or new build projects is to justify the need for large physical spaces at all, at a time when distributed access to information resources and learning materials may be seen to reduce need to visit academic libraries. Off-campus access to services is certainly growing quickly, with the development of networked information services and increased ownership of PCs; the development of virtual learning environments will accelerate this trend. There is already evidence that visits to academic libraries are being affected. In an article entitled 'The Deserted Library', it is reported that libraries in many parts of the United States have seen door counts and book circulation decrease while electronic access has dramatically increased:

> At the University of Idaho at Moscow, for example, door counts and book circulation have decreased by more than 20 percent since 1997, and reserve loans have plummeted by more than 60 percent. But since 1999, the number of electronic articles that Idaho students retrieved went up by about 350 percent, and periodical database searches shot up by almost 800 percent. Students are choosing to use dormitories, Internet cafes, bookstores, coffee shops, computer suites in other parts of the university to socialise and work. (Carlson, 2001)

The argument presented here is that this need not necessarily be the case. Students will continue to need access to extensive on-campus learning facilities, resources and services, which are centrally located and supported. Nonetheless, what these are and how they are managed needs to be rethought. The learning centre approach outlined below represents one particular response to this rethinking. Its distinctiveness will be drawn out from its underlying vision, its planning requirements, its design and operation.

The experiences of Leeds Metropolitan (LMU) and Sheffield Hallam (SHU) Universities are used as case studies throughout this chapter. Both have built new buildings that justify the name learning centres, rather than academic libraries. Both have extended and refurbished older libraries, relaunching them as learning centres. The experience of the University of Lincoln is also used to illustrate one particular response to changing student working patterns.

SHU opened the new Adsetts Centre in 1996 to replace the Eric Mensforth Library at the City Campus. Built on seven floors, it has a floor area of 11 000 sq. m. and provides approximately 1500 study spaces, 400 of which currently house networked PCs. Provision is also made for media production, including a TV studio and video-editing suites. Media viewing facilities are also available, supported by a broadband AV network. Individual, group and IT study facilities are provided within an open-plan environment. The University's Learning and Teaching Institute and Learning and Teaching Research Institute are also based in the building.

A more incremental approach was followed at the University's Collegiate Campus, where the library was expanded in two phases: firstly into an adjacent building in 1998 and then by means of extensions from 1999 to 2000. The result is a building that incorporates a similar range of facilities and resources to the Adsetts Centre but with a different character, one appropriate to the particular needs of academic programmes based at that campus. More than 500 study places are provided that meet individual and group study needs in more-discrete learning environments. Permanent open-access IT facilities are supplemented by more than 100 PCs located in a suite of IT teaching rooms; they are available for open access use when not booked for teaching.

At LMU, the new-build and conversion occurred the other way around, with the Beckett Park library initially being converted into a learning centre in 1995. The existing library space was substantially reconfigured, including demolition of the inner core, building a three-storey extension where one floor had been, and reconfiguring and refurbishing the perimeter rooms at all three levels. Apart from an additional 675 study spaces, the building now offers integrated teaching and learning space that incorporates library, media and IT facilities; extended IT facilities and teaching laboratories; group study rooms for project work; 50 audio-visual carrels with satellite links, a self-access video-editing suite, and audio-visual loans facilities. It provides a secure environment with access over extended hours, and 24-hour opening.

Almost immediately after this, as part of the University's long-term plan to improve accommodation, planning began in 1996 on a new learning centre at the City Campus, which opened in 2000. This is a purpose-built learning centre, merging two previous learning centres, with a variety of workspace on five floors, including 24 group study rooms, individual study carrels, some large tables and eight enclosed IT labs which can be used by students when not in use for teaching. There are 500 PCs available for student use on the open floors, in enclosed labs and in some specialist ones.

VISION

The learning centre rationale is geared primarily to institutional teaching and learning strategies; it anticipates the growing importance of communications and information technology (C&IT) to learning; it is concerned with learning activities, not just the supporting resources. It is not just the sheer breadth of role, in terms of resources and activities, which makes the learning centre concept distinctive. More fundamentally, it is how all of these resources and services interact. All of these characteristics, with a strong emphasis on integrated provision, are central to the visions of both SHU and LMU.

LEEDS METROPOLITAN UNIVERSITY

For the new-build project at the City Campus, the University's Executive Board charged the Learning Development Strategy Group with developing a set of guiding concepts for the building, that would ensure that its functionality supported the institution's teaching and learning strategy. It was to be an integrated learning centre with the widest possible range of facilities and media to support students' learning under one roof, including:

- provision of flexible space which could support the planned numbers of students with a range of information technologies, production and access methods and which could evolve over time to meet the changing needs of on- and off-campus students;

- provision of a study environment in which students could work individually or in a range of large and small group configurations;
- a physical layout which, supported by appropriate induction, guiding and documentation systems, increased the independence of students;
- a design that would enable the 24-hour opening of facilities;
- future-proofing;
- a design that complied with the Disability Discrimination Act and secured the welfare and convenience of disabled people; and
- a highly energy efficient building.

SHEFFIELD HALLAM UNIVERSITY

The situation at Sheffield was summed up as follows by Graham Bulpitt, Director of the SHU Learning Centre:

> It was clear when we were planning the building that there were changes happening in two key areas. There were changes in terms of new technology and it was clear that electronic information and multimedia materials would be important to the work that we would do. The other area that was changing was in terms of teaching and learning, and there has been a continuing trend away from classroom based work and towards independent work, by students working on their own or in groups. What we wanted to do with the building was to create an environment that allowed all those activities to happen and that is really rather different from a traditional library. (*Adsetts Centre Case Study*, 1996)

The development of these new approaches to teaching and learning needed a different kind of learning environment, which would allow students and teaching staff to work in an integrated way with a range of materials, equipment and services – and specialist staff. This statement of purpose encapsulated the rationale for the Adsetts Centre in 1996 but is equally applicable to all SHU learning centres, which are designed to:

- provide a high quality learning environment for students, which brings together a range of information resources, learning materials, equipment, accommodation and support;
- provide practical support for academic staff in the design and delivery of learning and teaching activities, and a testbed for experimenting with new approaches;
- provide an integrated working environment for all staff to exploit changes in technology and the convergence of information formats;
- increase access to learning support in a cost-effective and efficient way;

- provide a shop window for members of the University, client organizations and the local community that demonstrates the University's commitment to providing a high quality student experience; and
- establish the University as a centre of excellence in educational innovation.

PLANNING

Are there issues in planning the physical space for a learning centre that are in any way different to that of planning a space for a library?

CONSULTATION AND UNDERSTANDING

Academic staff

The predominantly academic rationale for learning centres means that an institution's academic staff must see themselves as important stakeholders. As an active learning environment, the learning centre must, as a minimum, match closely the approaches to learning that they will follow. More than that, however, it can play a more proactive role in encouraging staff to adopt new approaches to learning. This is more of a selling than consultative exercise, to create an understanding of the potential of what will be a radical new concept to many and persuading them to incorporate it into their individual learning strategies.

Learning centre staff

A similar process needs to be followed with learning centre staff, as it is they who will have to take the greatest ownership of the building, plan its internal layout and make it work. They have a good understanding of how students actually do learn and are likely to provide the most practical, productive and innovative ideas. They will require a sound understanding of institutional teaching and learning strategies.

Students

The top-down strategic approach to planning needs to be complemented by a more practical perspective, based on what service users need from a building. Involvement in the consultative process is necessary to raise awareness of its purpose and potential; user surveys, comments forms from students, feedback from course committees and from learning centre staff, will all provide a picture of evolving needs.

157

PROJECT MANAGEMENT

The distinctiveness of a learning centre is that it integrates a very wide and complex range of services and types of learning space. Planning for it, therefore, requires the involvement of a wide range of staff. It is unrealistic, as well as undesirable, to expect an architect and design team to provide a shell into which all these services will be poured. The architects, though well-qualified in their chosen profession, may start with little or no understanding of what a learning centre is trying to achieve and may need detailed briefing if they are to grasp the concept.

It is vital that all parties involved in planning – learning centre staff, estates staff, architects and project managers – have a clear and shared vision of what is expected from the building. Joint visits to other similar buildings with architects can be a useful way to start this process and help to develop a productive relationship. However, visits to other institutions may only involve a relatively small number of senior staff. The architect and design team also need a link to the staff who will best understand the demands likely to made of the building, and should be encouraged to hold meetings with learning centre staff groups to discuss their hopes and wishes. As with any major project, it is vital that the staff who will be managing the building take ownership of it through involvement at all stages of the project.

NEW BUILD, EXTENSION OR REFURBISHMENT?

New build can be easier to handle than refurbishment or extension. For example, with the range of services to be provided, the power and networking requirements may prove very difficult to install in any building designed before the IT age. At LMU Beckett Park Campus, the building of the new learning centre involved reconfiguration of the existing library space, including demolition of the inner core, building a three-storey extension where one floor had been, and reconfiguring and refurbishing the perimeter rooms at all three levels. This was further complicated because the building is listed and certain features had to be retained and incorporated – for example, stained glass windows, wooden panelling, brick walls and decorative plasterwork. Furthermore, this work had to be done while still running a library service! Refurbishment and extension also requires a lot more cooperation on a day-to-day level between building workers and learning centre staff who have to continue to provide a service to users throughout the project.

Whichever option is selected, it is of paramount importance that all parties affected should be included in the consultation process. This ensures that awareness and understanding of users' needs and concerns will be as full as possible. Care was taken to secure maximum stakeholder input at both Sheffield and Leeds.

Sheffield Hallam University: New build – Adsetts Centre

Academic staff An extensive programme of consultation and awareness raising was undertaken by SHU Learning Centre staff, both through targeted presentations and discussion in school of study committees. Unsurprisingly, feedback was limited, as the learning centre was a still a new concept and, without examples to refer to or previous experience, staff may have felt reluctant to comment. However, as at LMU, once academic staff had experience of one learning centre, demand for similar facilities emerged very quickly indeed from other sites and staff had a much clearer idea of what they did and did not want from a learning centre.

Learning Centre staff Faulkner Browns, the architect practice chosen for the Adsetts Centre, had a lot of experience of library design, but the Director of SHU Learning Centre has commented:

> It was absolutely a joint venture with the architect and people from the University working very closely together. The architect brought with him a lot of experience of library design and of designing social buildings and leisure centres and local authority buildings. What we were looking to do really, was to move the brief forward together and it really was an interactive process with us feeding off each other and respecting each other's expertise. We did not attempt to influence the architect unduly in terms of the creation of the building design and the use of materials and the relationships between spaces and so on. *I think the architect was very keen to get a clear idea of what we were trying to create in terms of a learning environment, which was new for him, too.* (*Adsetts Centre Case Study*, 1996; emphasis added)

Apart from the high-level steering groups that included staff from the University Estates division, the architects, the project management company, the Learning Centre and the IT department, there were a variety of Learning Centre sub-groups developing ideas for particular areas of the service and the building.

Students Students were directly involved through school-based consultation. Evidence from user surveys and user feedback also gave very clear messages from students on the sort of facilities they wanted.

Leeds Metropolitan University: Refurbishment and new build

For both the refurbishment and new-build projects it was important to gain input from the major stakeholders of the learning centres. Existing liaison and feedback methods with faculties, central University departments and students were sufficiently robust to allow the majority of the consultation and communication to be carried out through these routes. Direct student feedback, for example, influenced decisions about group study rooms, and the experience at the Beckett Park Campus indicated the number needed to be even higher at City Campus. As mentioned above, the University's

Learning Development Strategy Group guided the design of the City Campus learning centre, and the composition of this group – Learning and Information Services, the faculties, Academic Registry and Estates – ensured it was best placed to align provision with the teaching and learning needs of the University. At the initial planning stage, for example, input from faculties led to the decision to add another floor of specialist IT facilities to support specific teaching and learning activities.

Learning Centre staff In both projects, senior staff were involved at the design stage, while other Learning Centre staff were involved in varying degrees later on with issues related to the operation of the buildings. The Deputy Director of Learning and Information Services held a major planning role throughout both projects. Consultation and liaison with staff was handled more at local level, which meant that direct contact with the architects and contractors was minimal and on occasions relevant issues could have benefited from closer working, such as sharing the knowledge of Learning Centre staff about the needs of students. The design of the counter at Beckett Park, with insufficient space allowed between terminals for customers to place books was a case in point. Learning from this, at City Campus, Learning Centre staff were given responsibility for the design of the counter themselves. It was important in both projects for staff at all levels to feel involved and develop ownership of the new accommodation. They were encouraged to visit other libraries and learning centres, and found it particularly valuable to talk to other staff about issues and problems relating to their buildings.

DESIGN AND OPERATION

The distinctiveness of a learning centre can be seen in how it responds to the student learning needs identified in Chapter 4; in particular:

- the provision of the facilities, resources and services students need to support their learning;
- their accessibility at the times of day and days of the week convenient for their study, family and work commitments;
- their arrangement to support their learning needs effectively;
- staff support to facilitate their effective use; and
- an environment conducive to study.

FACILITIES, RESOURCES AND SERVICES

The range of learning activities that students undertake and the changed nature of their study now need to be supported by a wide range of facilities, resources and services. To research, write and produce assignments, students need access to print, audio-visual and networked information equipment and facilities. For many, assignments involve different media, such as video, and they may require media production facilities, such as TV studio and editing suites.

As more of the student learning experience takes place in virtual learning environments, dependence on C&IT facilities can only increase. This dependence on electronic access will grow even further with the development of comprehensive managed learning environments. Both Web-CT at LMU and Blackboard at SHU are used to deliver assessments, course materials and course resources. Take-up of this software has been rapid in both institutions. At SHU, for example, over 10 500 students are enrolled on at least one Blackboard unit and the software is averaging 34 000 hits a day in semester.

At the same time, there is an increasingly diverse range of options available to access these resources. The pervasive on-campus IT infrastructure undoubtedly makes access less dependent on centralized provision. The flexibility of the developing wireless networks will provide the potential to decentralize access further. With the spread of PC ownership, universities may question the need to provide PC facilities in learning centres or elsewhere. The future of the desktop PC is uncertain; UK universities may be a long way from requiring students to purchase their own laptops, but portable devices of various kinds seem to be the future.

Despite these developments, however, there will be significant demand for large-scale, central provision for the foreseeable future. Many students still do not have access to PCs and the Internet at home, and some find that their living accommodation is not conducive to study. While increasingly students live at their parents' home and study at an institution within commuting distance, it is still the case that significant numbers move away from home. Furthermore, ownership of laptops is still at a relatively low level.

Leeds Metropolitan University

Both learning centres at Leeds have a mix of networked PCs providing general software, along with some specialist IT provision for specific schools. General use PCs are provided in open areas, and in PC labs, which are used as both teaching space and open access. As much software as possible is networked to increase availability and accessibility, although some packages are restricted by licences or by networking issues to specific rooms. More advanced software and hardware is provided in a multimedia lab, although technology in this area is developing so quickly that needs for specialist and standard PC facilities change frequently; for example, demand for video streaming is widespread and it is no longer appropriate to restrict availability to one specialist room.

Both learning centres house facilities for media production for students to create presentation materials using video, audio and multimedia. At City Campus there are two video studios adjacent to a 15-station video-editing suite, with technical support for students on hand. These facilities are available to any student needing to produce video material as part of their studies, not just those on media courses.

A particular feature of the learning centres is designated space and facilities for specific user groups. For example, there is a Postgraduate Research Lab of ten PCs at the City Campus for the use of postgraduate research students, and at both campuses a specialized learning resources room with hardware and software for disabled and dyslexic students. On the top floor at the City Campus there are four rooms specifically for the use of schools using computer-aided design and Macs. This represents a gradual move towards centralized accommodation for specialized IT facilities, with the advantages of long opening hours and economical support arrangements. The Postgraduate Research Laboratory was designed to meet the needs of a group who tended not to study in the learning centre, which can be perceived more as an undergraduate resource in an institution where this is the majority activity. By allocation of their own space designated for their exclusive use, researchers are encouraged to feel they have a stake in the building and to articulate their needs more clearly.

Sheffield Hallam University

The Adsetts and Collegiate learning centres provide a similar range of resources and facilities to LMU, although there are differences in how they are arranged. Open-access PCs present a student desktop that gives access to all University general networked services, including the Internet, learning centre services such as the catalogue and databases, the virtual learning environment and a wide range of computer-based learning packages. An extensive range of software is available, including the Microsoft Office software, Oracle, Unix, some programming languages such as C++ and Visual basic, e-mail, maths and statistical packages such as Minitab, Derive and SPSS. Licensing and practical considerations mean that some specialist software does not run on the university-wide network and may only be available within schools of study.

Both learning centres make specialist media production facilities, such as video-editing suites, available to students; the Adsetts Centre also has a TV studio. Stand-alone and networked video presenters are also available in the open-plan areas of learning centres. Videos can be viewed individually or in a group set-up, where seating for up to four students supports a shared activity, to reflect the increasing trend of students working on group projects. Facilities are also available in small study rooms should a group of students want to work with video material without the restriction of headphones, and hold a discussion causing no disturbance to other users.

Networking technology is used to maximize access to audio-visual resources. The learning centres utilize a Broadband communication system to distribute signals. LCTV (Learning Centre Television) operates via this system, enabling a programme of videos to be shown throughout the day, seven days a week, during the academic year at City and Collegiate Campuses. There are two channels: one shows videos on key skills, such as presentation skills, team working, report writing; the second is available to tutors to request screenings of their choice to fit in with their timetable. LCTV can be viewed on any of the video presenters in the learning centres. The broadband system is also used to distribute European satellite TV. Planning is now under way to move from analogue to digital TV, satellite and terrestrial. A longer-term project is to investigate the central storage of digitized videos as the basis for viewing on any PC.

ACCESS

As growing student numbers have increased the pressure on accommodation, the operational times of many higher education institutions have lengthened; for many, the teaching day now extends from 9.00 am to 9.00 pm. And as the pressures on students themselves increase, both academic and otherwise, many now want to be able to access learning centre facilities, resources and services at any time of the day, on any of the seven days of the week. Students used to seeing some supermarkets open 24 hours a day may now perceive a learning centre as part of this service sector, which should strive to meet their needs at any time they wish.

The implications of these developments for library or learning centre buildings are twofold. First, as the only staffed buildings open for such long hours, they need to contain as many as possible of the resources, facilities and services that students need. Second, they need to be designed in such a way as to provide a secure environment and to facilitate adequate supervision with limited staff overnight.

Sheffield Hallam University

The general approach to learning centre design and operation is that as many facilities as possible should be available to students during opening hours; no distinction is made between information and IT resources. Chapter 4 describes the 24-hour opening operation of the City and Collegiate learning centres from the perspective of the student experience. The Adsetts Centre was designed with this extended opening very much in mind, with its open-plan design facilitating convenient supervision. At both campuses, security issues are given a high priority; extensive closed circuit television is used, with monitors being available to security staff and also placed in prominent areas in the main body of the buildings, so that users are aware of the presence of cameras. External security is more difficult to guarantee, in terms of the safety of students making their way in and out of buildings. While the Adsetts Centre exit opens onto a well-lit main road, the Collegiate exit is within the campus, leading to a footpath. The lighting around the site has therefore been improved.

Leeds Metropolitan University

Review of opening hours to meet students' needs is continuous at LMU, set alongside the resourcing and operational constraints. The move towards 24-hour access is an incremental process, with piloting and evaluation at each stage. Consultation and feedback has suggested that access to PC facilities is the majority need, and therefore resources have been concentrated on opening some PC labs at peak times of year. The new learning centre at City Campus was designed with 24-hour access to PC labs in mind, while at Beckett Park, adjustments to the accommodation have been necessary to allow overnight secure access. A separate entrance to these areas is used outside normal learning centre opening hours, which allows security of both users and facilities to be more closely monitored. At these times, the rooms have to become independent of other learning centre facilities, so as much equipment and software needs to be provided as possible. Staff support is not available overnight, so self-guided help needs to be designed to allow users to maximize their independence. The user population overnight is not necessarily the same as during the day, as students will make use of facilities that are convenient for their homes and travel arrangements, factors that are more important at night. For example, Beckett Park is close to student residences and has better car parking facilities.

ARRANGEMENT AND INTEGRATION OF FACILITIES

Book stock or reader spaces?

Predicting the medium- and long-term future of information provision is an inexact science. However, it is likely that printed collections will continue to take up significant learning centre space for the foreseeable future. For the next five to ten years at least, some book stock is likely to continue to grow, although probably at a slower rate. The space requirements of printed journals are already shrinking in some universities, as electronic versions replace current, and in some cases retrospective, issues. The balance of space between stock and other uses, particularly reader spaces, will continue to change and it is important that planning for new and refurbished buildings incorporates sufficient flexibility to accommodate changes in use.

The library services of the higher education colleges and post-1992 universities tend to have a different perspective to those of the older, more research-led, universities. The former are less likely to regard themselves as major repositories of paper-based research collections with a major archiving role and, except for a few special collections, they may take a fairly pragmatic attitude to stock that is not used on a regular basis. For example, both LMU and SHU took the view that their paper-based collections are unlikely to grow beyond a further 10 years and that hard copy will be progressively replaced by electronic information. Students will increasingly want access to electronic copies of materials and if they cannot have access directly, they will need access to databases, combined with an efficient interlibrary loans system; in other words an access, rather than a holdings, policy. Thus special care has been given to catering for increasingly diverse study requirements, particularly related to computer-oriented research. Providing user spaces with IT facilities or the capability of being linked to them has a higher priority than allowing for the physical expansion of paper-based collections.

Integration

The arrangement of information resources within libraries has always been a major source of debate and will continue to be so. Should all books be in one sequence, all journals in another, media items separate (or even in several sequences according to format) or integrated? Or should subject be the overriding factor, where broadly-based subject groupings bring all categories of material together? The same debate can take place about layout in learning centres, and arguments on either side are probably little different to debates about layout in libraries. However, a further complication of the debate concerns the degree to which all facilities and resources are integrated.

The basic rationale for an integrated approach is that during a single visit to a learning centre, students will need to use a wide range of resources and services and that these should, as far as possible, be located together. The result is a learning environment that can be substantially different from that of an academic library.

In practice, the biggest area of debate is the degree to which PC provision should be separate – either distributed throughout the building, or located together in one place? The proponents of an integrated model would argue that students are likely to use printed materials and IT facilities together, for example when word processing assignments. Electronic information services have become an increasingly significant part of information service provision, complementing and supplementing more traditional resources. The increasing use of word-processing, spreadsheet and other facilities as the basis of note taking and assignment composition require these facilities to be seen as an integral part of any study place and not as something special and separate from the use of information resources and services. From the users' point of view all of these resources and tools need to be used together.

(Of course, the debate about whether to adopt an integrated or separate approach may well become redundant if the combination of mobile devices and the installation of wireless networks within learning centres liberates access to networked services from the inflexibility imposed by complex cabling infrastructure.)

Group and individual work space

With the growing importance of group work to student programmes, provision of group workspace is a vital element of the learning centre concept and needs to be integral to any learning centre building, not just an add-on to individual study provision. However, this element of the learning centre vision is one of the hardest to plan for in practice.

The problem all learning centres face is how to provide such spaces and at the same time provide space for quiet individual learning. Getting this balance right is difficult, and more so as demands for different types of space can vary throughout the academic year; for example, although demand for group workspace will predominate for most of the year, during exam periods the demand for individual study space will expand. A further complication is that an increasing number of non-standard courses have exams and study periods outside the 'traditional' academic structure. The increasing pressure to allow courses to run timetables to meet the needs of different types of students and students in employment can produce a diversity of assessment and assessment periods.

Sheffield Hallam University

In the original vision statement for the Adsetts Centre the first paragraph stated:

> If we are going to make the Learning Centre more than just a building containing a library and computing facility, the starting point should be that the service provision and support should be integrated. The approach we should take, therefore, is to start from the premise that services and facilities should be integrated throughout the building and then to challenge that where we think it is not in the interests of service users. It is important that we avoid the position of having a separate 'computing area' in the learning centre, with only a token presence of IT facilities on individual subject floors. (*Adsetts Centre Case Study*, 1996)

The vision was therefore one of in-depth integration, with the fundamental organizational principle being subject, rather than format or function based. The aim was to bring together on each of the four subject floors a full range of information resources, facilities and study environments. These include group and individual work areas, extensive IT provision, individual and group video-viewing facilities, networked printing and photocopying facilities. While a small number of group study rooms are provided, mainly for activities such as practising group presentations, a fundamental principle of the Adsetts Centre is that group activity is as mainstream as individual study, and that it should take place in the main body of the building, rather than being enclosed and banished to the periphery.

Of course, the precise arrangement of a subject-based approach is itself contentious. How subjects are grouped is increasingly problematic, as many of the University's courses are interdisciplinary; engineers use legal and management materials extensively, for example. Size of stack and floors were also a constraining factor. A broad-brush approach was taken, which removed any explicit linkage between a school of study and a particular subject floor, to try to give the message to students that they need to use the whole of the building. The layout is designed to help encourage interdisciplinary exchanges. In addition to the underlying issues of principle about supporting student learning, there were practical considerations driven by site constraints: for example, in a six-storey building there is potentially a five-floor gap between different collections. Learning Centre surveys have shown that while students often identify with a subject floor and tend to go to 'their' subject floor, especially for group work, they will frequently use other floors. It may help here that the decision is often made on the basis of where there are most free PCs.

The incremental development of the Collegiate learning centre necessitated a different arrangement, as its size and range of discrete spaces imposed restrictions on adopting a purely subject-based approach. A somewhat different approach to the Adsetts Centre also needed to be taken to support the particular study requirements of its students, with greater emphasis on individual study. The PCs are available throughout the building, although perhaps a little less scattered than in the Adsetts Centre. However, learning from the experiences at the Adsetts Centre, greater provision has been made for small group workrooms, which are intensively booked. The physical nature of the site has made it more practical to separate group and individual study spaces and to provide a larger room for silent study that is more visible to users.

It is recognised that the availability of large numbers of PCs undoubtedly attracts a great deal of use, which may have no relationship with any other learning centre services. However, the view was taken that too many PCs located centrally away from other learning resources might reduce the effectiveness of integrated, subject-focused provision. In an environment where there is likely to be increasing pressure on IT resources, it is important to locate equipment to facilitate multi-purpose, flexible use. The Adsetts Centre has more than 400 networked PCs distributed across four subject floors. They are arranged both at single-use workstations and also at larger group worktables to reflect student requirements. There are more restrictions on PC distribution at the Collegiate learning centre, as the absence of raised flooring means that power and data access is wall-mounted.

167

Leeds Metropolitan University

In both learning centres, the principles of ease of use, user independence and integration of resources and facilities are followed as far as the accommodation constraints allow. The purpose-built City Campus building has therefore been able to take these principles further than the refurbishment at Beckett Park. To support both independent student learning and efficient staffing support, users are encouraged to be as self-reliant as possible in accessing and using resources and facilities. For example, consistent floor patterns, appropriate guiding and intuitive layouts allow users to learn quickly how to negotiate the building. Book collections are divided as simply as possible between floors and all journals are together in one alphabetical sequence, avoiding the subject grouping approach which may require more training and guiding. Responding to user feedback, a special concession was made to the law collection, where all materials are housed together, regardless of format. All audio-visual items are kept together at the beginning of the book sequence on each floor, so that they can be distinguished and are in close proximity to playback equipment.

The design of the physical layout took into consideration the major travel routes between high-volume services and facilities and attempted to shorten these pathways, so as to reduce traffic flows. Large open spaces with clear sight lines allow users to locate and access the facilities they need easily, while increasing the potential for security supervision. Cellular spaces, such as teaching labs and print/copying rooms, and enclosed corridors and stairwells, ensure noise is contained away from study areas.

While at City Campus PCs and printed resources are integrated in large open spaces, the physical restrictions of the building at Beckett Park make this impossible. The main provision of PCs is therefore on the top floor which houses all the teaching labs and a very large open-access space. The ground and first floors have a small number of PCs around the perimeter of the book shelving, and there are plans to extend PC provision to the mezzanine floor when networking can be provided. This means that the building is effectively divided into IT and printed resource areas, making integrated staff support more difficult, and necessitating two separate helpdesks.

Both learning centres have taken the approach to mainstream quiet study and provide dedicated accommodation for group work in bookable rooms, representing the reverse of the design of the Adsetts Centre at SHU. Quiet and group study are segregated in ways which are clear to users, and this has proved effective in reducing noise problems. It was quite clear at the planning stage that this was a critical issue for the building's design. The need for group accommodation has continued to increase over the past few years, and therefore many more group study rooms were planned at the City Campus, than at Beckett Park. To provide for maximum flexibility in student working requirements, some group study rooms are provided with PCs and some with video players. A number of the group study rooms may be configured as both four small rooms and one large room, to provide the option of other teaching rooms at peak times of the year.

STAFF SUPPORT

Student-centred learning encourages student autonomy and independence, and the reduction in class contact time with academic staff is likely to increase. However, student surveys within SHU consistently show that students value individual contact and help from staff. Students who have less contact with academic staff may wish to have more contact with Learning Centre staff. An evaluation of the Adsetts Centre during its first year of operation found that:

> Information desks were a major source of support for students working in the Adsetts Centre on general information gathering tasks. (From the questionnaire 38.2% most often go to information desk, followed by 12.5% ask friend or lecturer. This trend was reiterated in the Focus Group.) (Learning and Teaching Research Institute, 1997)

There seems to be no lessening of demand for help from staff in a learning centre. Information or helpdesks are still a vital service and of course the range of enquiries broadens out with the inclusion of extensive IT facilities. In addition to the staffing related aspects of helpdesk support (discussed in Chapter 3 particularly), there are also issues of operation that can be usefully discussed as part of the operation of learning centre accommodation. There are different models for helpdesks – single helpdesk with staff then roaming the building, or perhaps subject area helpdesks, for example. There is also debate about whether to have separate IT and information desks, or single helpdesks with separate IT and library/information staff sitting side by side, or to integrate support fully with no distinction visible to students.

Leeds Metropolitan University

The design of the building is fundamental to how help services are staffed; integrated facilities make integrated support services both necessary and efficient. The constraints at Beckett Park have already been mentioned, but at City Campus the opening of a truly integrated resource was aligned with the development of a pilot integrated information and IT helpdesk, which is now consolidated as a permanent service. Staff support for the five-storey building is provided from a single information desk on the ground floor, which has available all kinds of support required by users. The need for a more distributed form of help in such a large building was anticipated by providing 'nurse phones' – telephones in open areas and PC labs linking directly to the information desk – and by introducing a 'roving' help assistant role. Help can therefore be both centralized and distributed, as user needs and staffing levels dictate.

At Beckett Park site, the information and IT helpdesks remain separate, but the roving help assistant role is also used to overcome the problems of large unstaffed spaces.

Sheffield Hallam University

Because the SHU vision was one of integration of services, information desks and the people who staff them make no distinction between information and IT enquiries. Public services in the Adsetts Centre operate from six floors, four of which are subject-based. There are two information desks, each of which supports two adjacent subject floors. This arrangement works well within the overall design of the building and matches the subject team structure. However, the subject of enquiries brought to a particular desk can be very diverse, as many queries are linked to e-resources and students may sit anywhere where there is a free PC. There is one information desk at the Collegiate learning centre, situated close to and visible from the building foyer. This provides frontline support for both information and IT enquiries, but also has access to a technical support desk that is associated with IT teaching facilities located within the learning centre, at least during the core parts of weekdays.

AN ENVIRONMENT CONDUCIVE TO STUDY

Physical design

The exterior design of a building may make an important architectural statement for the institution and the surrounding city; it may even attract students into it for the first time. Both LMU and SHU have striking new buildings and have enhanced the appearance of their refurbished learning centres. However, it is the interior design and environment that is important to students and must be attractive and comfortable to support and encourage lengthy periods of study. Many issues, such as colour, temperature levels, or whether the environment is open plan or not, do not change. Learning centres introduce new ones, particularly those associated with the presence of large numbers of PCs; they sharpen the focus of others such as noise management. However, these are very subjective areas and no approach will ever satisfy everyone.

Lighting

Lighting has always been an important issue in the design of libraries but becomes even more important in planning a new building, especially if PCs and media equipment are to be distributed throughout the building, rather than being kept together in discrete zones. It must support a wide range of often conflicting requirements. While natural light may be enjoyed by readers of print materials, there can be problems with direct sunlight for users of display screens. Furthermore, general lighting levels suitable for reading material on a desk, for finding books on a low shelf and for reading a PC screen will differ.

Furniture

Furniture design is a particularly important aspect of modern buildings because of the more varied demands it will be expected to satisfy. Individual study places may need to provide space for books and learning materials as well as the PC. It is not just a question of space, or of cable management, but one of design principle: to what extent is furniture customized to accommodate information technology?

Some specialist furniture will be required, for example, to view video material in groups, as well as on an individual basis. Extensive group work requires properly designed furniture if it is to be facilitated effectively. This increasingly includes provision for PCs, as groups of students will wish to use them to work together on writing reports, creating presentations or finding information. So group work furniture needs to be capable of housing PCs and cables.

Above all, however, furniture must be flexible to accommodate changing needs; getting the balance right between the different types of workspace may prove difficult and adjustments may need to be made. It is unlikely that layout will be correct the first time or that demand will stay the same: the number of PCs in the building is likely to increase, for example.

Noise levels

Noise remains a major problem for every library, one that has been exacerbated in the last five years by mobile phones. However, for learning centres at least, it is now a more complex issue, in that some kinds of noise, for example that generated by group work, are not just tolerated but encouraged. Even mobile phone use is not so straightforward. From the perspective of students working in groups and talking, they often do not see a problem with talking on a mobile phone as well. They may be using it to contact fellow students for information or to phone companies for data for a project. Part-time students may need to be contacted by work, or if they have children may need the security of knowing they can be called at all times. Some University teaching and school administrative staff have started to phone students' mobile numbers as a means of contacting them. The idea of a total ban on mobile phone use within a learning centre is frankly unrealistic.

How can noise be controlled, to keep in balance the different user requirements? There are fundamentally two approaches within a learning centre building. Firstly make most of the open areas a group work space and create silent zones or silent rooms, the other is to make the open areas quiet and then create separate group work rooms.

Sheffield Hallam University

The internal layout of the Adsetts Centre is open-plan, using very few solid walls. This produces large open spaces, whose use can be changed easily, allowing for maximum flexibility. This open design also allows good vertical and horizontal views and thus supports the principle of high visibility: to make its users aware of the potential of the building, in terms of resources and facilities.

The incremental approach to developing the Collegiate learning centre produces an entirely different physical space, which may not have the same degree of flexibility but does accommodate discrete spaces to support different learning styles. It provides a study environment appropriate to, and appreciated by, the students based at that campus.

Power and data distribution The benefits of a new build can be seen at the Adsetts Centre, where the power and data transmission framework has been designed and spatially coordinated to cover the whole floor area. The aim was for as much flexibility as possible so that, as user spaces changed in number and location, it would be possible to extend power and the IT network to any user space, which in effect means almost any part of the building.

This had a major influence on the design of the building – the architect, Bill Cowen, has commented that it was in many ways the driving factor. The floor design is based on a raised, load-bearing floor, all of which will support shelving as well as seating. Cabling is delivered to floor boxes attached to flexible hosing so that they can be very easily moved, particularly as all carpeting is laid as tiles. Most parts of the building have a box nearby and new boxes can be installed relatively easily.

In the architect's view:

> [The] floor is cost effective, and I think it will serve the university well, because at any point in this building you can change the density of occupants, you can change the density of computers, you can deliver the building environment to those areas and you can deliver power, voice and data cabling. And, who knows, whatever new technology might come along, will be suited to that sort of distribution. (*Adsetts Centre Case Study*, 1996)

In addition to power, data and voice cable, the floor cavity is used as part of the system that circulates air through the building. This avoids the need for a suspended ceiling to conceal metal ducts, although the downside to this is that the ceiling throughout most of the building is of sprayed concrete. It is therefore not possible to suspend signage from it; nor can lighting be set into the ceiling but has to be suspended from it.

Lighting At the City Campus the previous Eric Mensforth library had very little natural light and feedback given from staff to the architects was that for many staff an increase in natural light would be very high on their wish list for improvements to their working environment. The architect's solution, the 'Gull Wing' on the southern side of the building, is the most distinctive external and internal feature of the new building. It extends over reading areas to provide a high level of natural illumination, yet protects against direct sunlight falling on to PC screens. The main stairways through the building and the separate light well contribute to the sense of openness and accessibility, and also to help diffuse natural light from the large window running the length of the roof at the top of the building.

At an early stage of planning, a very flexible – and expensive – lighting system was specified but its specification had to be lowered to contribute to cost reductions. The lighting system installed does provide good overall coverage and is particularly good for PC use, although the reduced flexibility over shelving areas can cause problems when shelves are moved.

Furniture All student desks are IT-capable, although they have not been customized to hold PC hardware, apart from cable management. This decision has already been justified, as furniture and PCs have been rearranged most years since opening – to help noise management and to create specialist areas, such as assistive technology resource areas with equipment and software for users with disabilities and a learning skills area where materials and tutorial help is available on, for example, maths. Group study tables were specially designed for the Adsetts Centre. The response from students has been extremely favourable, although smaller, more flexible tables were specified for Collegiate.

Noise management The design of the Collegiate learning centre means that its series of discrete areas allow the physical separation of different activities and thus contain noise effectively. The design of the Adsetts Centre was more challenging and deserves more detailed examination.

It was recognized from the early planning stages of the Adsetts Centre that the open-plan design would require a different approach to noise management. In some parts of the building, noise is encouraged. Indeed, when visitors come to visit the Adsetts Centre one of the most obvious differences that they notice is not the number of PCs scattered around but the number of students working in groups.

The feedback after the first year of the Adsetts Centre operation noted:

> The Adsetts Centre was perceived as being most conducive for group work – the group work facilities were rated as excellent and the large curved desks were seen as particularly conducive to effective group working This represents a shift away from the traditional 'quiet study' associated with libraries. (Learning and Teaching Research Institute, 1997)

However, the building must also provide an environment supportive of individual study. At the planning stage, it was accepted that noise transmission would be a consequence of an open-plan study environment, as the different types of use had in-built conflict, principally between group work and individual study. The fabric of the building itself was therefore designed to reduce this problem, with sound-absorbent materials being used and an acoustic coating applied to ceilings.

Noise transmission across areas has been managed in a variety of ways:

- The initial layout design was based on a progression across each subject floor from group work space, through a quieter zone where individual workspaces for PCs would be clustered, to an area where individual non-PC study spaces would be grouped together for silent study. However, the demarcations between the different areas were not sufficiently distinct, signage was largely ineffective; activities and associated noise, tended to spill across boundaries.
- The different zones were then rearranged to sharpen demarcation and alter the balance between them to match changing demand.
- Most recently and effectively, one floor has been designated as a completely silent area and is patrolled at busy times of the year by student noise monitors. A large office on another floor has also been turned into a silent study area. While this is used, it is never full, as most students, most of the time, seem to be comfortable working with background noise.

Noise still features as an issue in responses to the Learning Centre's annual user survey, although as can be seen from Chapter 4, it is becoming less so. Mobile phones have been the biggest single cause of complaint but the learning centre has now moved to a policy of mobile tolerant areas where students are encouraged to go, or to work if they feel they cannot switch their phones off. Evidence to date suggest that this arrangement works much better for both staff and students.

Leeds Metropolitan University

The environmental design principles of openness, flexibility and accessibility employed for the City Campus learning centre by the Bowman Riley Partnership have been mentioned above. The large open areas allow both integration of facilities and a pleasant working environment for users. Large windows allow plenty of natural light, and are designed to maximize light transmission and minimize radiant heat transmission. Lighting within the building is a combination of ambient lighting provided by uplighters reflecting off the ceiling arches, and downlighters in the shelving areas activated by infra-red presence detectors. Arc lamps in individual study carrels allow users to switch on additional lighting if required, and presence detectors, which switch off when the user leaves, also control these. Lighting in teaching rooms and offices is also controlled by presence detection, which requires some retraining on the part of staff to resist switching lights on and off manually. There was some apprehension at introducing such a radically different lighting system, but it has proved effective once users and staff become familiar with it. Energy efficiency was a specific design objective; this is also achieved through the heating system, which moves heat generated by high PC usage into lower temperature areas.

Furniture and fittings Furniture throughout both learning centres is standard office and library design, which has been found to be adequate to support users' needs. The exception is the design of service points, which have very specific localized requirements. Staff have been thoroughly involved in specifying and designing information desks and counters from both a user and staff perspective.

Noise levels Noise control was flagged up as a crucial design factor at both learning centres from the start, based on the experience of the previous accommodation and of elsewhere. The approach to group work has been outlined above, but it was also recognized that individual PC use creates a certain amount of noise, and so in the large open areas PCs are separated from silent study spaces by rows of book and journal shelving. This is reasonably effective, but there is still a low level of demand for completely silent accommodation, which is provided at Beckett Park, but is more problematic at City Campus. A part-time security assistant patrols the quiet areas to provide some noise control, and at peak times employing student 'quiet patrollers' has been trialled. As for mobile phone noise, this has been managed by allocating 'phone zone' areas in the enclosed corridors and stairwells. Although this system has not entirely eradicated the occasional ringing of mobile phones in quiet areas, it does provide a convenient nearby location for users to move to, and they have adapted to it with enthusiasm.

A SOCIAL ENVIRONMENT?

A learning centre is designed to provide a welcoming, relaxed atmosphere and the computer environment is designed to be welcoming and user friendly. As a result, many students see the academic computer network and the learning centre itself as social space as well as workspace. They may not see a clear distinction between work and social space, and the design of a learning centre building may not always make an obvious distinction.

The boundaries between work and leisure are also blurring in the workplace:

> As Riehle notes, the *work* ethic is not collapsing so much as the boundaries between *work* and *leisure* are blurring – a combination that often produces stress and confusion. According to a new Ipsos-Reid poll, about 43 percent of workers say they bring *work* home or are 'on call'; similarly, 30 percent admit using the Internet or e-mail at *work* for play or personal matters. (Samuelson, 2001)

175

If the boundaries between work and leisure are getting fuzzy, it is not surprising that the use of a learning centre reflects this and that some students regard social use as one function of the one-stop-shop. There is undoubtedly considerable variance in the extent to which libraries permit and make specific provision for this use.

It is a particular issue for learning centres. Students may spend long hours there, using the wide range of resources. Between the work they may socialize, meet their friends, surf the Internet or e-mail friends and family. It is the presence of large numbers of networked PCs that highlight social use as an issue, as they have extended its possibilities and are often under pressure for academic use. At the same time, they make one type of social use almost impossible to stop. Enforcing 'academic work only' rules is increasingly difficult; on seeing a member of staff approach, students have only to switch to Excel or Word. With so much teaching material being delivered electronically, and students increasingly interacting with staff and fellow students by e-mail, it is not possible to limit e-mail usage. Many networked packages now deliver sound and it is difficult to tell if a student with headphones is listening to work or an Internet radio station.

There may be other factors driving social use. The Students Union may be seen by students who do not drink alcohol as an unsympathetic social space. While parents may disapprove of them spending time there, few would object to them going to the library or learning centre.

Bookshops, libraries and learning centres have attempted to create a welcoming social atmosphere, viewing some types of social use not as problem but as a benefit. Their aim is not to discourage social use but to permit or even encourage it, without detracting from their primary focus of being centred on learning. The experience of the University of Lincoln in particular illustrates how this sort of positive approach can be accomplished successfully.

Leeds Metropolitan University

Shortage of social space in certain areas of the University is a general problem, and inevitably social noise and activities do impinge on the learning centre environment. The layouts of the centres, however, help to encourage users to recognize when they are moving from reception and traffic zones to quiet study areas and teaching labs, where social activities and noise are not appropriate. The entrance foyers, corridors and stairwells are almost all separated from study areas by walls and doors, which help contain noise, but also betoken passing into a different type of space. Much of what may be termed social activity therefore takes place in these traffic and circulation areas, where it is not such a significant problem. At both campuses, the need for refreshment facilities near to the learning centres has been recognized, and at the City Campus development a commercial coffee bar has been introduced next door to the centre. It is still increasingly difficult to keep food and drink out of the centres, as students appear not to distinguish between traffic/group areas and social space, or to recognize the need to keep food and drink away from resources and equipment. At many times of day, however, the learning centres are the only areas open for use and therefore they seem to become a microcosm of all University activity.

Sheffield Hallam University

SHU user survey forms reveal a diversity of opinions:

'This is just a cyber cafe' – Disgruntled user!

'It's great, free Internet all over the place' – Happy user

As part of the development of the Collegiate learning centre, provision was made for social use in what is called 'the Street', a space linking two parts of the building. Here, students can get snacks and hot drinks and socialize. The introduction of a similar facility at the Adsetts Centre is one of the frequent requests coming out of Learning Centre surveys, especially of overnight users. Staff do have concerns about food and drink in learning centres, some of which are about possible damage to books and PCs, while others are about the different atmosphere created. However, the trend is to adopt a more pragmatic approach based on what is actually being brought in. Staff recognize that social space elsewhere on campus is limited. If most students are unconcerned about food and drink in learning centres, then perhaps this new atmosphere should be embraced.

In practice, it is not feasible to keep any tight control of PC use. Some time ago, attempts to restrict non-academic social use of the University e-mail system were frustrated by students opening Hotmail accounts. Use of chat facilities was banned but this became increasingly difficult to enforce, as some students find it hard to meet any other way than electronically.

To those users whose experience is of more traditional libraries, the learning centres can be something of a shock; the sight of students sitting around a large table talking, or gathered round a PC can seem incongruous. They find the atmosphere, the noise, the group work and even the PCs difficult to come to terms with. Others hear the noise and regard it as the sound of students working. Learning Centre staff have had to accept that parts of the building will have a more social atmosphere, that activities beyond traditional academic work will take place and that their role is not to suppress this but to hold a balance between the different needs of the users of the building. The learning centre attempts to facilitate learning in all its different forms and to provide a space for students to come together as a community and not just as a collection of isolated individuals.

University of Lincoln

Lincoln's view of student working in the learning centre was informed by observing different study patterns and it soon became clear that students now spend large amounts of time in the learning centre mostly, but not exclusively, working. A variety of study spaces are provided, including informal areas for students to meet friends, relax and have something to eat.

In response to these new student working patterns the 'no eating' policy was revised in favour of allowing students to bring snacks and drinks into working areas. The learning centre has water fountains and vending machines selling hot and cold drinks as well as chocolate bars and crisps, and from mid-morning to mid-afternoon there is a service for sandwiches and snacks provided by the catering department. The extended opening hours were not matched by other University departments and, as the campus is some distance from city shops, it was felt to be crucial to provide these facilities so that students could work effectively during their study times in the centre.

Of course, these initiatives were not fully welcomed by all staff or students, some of whom perceived a conflict between the role of the learning centre in creating a comfortable learning environment and the need to protect learning resources. In reality, Lincoln's experience has been that students have embraced this initiative and respected their surroundings. There have been no major spillages or accidents and the provision of much larger waste bins together with increased cleaning of the building and waste removal has meant less mess hidden in corners. It is felt that this initiative succeeded in part, not only because the new learning centre allowed gave an opportunity to look at operations differently and perhaps more creatively, but also because the student population at Lincoln was initially very small and the culture was therefore more open to change and more appreciative of new initiatives.

CONCLUSION

The learning centre concept is undoubtedly distinctive in the way it contributes to institutional teaching and learning strategies and supports student learning. This is reflected in the breadth of resource and service provision and the learning activities its buildings support. These factors combine to create an atmosphere different to that normally associated with an academic library. So, against the background of increasing virtual access to information resources and learning materials described in the introduction to the chapter, have learning centres justified the investment placed in them?

It is true that there is a growing use of the virtual library. At Sheffield Hallam University, the Learning Centre user survey in 2001 indicated a growing use of services outside the learning centres and also growing use from outside the University. Of the users surveyed, 60 per cent accessed learning centre services from outside the learning centre – a 14 per cent increase on the figures for the previous year. There was also a 22 per cent increase in students accessing services via the Internet from outside the University.

One conclusion might be that the increasing availability of student access to a wide range of services off campus and the increased ownership of PCs is reducing the need for large central facilities on campus. However, this is not supported by the experience of learning centres at Leeds Metropolitan and Sheffield Hallam Universities, where use nevertheless remains high.

LMU experienced a considerable increase in use at both campuses after relaunching libraries as learning centres. For example, in the City Campus learning centre's first year of operation, the number of users entering showed a dramatic increase of 42 per cent compared to the combined totals of the two previous facilities it replaced. At SHU, visits to the Adsetts Centre showed a 17 per cent rise during the first year of operation and a similar pattern was seen at the Collegiate site. Some initial increase may be ascribed in both cases to the novelty factor, yet usage of the learning centres at the two universities remains high. At SHU, for example, the Learning Centre annual user survey in 2001 indicated that 64.5 per cent of users visited daily, 32.1 per cent weekly and 2 per cent monthly; figures that have remained consistent for the past five years.

The different types of study spaces and the range of facilities available in learning centres are attracting students and it may be that libraries or learning centres that do not meet this need for different kinds of space may find that students go elsewhere. The book and journal collection may no longer be sufficiently attractive to ensure high usage, if other facilities are not available in the same space. Experience at LMU and SHU demonstrates how enhanced accommodation encompassing careful design, consultation with stakeholders and alignment with institutional teaching and learning strategies can meet the needs of students for different forms of learning activity.

REFERENCES

Adsetts Centre Case Study (1996), [CD ROM]. Sheffield: SHU Press.

Carlson, S. (2001), 'The Deserted Library', *Chronicle of Higher Education: Information Technology*, November 16, at http://chronicle.com/free/v48/i12/12a03501.htm

Learning and Teaching Research Institute (1997), *An Evaluation Of The Functioning Of The Adsetts Centre As An Integrated Learning Centre*, Sheffield Hallam University, at: http://www.shu.ac.uk/services/lc/cmeweb/accs/contents.htm

Samuelson, R. (2001), Fun Ethic vs. Work Ethic?, *Newsweek*, **138** (11), 9 October, p.43.

New environments: the environment for learning

7

Edited by Alison Hudson

Contributors:
Sheffield Hallam University

Phil Bannister,
Sue Clegg,
Madeleine Freewood,
Julie Hanson,
Alison Hudson,
Sadie Parr, John Steel
and Stephen Wan

CHAPTER OVERVIEW

This chapter will explore some of the broader issues confronting higher education systems by looking towards the future on the basis of an analysis of current trends. It therefore begins with a broad overview of the emerging new environments for learning and goes on to reflect on the consequences of those environments by considering their impact on learners, and their response to changing needs. The key argument is that the main issue confronting all higher education institutions (HEIs) is that of responding to change. It is, therefore, necessary to understand the drivers and barriers to innovation and reorganization. In this context, how the Sheffield Hallam University Learning Centre model works in supporting innovation and change by considering cross-departmental roles is examined through three case studies. These studies are not designed to be exhaustive; rather they are a way of exploring some of the complexities relating to change and the emergence of new roles and new relationships. Institutions in the UK and internationally have different cultures, purposes and histories. The answer to the question *What Kind of University?* (Brennan et al. 1999) yields no unitary response; however, we hope that by critically reflecting

181

on our experience at SHU we can offer readers an insight into strategies that can work, as well as pointing to some of the difficulties.

EXPANSION, EXPECTATIONS AND SUSTAINABILITY

The most notable feature of modern higher education is that it is no longer confined within the boundaries of the traditional post-compulsory education sector. Drivers to exploit the new capabilities of communications and information technology (C&IT) come from the international market of education providers (Cunningham et al., 1998), policy-driven initiatives to promote lifelong learning (Coffield, 1999) and business investment to meet the needs of the knowledge economy. The centrality of learning as a focus for assessing the impact of C&IT is recognized in the government's Foresight consultation (Foresight, 2000). Policy is being shaped by the perception that new media can extend learning to everyone regardless of location. Any appreciation of new environments for learning therefore needs to be understood in the context of the government's orientation towards globalization and its view that the competitive position of the UK can be enhanced through the development of a highly skilled and trained workforce.

One of the clearest expressions of the UK government's assessment of the changing learning environments was the speech delivered by David Blunkett, then Secretary of State for Education, at the University of Greenwich in 2000. This set out his views on the future of higher education and has become known as the 'Greenwich Speech'. Blunkett frames the whole of the higher education agenda in terms of the likely impacts of globalization:

> ... this change is related to the fundamental socio-economic development of the last quarter of the 20th century: globalisation. It is therefore with the challenge of globalisation that higher education policy now starts. (Blunkett, 2000, para. 7)

HEIs are exhorted to open up to business in order to play their role in the knowledge economy and to provide students with 'a flair for enterprise' as well as C&IT and other skills.

Delivering this vision involves multiple institutions: some especially created (such as the University for Industry); and some based on an expanded model of traditional HEIs using new media to extend their delivery (Laurillard, 1993) and through companies with their own training programmes – for example, Motorola (Motorola, 2000), British Airways (Lancaster University, 2000), British Telecom (Solstra, 2000), and Unipart (UCG, 2001) – and newer global market entrants concentrating specifically on e-learning (Online learning, 2001; Hungry Minds, 2000). The pressures on HEIs in the creation of new learning environments are therefore wider than those associated with the traditional higher education sector.

THE NEW IMPERATIVE

As well as global competitiveness and a flexible workforce, new ideas about lifelong learning have come to the fore. Learning is no longer conceptualized as taking place at the beginning of a career; rather, changing economic conditions necessitate constant updating of skills. As Malcolm Tight (1998) has observed, 'Lifelong learning for all is the new imperative'. HEIs are no longer solely concerned with providing under-graduate courses. They are also involved with the provision of a range of skills and courses at various stages in a person's career. Lifelong learning meshes with the government's widening participation agenda. It is accepted that it is no longer possible to contemplate a future in which only a minority of the population receives education. The need for a highly qualified workforce, widening participation and lifelong learning all fit together as a way of envisaging the future of higher education.

In the higher education sector today, an increasing emphasis is therefore being placed on the need for HEIs to help develop a set of personal and non-academic skills in their students that may be transferred to various work-related contexts. This enterprise is broadly termed the development of key skills – a term that is often used interchangeably with 'core competencies', 'transferable skills', 'employability skills', and 'enterprise skills'. The most commonly used definition of such generic, transferable skills or 'key skills' is the one developed by the Qualifications and Curriculum Authority (QCA, 2001) which identifies the six 'key' skills as

- *communication*
- *IT*
- *working with others*
- *application of numbers*
- *improving own learning and performance* and
- *problem solving.*

This emphasis on what has been termed the 'skills agenda' (Holmes, 2000) has been supported by a wide variety of 'stakeholders'. The Association of Graduate Recruiters (AGR, 1995), for example, has recommended that HEIs should focus on the need for all students to be taught career management and effective learning skills from their first year at university. Both government and employers have encouraged the notion that all degrees should work to aid students' acquisition of key skills, which is deemed essential for successful lifelong learning and for a flexible, adaptable workforce. Academic research has supported such calls, and suggests that large companies and SMEs do indeed expect evidence of transferable skills, and that such skills play an important role in the employability of graduates (Harvey, 1999).

The notion of employability has gained even more prominence in light of the changes to tuition fees and grants. While most governments internationally have been keen to develop supply side economics, based on skilling the labour force, few have

183

been willing to fund this expansion from taxation. In the UK as elsewhere therefore, a greater burden of cost has been shifted to students and their families (CVCP, 2000; Barke et al., 2000; Sorensen and Winn, 1993; Stevenson and Winn, 1997). Yet graduates are reluctant to accumulate large debts without reasonable prospects of gaining satisfactory employment following their graduation (Ashworth, 1997). Faced with these pressures, together with the demise of traditional graduate jobs, HEIs have moved to include more skills-based units in their degree courses in order to prepare university leavers for the graduate labour market and employment. These changes have been accelerated by changing forms of governance involving a move away from an emphasis on providers and towards students as 'customers' (Salter and Tapper, 2000). Meeting student needs has therefore taken on an economic and organizational imperative.

The issues for how best to teach key skills have risen swiftly up the higher education agenda as various government-funded initiatives are implemented across HEIs. This has become even more important as the number of students has increased, and their backgrounds have become more diverse (see Figure 7.1). Providing a higher education system for a diversity of students who may differ in educationally relevant ways from the traditional model of the full-time, white, young and (until recently) male undergraduate, necessarily requires effective learning and teaching strategies, if diverse groups of students are not to be disempowered, alienated or marginalized.

- Students from countries other than the UK numbered 224 660 and represented 12.1 per cent of the total student body.
- Ethnic minorities constituted 13.0 per cent of all first-year, UK-domiciled students whose ethnicity was known.
- Women made up 54.6 per cent of the student population and 56.5 per cent of UK-domiciled undergraduates.
- 60.6 per cent of part-time first degree entrants were aged 30 or over (1998/ 99: 59.8 per cent).
- The proportion of undergraduates on sandwich programmes rose from 8.2 per cent in 1998/99 to 8.6 per cent.
- Of classified first degrees awarded to women, 8.2 per cent were first-class honours, compared to 9.6 per cent for men.
- Part-time students obtained a higher proportion of first-class, first degree honours (10.1 per cent), than full-time students (8.7 per cent).

Source: HESA (2001)

Figure 7.1   Diversity in higher education (1999/2000)

LEARNER DIVERSITY: RESPONDING TO NEED

The parameters outlined above set the agenda for institutional responsiveness in relation to learners, diversity and responding to need. All the drivers point to putting students at the centre of initiatives to improve student learning. Moreover, we should not see this agenda as only top-down. There are trends within educational research and in pedagogic scholarship which have also influenced the move towards more student-centred pedagogy. As will become clear from the case studies, there is a genuine desire to innovate coming from some lecturers. Innovation has in part been inspired by the growth of the new media, but also from an interest in learning and teaching strategies and student-centred models of learning. The rest of this chapter will explore the model of support developed at Sheffield Hallam University to encourage innovation and improvements in students' learning demanded both by the broader policy agenda, new more diverse and local paying students and by lecturers themselves engaged in improving student learning.

The Learning Centre model at SHU is underpinned by research into educational practice. Departmental changes in policy, practices and infrastructure have drawn together a variety of professional academic activity that reflects some of the complexity at the heart of a modern HEI. Although the climate has moved heavily towards accountability, the constituent groupings that make up the Learning Centre allow the Department to accumulate evidence and to evaluate a wide range of academic activity directed towards improving educational processes.

LEARNING, TEACHING AND ASSESSMENT

The Learning Centre model combines information services with support for learning, teaching and assessment, and with educational research. The role of the Learning and Teaching Institute within the Learning Centre is distinct in that it works closely with staff and senior management across the institution to identify and implement learning, teaching and assessment strategies.

The Learning and Teaching Institute (LTI) provides a focus for supporting developments in learning, teaching and assessment within the University through research, staff development, educational development projects and educational research. The Institute's direction is determined by the University's Learning Teaching and Assessment Strategy and by its involvement with activities undertaken both within the University and in other organizations.

Staff in the LTI work with other colleagues in the Department and schools of study on core activity in the following ways:

- supporting schools in their bids for external Learning, Teaching and Assessment funding

- developing links with key external Learning Teaching and Assessment agencies
- organizing a wide range of forums
- organizing dissemination events such as workshops, an annual conference, mini-conferences
- supporting course planning and course validation
- supporting national initiatives such as Academic Review
- contributing to the new staff course.

Central to the developmental activities undertaken in the Department are the three key learning, teaching and assessment priorities of the University:

- flexible delivery with time, pace and, increasingly, place chosen by students;
- support for a diversity of students within a culture of lifelong learning; and
- opportunities for realizing the potential of the appropriate use of technology to enable and facilitate learning.

These arose out of early drafts of the University's Learning, Teaching and Assessment (LTA) strategy and were defined in response to the external national and international drivers discussed in the Overview section to this chapter, such as diverse student population, lifelong learning, integration of key skills and so on.

These priorities and the related strategy were devolved to schools for reinterpretation within their specific context. The strategy documents are organic and change to reflect current priorities in schools. This process of devolution was intended to develop ownership of change and innovation for quality enhancement among the staff in schools. Each school has LTA Coordinators who work within their respective school and belong to the University-wide LTA Coordinators Group, which is managed by the LTI. The development of LTA activities defined in the strategy documents is based very much on an Action Research approach to change and innovation.

Out of this process of redefinition, a collaborative model of working has been created in which Learning Centre staff – LTI academics, research assistants, courseware developers and Information Specialists – support school-owned developments. Developmental activity, defined by schools and supported by the LTI, is disseminated both internally and externally, in order to share experience and forge links across disciplines and other institutions and prevent duplication of effort. There is much emphasis on developing activities that are transferable across schools and are suitable for adaptation to the context of a particular school. Furthermore, there is regular feedback to the Pro Vice-Chancellor for Academic Affairs, which aims to ensure that senior management is well informed about activity within schools, allowing the situation within schools to influence the development of central policy within the University.

This model of working acts in practice to place the LTI staff in a position where they mediate between institutional, school and individual staff priorities in the actualization of research, curriculum development and innovation. LTI and Information Services staff (who have frontline responsibility for information and IT services and support) play key roles in the negotiation between the policy-driven concerns of management and the specific needs of tutors and students. They work to identify a balance between the needs of the institution to support developments, without over-regulating activity and thus limiting the scope for innovation.

The following are indicative of the priority areas which schools have identified in their LTA Strategies:

- information and communication technology,
- student-centred learning,
- supportive tutor-led environment,
- flexible learning opportunities
- active and experiential learning
- integration of key skills
- learner autonomy – the independent learner.

Many of the activities which schools have undertaken, with the support of the Learning Centre, incorporate more than one of the areas set in their targets.

For example, information management skills have become an important topic within HEIs as the need to educate information-literate students becomes more widely recognized. There has been much written, particularly in American publications, about the importance of information literacy as a core skill for students in higher education (Wiggins, 1999; Breivik, 1999). In the US, the Association of College and Research Libraries has formally defined standards, performance indicators, and outcomes for student information literacy (Association of College and Research Libraries, 2000). In the UK, a 'national framework of qualifications' has been established which is underpinned by the six key skills (QCA, 2001).

The InfoQuest project (presented as a case study in Chapter 5, pp. 138–41) typifies many developmental initiatives which draw upon expertise from schools and departments to work collaboratively to benefit student learning. The InfoQuest initiative is also an example in which school Learning, Teaching and Assessment (LTA) strategies can be aligned with central departmental targets to meet the overall University priorities of enabling flexible, student-centred and computer-based learning.

Aligned with the University LTA strategy, the web-based package was used to encourage flexible and student-centred learning. This development subsequently took shape to meet the Learning Centre's objectives, while simultaneously forming part of the school's action plan in addressing priorities for the use and enhancement of C&IT, flexible learning opportunities and student support.

The development highlights the effect of new working partnerships and is an example of Information Specialists and Advisers working collaboratively with tutors in schools, staff from the LTI and the Centre for Multimedia in Education. This kind of unique working relationship has been advocated by Breivik, who argues that librarians (and therefore Information Advisers/Specialists) 'need to collaborate more with instructional designers and media producers', so that they are able to 'contribute their information literacy expertise just as faculty members bring their subject expertise to a course or project production team' (Breivik, 1999). In this project, the role of the Learning Centre staff was central to the whole development process.

Many schools have identified the use of C&IT among their targets, partly as a response to the University's own priorities and its setting of C&IT targets for schools. In one subject area, support for final-year dissertation students is being provided through the virtual learning environment as well as by individual supervisors. In addition to providing guidance on all stages of researching and writing the dissertation, the virtual learning environment is used to give students the opportunity to share ideas, resources and experiences with their peers through what can be a very solitary part of the degree course. This clearly encompasses many of the priorities listed above: C&IT, student-centred learning, flexible learning opportunities, and the integration of key skills and learner autonomy.

E-LEARNING

The LTI further attempts to achieve a balance by commissioning its own research; one such research project examined the experiences and perspectives of both academic and technical staff on e-learning. A number of recurring, and often linked, issues were identified. The need for e-learning to be perceived as being pedagogically driven and the importance of dedicating resources, not just to technical provision but to what was termed 'hearts and minds' work, became apparent. Staff were more comfortable and more interested in pursuing a mixed mode of delivery – that is, where e-learning is used alongside more traditional teaching methods such as lecturers, seminars and tutorials. In addition, staff felt that there was a lack of effective forums at which academic staff could share and generate ideas for e-learning; in general terms, they wanted to be kept better informed about the e-learning resources available within the University as well as innovations such as the e-learning forum, recently established to allow staff to share ideas. The commissioned research has influenced other innovation, not least the implementation of a virtual learning environment at the University. This development is being managed in the Department by the LTI, with members of academic staff, who have the advantage of being e-learning practitioners, being seconded part-time from schools to act as e-learning coordinators.

The development of an e-learning strategy, which has pedagogy and technology at its core, has a fundamental implication that central departments work together and that the most appropriate support and staff development activities are identified to assure quality and stimulate innovation. The LTI's central position within the

Learning Centre and its overview of institutional activity and strategy across the schools puts it in a primary position to identify the needs of staff and students and to respond accordingly. The role of the LTI in this key strategic area means that the Learning Centre is involved in e-learning in all schools.

Working relationships are interwoven with a common understanding and a shared vision across the central departments. Although roles are embedded in established departments, many are innovative. Some are newly created, others are established roles that have been extended, developed or refocused. The scale of the development requires staff to draw their experience and skills together in order to be able to respond to new agendas in learning and teaching. In supporting the initiative, staff are involved in identifying the agenda, developing strategy in response to the agenda, and working with colleagues across the University to respond to change.

EMERGING ROLES AND INTERDEPENDENCE

Researchers in the Learning Centre have worked alongside teaching staff, support staff and students to document and support decision-making processes by providing data to help shape learning, teaching and assessment strategies.

The following case studies have been chosen as indicative of a range of research and development initiatives that have been undertaken in the Department. They are examples of the Department's proactive role in commissioning research that, as well as feeding back to the schools involved and the Learning Centre, can also be disseminated across the institution to influence future developments. As well as reflecting some of the priority areas that the schools and the Department have identified in their LTA Strategies, they also manifest the three key learning, teaching and assessment priorities for the University listed earlier:

- flexible delivery with time, pace and, increasingly, place chosen by students;
- support for a diversity of students within a culture of lifelong learning; and
- opportunities for realizing the potential of the appropriate use of technology to enable and facilitate learning.

The case studies illustrate the diversity of the developments and highlight the interdependence between tutors in schools, Information Specialists, researchers, and multimedia courseware developers, and the integrated relationships within the Department between Information Services, the LTI, the Learning and Teaching Research Institute and media production. They also contextualize some of the new emerging roles that staff in the Learning Centre play.

189

CASE STUDY 1: THE ROLE OF ACTION RESEARCH IN PLANNING FOR CHANGE

The process of change management can be a fraught and complex one. Drivers and barriers to innovation and reorganization can emerge from a range of sources, and range from broad economic or institutional factors to complexities arising from circumstantial or individual dynamics. A useful way of orchestrating and managing the change process is by attempting to ensure that the key stakeholders within this process are not only informed about change, but are also involved in the decision-making process itself. This can be accomplished via an action research strategy. This section will briefly outline such a process and demonstrate how action research can be a useful means to orchestrate and implement the change process within the new environments for learning. This case study sought to address specific problems within the context of shifting expectations of students; a transformation of learning dynamics; changing infrastructural factors, and the changing contexts of higher education.

The action research process is highlighted by Kemmis (1997) as: 'collective self reflective enquiry undertaken by participants in social situations in order to improve the productivity, rationality, and justice of their own social or educational practices and the situations in which practices are carried out.' The central feature of the process is that all participants are involved in the focus and direction of the research with a view to engendering a sense of ownership and inclusion in the change process. Furthermore, a feature of action research stems from the belief that the researchers themselves are actively engaged in a process of reflection and re-evaluation about their own activities and objectives within the research. The result is a *continuous* process of reflection and reappraisal.

Context

This example of action research focuses on a Level 1 unit that had been taught 'traditionally' via lectures and tutorials. In the years preceding the action research process, a problem of student 'fall-off' was identified, in that student attendance and retention rates were low and becoming increasingly lower year by year. Also, on a broader level, the changing learning landscape with its increased emphasis on learner autonomy, the move towards student-centred learning, and the advances in learning technologies, highlighted shifts within the context of higher education which necessitated a reappraisal of current practice.

Course of action

In attempting to address the problems of the course and take into account the changing context of higher education, the unit leader, in collaboration with research

190

staff in the LTI, reflected on the issues and problems within the course. A broad set of 'solutions' was proposed with a view to involve the students as much as possible in shaping change within the unit. Firstly, as face-to-face contact with the student body was a problem, it was considered that, when contact did occur, it should be of a high quality, engaging the students in a more meaningful way and involving them in the learning process itself. The number of lectures were reduced, providing space for more-meaningful, smaller-scale face-to-face interaction, in which ideas and issues could be explored in greater depth by the students and the lecturer. The bulk of the lecture material was dropped, in favour of utilizing a broader range of learning experiences for the students. It was hoped that, by realigning the focus of teaching to provide students with a greater range of learning experiences, the main elements of the course would be provided for the students with an added impetus for them to engage.

However, we only have one side of the action research picture so far; in order to fully engage the students within the action research process, some mechanism was needed for them to provide feedback on their experiences of the course. Although it would have been easy to set up focus groups or interviews with the students, it was considered that this might lead students to feel dislocated from the whole process itself, in that they might lose the sense of ownership that the researchers were intending to provide. So, in order to provide students with a greater sense of involvement in the way the course was being conceptualized and rethought, the view was taken that they might like to express their perceptions and experiences in a way that was relatively unconstraining and within the context of the learning process itself. In short, the aim was to provide the students with a means to express their views of the course and the various media employed to deliver it, in a way that would also enable them to reflect on their learning as well; thus providing a vehicle for learning and feedback at the same time.

Woodward (1998) and O'Rourke (1998) highlight the potential learning and teaching benefits to be found in learning journals and portfolios, in which students reflect on their learning process throughout a given course. They argue that a sufficiently directed form of reflection can occur that improves the students' understanding of their learning while at the same time producing assessable work from the students. This process can also provide meaningful research data and a sense of ownership in the developmental process of the course. However, this type of reflective assessment practice is generally not suitable for Level 1 students, although an adapted version of this learning process might be, if it were incorporated into a formal, structured piece of work. Thus, within the context of their assignments, the students were asked to express openly and honestly their views of the course. In other words, a reflective space was provided within the context of their main assessment, in which the students could reflect not only on their learning, but also on what they found useful and not so useful within the context of the unit.

Response

This provided the unit team with a wealth of feedback and raised a number of issues, some of which were expected, some surprising. One of the strongest themes to emerge from the discourses was a current of instrumentalism and vocationalism, which was expressed in students' willingness to engage with a broader range of media; it was clear that students valued the wider variety of learning experiences on a number of levels. In particular, the students noted that the change to a 'mixed mode' system of course delivery provided them with a richer variety of learning experiences, which helped them engage more fully with the learning materials on the course. This shift from 'traditional' lectures and seminars to a more varied set of learning experiences seemed to generate a new level of enthusiasm from the students, with attendance rates in seminars growing from 50 per cent to over 80 per cent and referral rates dropping to 4 per cent. Moreover, the addition of the technology component into their learning was perceived as facilitating a further range of abilities with which the students could relate more closely to the subject matter, and the wider world of work.

Conclusion

As noted, a key component of the action research process involves continued reflection and reappraisal of activities and feedback. Shifting the mode of teaching necessitated a balanced approach from the more traditional to newer types of learning experiences. If this type of change is to be successful for the students and the staff involved, it needs to be managed and negotiated through dialogue and reflection between support departments and the schools. Thus, a new type of learning scenario is developed: one that is negotiated with, rather than being imposed on, students. This case study demonstrates that, in order to facilitate change within the context of changing expectations of teaching staff, support departments and students within these new environments for learning, the process of change has to be managed sensitively, appropriately and continuously, with all stakeholders influencing how change is managed. As we have demonstrated, the action research process can be employed to negotiate change from the learning context itself, rather than being imposed.

CASE STUDY 2: SUPPORTING STUDENTS' SELF-MANAGED LEARNING

Throughout higher education in the UK, the amount of formal contact between tutors and students is reducing, with the learning that takes place outside class contact hours becoming more significant. In most instances, this learning is 'tutor-directed' in that it is the tutor and not the student who is responsible for setting the unit learning outcomes, format of the assessment(s), assessment criteria, deadlines and so on.

Although the tutor *directs* this learning, it is the student who *manages* it – ultimately a student decides which activities he or she wishes to undertake.

Accordingly, there is pressure on tutors in conjunction with Learning Centre support to take account of and respond to this situation. The Dearing Report on higher education recommended that 'all institutions encourage staff to plan for the learning time of their students' (NCIHE, 1997, para. 8.18). The increased amount of time which students are expected to study away from tutors has implications for the learning environment, as this reduction in contact must be taken into account in the planning of the learning experience. Within Sheffield Hallam University, the term 'directed learning', which has been adopted to refer to out-of-class learning, anticipates that the tutor *will* provide students with guidance on the study which they are expected to do outside formal teaching situations. The large proportion of study time which students spend in directed learning also has implications for their use of resources and is something that needs to be considered in terms of the provision and types of support offered.

Context

The research undertaken by the Learning Centre on the issue of directed learning is one of the larger projects to have emerged from school LTA strategies. The purpose of the research was to explore how best to support students in making effective use of their self-managed learning time, in the context of developing student independence. Issues of student-centred learning, supportive tutor-led environments, flexible learning opportunities and learner autonomy (the independent learner) all feature in the research. It provided an opportunity for collaboration between the Department and one of the school-based research centres on a topic which has important implications for the role of the academic and the relationship between tutor and student.

Course of action

It was felt that to gain some understanding of the topic area, it was important to begin with the tutor perspective. The first stage was to map the range of approaches adopted within the school to guide students in the learning they undertake outside of scheduled classes. An analysis was conducted of the documentation which students on courses receive for each unit they study. Every unit within the school is required to produce a *Unit Learning Scheme*, which is meant to provide students with very clear guidance and support for the whole of their learning time, and to explain and enhance the relationship between directed and face-to-face learning. This documentation provided a good starting point for the research in that it is, perhaps, the primary means through which tutors advise students on their out-of-class studies.

The focus of interest was the overall extent and the precise nature of the guidance given on directed study within this documentation. Analysis of selected Unit Learning Schemes indicated the degree of diversity that existed in terms of the amount of guidance that students were given, and highlighted some key themes to be explored further with staff. Subsequently, a small number of in-depth interviews were undertaken with tutors.

Response

Below is a very brief summary of key themes that were identified and discussed during the interviews. (Interestingly, there was much discussion among tutors about how much time students should be expected to spend in directed study.) It did, however, become apparent that directed study is not considered simply as 'stand-alone' learning, but rather is integrated, in various forms, into course structures and class contact time. The extent of the guidance on how to use directed learning time, provided by tutors to students within a given unit, was influenced by a number of concerns. Indeed, tutors made decisions in this area on the basis of individual units, rather than assuming a single, overarching approach to all of their teaching. The following factors influenced tutor 'philosophy' in terms of the extent of guidance that it was regarded as appropriate to provide:

- The level of a unit was important. Tutors explicitly stated that guidance to students varies according to level of the unit.

- The substance of a unit. Some areas in particular, such as finance, involve subjects which can change daily and this makes some tutors feel that they must not be overly prescriptive in the guidance relating to directed learning to allow them to ensure that the substance of the unit is kept up to date.

- A desire not to patronize students. Although staff felt they had a role in motivating students to study, this should not be all encompassing – it would be patronizing to tell students exactly how to use their time.

- The experience of individual tutors also influenced the extent of the guidance given. Three main areas of experience were significant:

  - The experiences and preferences of staff as learners – tutors adopting an approach which they had liked as students.
  - The tutors' experience of student performance: the approaches they took to supporting learners reflected some of the problems that had been encountered (for example, low student engagement or, unacceptably high fail rates).
  - Staff felt that exposure to educational theory through various courses had also influenced them.

194

Implications

- What is the level of responsibility it is reasonable to expect a tutor to exercise? This is one of the key issues. If the amount of directed learning is increasing (at the expense of face-to-face learning) and a tutor does not accept responsibility for this part of a student's time, is a tutor's influence being reduced?

- What message does the reduction in face-to-face contact send to students? Does a relatively minimal timetable suggest to students that less study is required of them? The tutor interviews highlighted the emergence of activities that are formal, in the sense that they are incorporated into the timetable, but do not require the presence of the tutor. This would include group work based on projects and case studies that aim to bridge the gap between face-to-face contact with a tutor and a student studying 'in private'. Such activities are increasing in popularity as face-to-face contact is reduced, but there are huge implications for resources, timetabling and notions of offering flexible learning.

- What is the potential of C&IT in supporting students as the amount of directed learning increases? Can it provide a way of supplementing face-to-face contact as tutor–student contact is reduced? This type of activity might include students being required to undertake work on electronic resources in the Learning Centre without tutor support (perhaps the provision of a helpdesk).

- Is there a need for a strategic approach? Many staff stated that the level of guidance regarding directed learning must be appropriate to the level of a unit (i.e. declining as a student progresses through the levels). This raises the question of how students should be supported as they move away from dependence and towards independence. Furthermore, who should equip students to manage this transition? Should there be a standard approach adopted within the school on the extent of guidance on out-of-class study – perhaps for each level? However, if this brings clarity and cohesion to the student experience, is it at the cost of variety of educational experience for the students and academic freedom for the tutors? Should staff at least be expected to explain at the beginning of a unit the pedagogic philosophy that underpins the approach to teaching and learning within it?

- What are the implications for Information Services staff? Clearly, as students study more away from tutors, there need to be changes in both the material resources and other forms of support provided for them. In the context of reduced face-to-face contact time, it seems likely that Learning Centres and their staff will be placed under growing and changing demand. There is a trend at Sheffield Hallam University for closer working relationships between tutors and Learning

Centre staff, and this is something to be nurtured if a holistic approach is to be adopted in the provision of a supportive environment for students.

Further interviews are planned with staff to explore their attitudes and beliefs concerning directed learning. So far, the interviews and the analysis of the Unit Learning Schemes have focused on the staff perspective; the next stage is to look at the student perspective – to investigate how much time students are able to devote to directed learning; how useful they find the types of guidance which tutors provide; and what does or does not motivate or enable them to use their time effectively.

This study has focused upon only one school within the University, although the issues involved clearly have implications across the institution as a whole. Dissemination of this project is felt to be important and to that end the issues surrounding directed study ought to be discussed within the University as a whole.

CASE STUDY 3: THE SKILLS AGENDA AND PROGRESS FILES

The University's commitment to delivering on the skills agenda has a number of wide-ranging implications for educational practitioners. In light of the shift in emphasis towards increasing employment prospects for students, key skills are now embedded in all undergraduate courses across all schools. One of the many forms this has taken has been the introduction of a Quality Assurance Agency (QAA) requirement for universities to implement the use of Progress Files by 2005/06 (QAA, 2000).

Context

One school of study approached the Learning Centre, seeking support in delivering an introductory Level 1 skill-based unit, which aimed to enable students to develop problem-solving strategies, to research a contemporary area of study, and to support students' personal and professional development throughout the course. The last of these objectives is synonymous with QAA's advocation for Personal Development Planning (PDP), a term being used to reflect Dearing's recommendation of a 'means by which students can monitor, build and reflect upon their personal development' (NCIHE, 1997, recommendation 20). Dearing's definition of Progress Files describes two components: PDP and 'transcripts', which record student achievement following a common format. Progress Files aim to provide students with a record from which they can construct their curricula vitae to communicate their achievements to prospective employers or further education and training providers.

In preparation for QAA's deadline for implementation, the unit leader for the skills module sought support in evaluating the newly implemented concept of a Progress File for students enrolled on Level 1 units. The work feeds into the philosophy of attempting to create an educational environment that promotes the idea of the autonomous learner by encouraging students to take ownership of their learning through proactive and reflective exercises of identifying goals and reflecting on performance and achievement.

Course of action

A small-scale project was undertaken by the LTI with a localized focus at unit level, but with a potential for school-wide benefits. The main objective of the research was to gain feedback from the students on the concept of Progress Files themselves and the manner in which they had been introduced and delivered in the unit. The implementation of skill-based booklets and exercises, and developing the idea for the Progress File had been discussed amongst the unit tutors, and a systematic incremental approach to delivering skill-based material and exercises was undertaken. Students were introduced to the concept of the Progress Files to complement the work undertaken in the unit, which included developing a practical ability in completing a project, researching a contemporary area of the field of study and weekly core-skill exercises such as developing report writing skills.

Students were interviewed in groups of three or four. The research was divided into two sections:

- A short set of close-ended, structured questions were designed and used to obtain specific factual information from a narrow set of possible responses (Allison et al., 1996, p. 103) to establish the actual students' experience of personal tutor meetings that took place to introduce the concept of the Progress File. Students were asked to briefly comment on the structure, length and content of the dialogue with their tutors, and also the time devoted to the topic of Progress Files.

- A series of open-ended questions were then employed for the main bulk of the interviews, to provide students with an opportunity to air their views, feelings, ideas and attitudes (Allison et al., 1996, p. 103) towards Progress Files. This section of the research featured discursive feedback among student participants who shared the common experience of being introduced to and developing their Progress Files, and hence formed the basis of mini-focus groups (Anderson, 1998). This form of group interviewing obtained students' impressions of the overall concept of the Progress File and what it meant to them in the wider context of their academic, professional and personal development.

One of the main features of the report was to provide an element of quantitative information in relation to student opinion. The report was used by the unit leader for reflection and to inform any necessary change to the introduction and integration of Progress Files.

The student feedback suggested that there was some requirement to modify the way in which the core skills work and Progress Files were combined and delivered. The main issues that arose from the interviews pertained to the students' understanding of the Progress File in relation to their personal and professional development. It became evident that the general student perception of Progress Files was one of academic requirement confined to a single unit. There was little indication of any student notion of seeing the Progress File in a wider context of independent learning or lifelong learning. The qualitative evidence gathered suggested that students had not reached a stage in their courses where they could engage in such discourse.

Positive action

On completion of the evaluation report, the researcher worked with the tutor to discuss remedying the issues that were highlighted in the interviews. In an attempt to encourage students to consider the Progress File beyond the remit of the unit itself, plans for newly validated courses include continued assessment of *elements* of the Progress Files at Level 2 and Level 3. This is planned to work in conjunction with a proposed new formal programme of personal tutoring. The meetings will act as a support mechanism for students to discuss their Progress Files, and set goals and action plans to develop, monitor and review their own progress. Another measure to improve student engagement of skills development will be to use fewer skills booklets in the unit and make more use of other media such as 'Key Skills Online' (Key Skills Online, 2001), interactive, web-based material developed and produced in the Learning Centre. Furthermore, attempts will be made to take a coordinated approach with other course units in identifying opportunities for students to contribute to their Progress Files and perhaps find more suitable times for students to complete skill booklets in the context of the work they undertake in other units.

This idea was echoed when the LTI facilitated meetings with other schools to share experiences and ideas around the introduction of Progress Files. An outcome of the meetings between schools was that other examples of different approaches emerged – such as an explicit grid of units that students undertake on their courses, to map out specific key skills that students were expected to use in particular units. Tutors can use the matrix to introduce skill-based support material at more appropriate stages of the course. As part of the ongoing support for schools, the Learning Centre actively encourages them to collaborate further on the development and implementation of Progress Files. Future work to evaluate the overall approach taken to the implementation of Progress Files is being planned.

CONCLUSION: SUPPORTING COMPLEXITY AND FLEXIBILITY

The Dearing Report (NCIHE, 1997) recommended that 'all higher education institutions in the UK should have in place overarching communications and information strategies by 1999/2000' (Recommendation 41). Increasingly, however, academic staff are coming under pressure from government bodies and university management, to show innovation in the use of C&IT in the new educational and political context of a mass education system (Clegg et al., 2000; Scott, 1995).

The desire to embrace new media is far from all-pervasive among academic staff. A recent enquiry by the Joint Information Systems Committee (JCALT, January 2001) into the roles and functions of UK higher education staff involved in the development of learning and teaching through the use of C&IT identified both the growing numbers of staff involved in using learning technologies and the diversity of their work. Among the groups of staff which the report identifies, it classifies only 10 per cent of all academic staff as innovative in terms of their use of learning technologies.

The current JISC Five Year Strategy (JISC 2001) reports that the provision of resources and technology infrastructure is in danger of outstripping the skills of the community to exploit it. This concern is supported by the JCALT Audit of Learning Technology Staff (JCALT, 2001) and is echoed in the Campus Computing Survey from the United States (Green, 1999) which found that:

> Two decades after the first desktop computers arrived on college campuses, we have come to recognise that the campus community's major technology challenges involve human factors – assisting students and faculty to make effective use of new technologies in ways that support teaching, learning, instruction and scholarship.

If a high-skill strategy is at the heart of 'the productive capacity of the new economy and the prosperity of our democracy' and if policy is being shaped by the perception that new media and C&IT can extend learning to everyone regardless of location, the effective and innovative application of C&IT to learning will have a major impact on the future of higher education and learning in general.

The Learning and Teaching Career Development study carried out by the JISC Committee for Awareness, Liaison and Training identifies 11 distinct roles of learning technology staff within higher education. They are summarized under three categories.

- *New specialists*, which include educational developers, educational researchers; technical researchers/developers; materials developers; project managers and learning technologists.
- *Academics and established professionals*, which include academic innovators and academic managers.

199

- *Learning support professionals*, who include library/resource professionals; technical support professionals and C&IT skills professionals.

The study indicates that the effective coordination and collaboration of staff involved with learning technology influence the successful exploitation of good practice across an institution. At an institutional level, the JCALT audit showed two distinct development trajectories:

- A focus on factors associated with *institutional expertise* in the use of learning technologies: staff C&IT skills, student C&IT skills, electronic/multimedia resources and networks and collaborations.
- A focus on factors associated with *institutional infrastructure* (C&IT management, C&IT infrastructure, learning technology support, learning technology funding and administrative systems) and *institutional strategy* (learning and teaching strategy and research and development).

Only 19 per cent of the institutions audited provided a full range of support: support for teaching staff in embedding the use of learning technologies; support for students in accessing and using technologies; and support for the development of new materials and applications.

In response to the short-term social and cultural dimension, human and organizational issues relating to the deployment of new technologies in HEIs are likely to dominate all aspects of educational activity. The EFFECTS Project (2000) investigating frameworks for embedding C&IT and the JCALT Audit identified that:

- Role-specific C&IT skills required by individuals and groups of staff are undergoing continual change as both their roles and the technologies available evolve to meet new institutional demands.
- New roles are emerging – particularly in the broad area of learning support – for which C&IT skills are often crucial.

NEW ENVIRONMENTS: NEW ROLES AND RELATIONSHIPS

This chapter goes some way towards illustrating how the Learning Centre at Sheffield Hallam University is involved in the development and implementation of wide-ranging institutional strategies and how research and development carried out in the Department help staff to understand the drivers and barriers to innovation and change. The case studies illustrate the range of activity supported by the Department, including developing innovative approaches to areas such as information skills, key skills, managed information systems, the development and production of learning material, educational research, learning, teaching and assessment, e-learning, staff development and student support.

The effective integration of a wide range of staff expertise within the Learning Centre, combined with a receptive approach to staff development, creates an environment that is responsive to change. The central position that the Department occupies is essential in terms of influencing both academic and social and cultural development. By engaging proactively with the institutional agenda, school-based learning and teaching strategies and educational research, the Department can put learning and teaching, and student and staff support, at the forefront of its strategy and actively engage in the creation of new learning environments and new learning communities.

The Learning Centre, the Learning and Teaching Institute and the Learning and Teaching Research Institute collectively and independently help to inform institutional strategy, manage cultural change and help to embed and promote educational research and critical reflection, both within the department, and across the institution.

Without knowledge of the attitudes of academic staff as a whole to learning technologies, it is difficult to develop strategies that will encourage staff to explore and take up the new media available to them. Researchers in the Department have worked alongside teaching staff, support staff and students to document and support decision-making processes and provide data and information to help shape learning, teaching and assessment strategies.

The case studies in this chapter identify some of the drivers and barriers and reflect a complex set of working relationships that are both broad, working across the University, and deep, working with individual tutors, course teams, senior managers in schools and senior management at an institutional level.

The Learning Centre is at the core of activity in terms of responding to the increasing emphasis placed on HEIs to integrate the skills agenda, to provide flexible delivery of programmes, to support a diversity of students, and to realize the potential of technology. In response to issues confronting the higher education sector and the rapid expansion and increase in the utilization of new technology, the greatest pressures for the future are around managing change, building on experience and developing staff expertise.

As we set our vision for the future and define our business plans the outstanding challenge is the rate of change and the potential effect that technology will have on the student experience. What will the student experience be in five years' time? Will our students be communicating with their tutors, peers, Information Specialists and 'experts in the field' through student portals on laptops or wireless technology? Will HEIs be able to respond to different learning styles, different work rhythms and different personal paths? Will students and tutors be able to benefit from the real meaning of 'flexibility', 'mixed mode' and 'distributed learning'? Will the notion of the Meta Campus be realized, connecting the University to Global and World Wide perspectives?

The Learning Centre is at the heart of the University. The future for all learning centres lies in their staff in terms of experience and expertise, being able to be both supportive and proactive, being able to identify change, respond to change and support change, being able to collaborate and forge new relationships and also being able to engage as a reflective practitioner. The future calls for a culture that:

- recognizes and rewards essential experience and expertise,
- provides opportunities to develop experience, expertise, skills and knowledge,
- strengthens working relationships,
- identifies new roles and responsibilities,
- recognizes the importance of communication and collaboration, and
- harmonizes interdependence across different departments, different institutions and different professional sectors.

REFERENCES

AGR, (1995), *Skills for Graduates in the 21st Century*. Cambridge: AGR.

Allison, B. et al., (1996), *Research Skills for Students*. London: Kogan Page.

Anderson, G. (1998), *Fundamentals of Educational Research*. 2nd edn. London: Farmer Press.

Ashworth, J. (1997), A Waste of Time? (Private Rates of Return to Higher Education in the 1990s). *Higher Education Quarterly*, **51** (2), pp. 164–88.

Association of College and Research Libraries (2000), Information Literacy Competency Standards for Higher Education at: www.als.org/acrl/ilcomstan.html

Barke, M. et al. (2000), *Students in the Labour Market – Nature, Extent and Implications of Term-Time Employment Among University of Northumbria Undergraduates*. DfEE Research Brief. 215. Nottingham: Department for Education and Employment.

Blunkett, D. (2000), Greenwich Speech, Department for Education and Employment, at: http://cms1.gre.ac.uk/dfee/#speech

Breivik, S. (1999), Take II – information literacy: revolution in education, *References Services Review*, **27** (3), pp. 271–5.

Brennan, J., Fedrowitz, J., Huber, M. and Shah, T. (eds) (1999), *What Kind of University? International Perspectives on Knowledge, Participation and Governance*. Buckingham: SRHE and Open University Press.

Burley, G. and Moreland, N. (1998), *A Practical Guide to Academic Research*. London: Kogan Page.

Clegg, S., Konrad, J. and Tan, J. (2000), Preparing academic staff to use iCTs in support of student learning. *International Journal of Academic Developments*, **5**(2), pp. 138–48.

Coffield, F. (1999) Breaking the Consensus: lifelong learning as social control. *British Educational Research Journal*, **25** (4), pp. 479–99.

Cunningham, S. et al., (1998), *New Media and Borderless Education: A Review of the Convergence between Global Media Networks and Higher Education Provision*. Australian Department of Training and Youth Affairs at: http://www.detya.gov.au/highered/eippubs/eip97–22/eip9722.pdf

CVCP (2000), *Student fees and loans in UK higher education*. Briefing Note. July.

EFFECTS Project (2000), The Effective Framework for Embedding C&IT Using Targeted Support. TLTP Phase 3, at http://sh.plym.ac.uk/eds/effects

Foresight (2000), *The Learning Process in 2020 task Force: Point and Click; learners in the ICT driving seat*, at: http://www.foresight.gov.uk./default1024ns.htm

Green, K.C. (1999), *The Campus Computing Project*, at: www.campuscomputing.net

Harvey, L. (1999), New Realities: the relationship between higher education and employment. *Centre for Research into Quality*, at: http://www.uce.ac.uk/crq/publications/eair99.pdf http://www.uce.ac

HESA (2001), Press release: 1999/2000 higher education student data, at: http://www.hesa.ac.uk/Press/pn47/pn47.htm

Holmes, L. (2000), Reframing the Skills Agenda in Higher Education: Graduate Identity and the Double Warrant, at: http://legacy.unl.ac.uk/relational/papers

Hungry Minds (2000), at: http://www.hungryminds.com/

JCALT (2001), *National Audit of Learning Technology Staff*, at: http://sh.plym.ac.uk/eds/effects/jcalt-project/index.htm

JISC (2001), *Five Year Strategy 2001–2005*, at: www.jisc.ac.uk

Kemmis, S. (1997), Action Research, in Keeves, P. (ed.), *Educational Research Methodology and Measurement*. Oxford: Elsevier Science Ltd, pp. 403–13.

Key Skills Online (2001), at: http://www.shu.ac.uk/keyskills/entersite.html

Lancaster University (2000), News page: BAe Virtual University Attracts Press Comment at: http://www.lums.lancs.ac.uk/mdd/news/Baenews.htm

Laurillard, D. (1993), *Rethinking University Teaching: a framework for the effective use of educational technology*. London: Routledge.

Motorola, (2000), Motorola University at: http://mu.motorola.com/

National Committee of Inquiry into Higher Education, (1997) *Higher Education in the Learning Society* (Dearing Report). London: HMSO

O'Rourke, R. (1998), 'The Learning Journal: From Chaos to Coherence', *Assessment and Evaluation in Higher Education*, Vol. 23, No. 4, pp. 403–13.

Online Learning (2001), at: http://www.onlinelearning.net/Index.html

QAA (2000), *Guidelines for HE Progress Files*, at: http:www.qaa.org.uk/crntwork/progfilehe/guidelines/guideline.pdf

QCA (2001), at: http://www.qca.org.uk/

Salter, B. and Tapper, T. (2000), The Politics of Governance in Higher Education: the Case of Quality Assurance. *Political Studies*, 84, pp. 66–87.

Scott, P. (1995), The Meaning of Mass Higher Education, Buckingham, SRHE & Open University Press.

Solstra (2000), Online Learning, at: http://www.solstra.com/Solstra2000/mnframes.htm

Sorensen, L. and Winn, S. (1993), Students Loans: A case study. *Higher Education Review*, **25** (3), pp. 48–65.

Stevenson, R. and Winn, S. (1997), Student Loans: are the Policy Objectives being Achieved? *Higher Education Quarterly*, **51** (2), pp. 144–63.

Tight, M. (1998), Education, Education, Education: The Vision of Lifelong Learning in the Kennedy, Dearing and Fryer Reports. *Oxford Review of Education*, **24** (4), pp. 473–85

UCG (last accessed 2001), The Learning Organization, at: http://www.ugc.co.uk/learning/lea_0100.htm

Wiggins, M. (1999), Instructional design and structured learning. *References Services Review*, **27** (3), pp. 225–8.

Woodward, H. (1998), 'Reflective Journals and Portfolios: Learning Through Assessment', *Assessment and Evaluation in Higher Education*, Vol. 23, No. 4, pp. 415–23.

8

Looking over the horizon: a future perspective

Graham Bulpitt

FUTUROLOGY

Anticipating the future is a notoriously risky business, and predictions made now can easily be overturned by developments coming from unexpected directions. For example, who would have expected the Internet to transform the information world so quickly in the mid-1990s? Alternatively, technological developments – seeming sure-fire certainties at the time – may fail to have the impact that was confidently predicted. Audio-visual media, so well established in the entertainment sector, failed to transform education in the 1970s in the way that Richard Fothergill predicted in *A challenge for librarians* (1971), while Brian Enright's advocacy of the term *metabook* (1970) to encompass new formats within conventional terminology, now sounds a curious anachronism.

Yet, anticipation and prediction help to build the future too. All the developments outlined in this book have been made with an eye on the future, particularly the changing educational landscape where learning centres are located. Having stated the health warning about the risks of making predictions, it should nevertheless be possible to identify some key trends and to consider their implications. What is perhaps more difficult is to predict the pace of change, or the cumulative impact of a variety of changes across different sectors.

LEARNING CENTRE RATIONALE: EFFECTIVENESS AND EFFICIENCY

Much of the rhetoric from politicians and senior figures in the education world emphasizes the potential of new technology to make education more effective and efficient. The Dearing Report noted 'There is scope to reduce costs in the future and the potential is great' (NCIHE, 1997, p. 202 para 13.1) and the substantial investment in libraries and learning centres in the UK in the 1990s partly reflects the continuing

205

pressure on institutional budgets as tutor contact time is reduced and students spend more time working independently. Some efforts have been made by higher education institutions to protect learning centre budgets, recognizing the increasing demands on their provision.

Although the learning centre model has been partly driven by an educational philosophy which recognizes that students learn best when they are actively engaged in learning, there has been a financial imperative driving the model too (and this has been viewed with suspicion by many tutors). It is certain that government ambitions to increase participation in higher education are unlikely to be matched by corresponding increases in institutional budgets, so the pressure for gains in effectiveness and efficiency is likely to continue.

Experience of learning centres so far suggests that the initial focus on efficiency gains may be misplaced, and that their real impact is on learning effectiveness. Early studies carried out at Sheffield Hallam University suggest that students who are provided with an enriched learning environment are likely to be more successful than those who are confined to a prescribed programme of study (SHU, 2000). The evidence is based on small-scale studies, so the results must be treated with caution, but common sense would suggest that the results are sensible: students are more likely to succeed when they have the maximum number of opportunities to engage in learning.

The provision of a range of learning experiences, using a variety of learning and teaching styles and different media, means that each individual is more likely to find something that engages them – an article written in a way that reflects their intellectual approach, a multimedia programme that engages their senses, a problem-based case study that relates to their experience.

The continued expansion of higher education will mean an increasingly diverse student community, which will challenge institutions to meet the variety of individual needs, particularly in learning styles. The trends identified in Chapter 1 will undoubtedly continue. The boundary between full-time and part-time is likely to disappear as individuals increasingly combine higher education courses with careers, part-time work, family commitments, leisure pursuits and retirement. Institutions will need to make programmes of study as flexible as possible. In this environment, learning centres will have an increasing role to play in providing accessible learning, through long opening hours, a wide variety of learning and information materials, a wide range of facilities and high-quality student support.

REAL AND VIRTUAL LEARNING

The learning centre study environments described in Chapter 6 are quite different from a conventional academic library. Newcomers are struck by the activity and

206

movement in these contemporary buildings, rather than the quiet and tranquillity that they associate with traditional studies. The design of learning centres draws on the experience of department stores, leisure centres and civic buildings as well as libraries. Certainly, there are echoes of the grand Victorian department stores in the sense of vertical and horizontal space in many learning centre buildings.

Social attitudes and behaviour are also reflected in the design of buildings, and the openness and accessibility of learning centres attempts to capture the interest and imagination of students. Learning should be an exciting experience, and learning centres should aspire to convey this sense of excitement through their architecture. Learning styles also reflect changing social behaviour and this is evident in the way in which students use learning centres. Group work and conversation, aided by regular intakes of drinks and snacks and mobile telephone calls, are becoming the preferred way of working for many students. Flexible work areas and mobile-tolerant zones are the way forward for many institutions and it may be the Internet café that provides an additional model for the future.

It is this sense of activity which is the dominant feature of learning centres and which is attractive to many students. One senior education figure has commented that the practical activities that occupy students in learning centres are exactly in line with what they will find when they start their careers: working with other people to find information, solve problems and communicate the results. Since many students will have been used to this practical approach in earlier studies at school or college, there is a sense of continuity in developing it in higher education before going on to use it in employment.

Flexibility is the key requisite in building design, and most learning centres provide a variety of study environments to accommodate the working styles of individuals and groups. Flexibility to meet changing requirements over time is also essential. Small-scale reorganization is necessary from year to year to respond to changing patterns of use – for example between individual and group study, print collections and PC clusters.

Over the longer term, there are likely to be significant shifts in the use of space in learning centres. The size of print collections is likely to decrease as electronic information sources become more prevalent. A decline in the physical use of print collections has been reported by many institutions as information is delivered to researchers' desk-tops (Carlson, 2001). Conversely, the increase in independent study has increased the demand for access to study space, particularly space which is equipped with PCs (in spite of the steady increase in the proportion of students with their own PCs and Internet access). It is also likely that savings in the space taken up by conventional services could be offset by the requirement to house activities which develop and support virtual learning environments.

The Internet and networked learning will increasingly be regarded as an alternative for building projects in the future. However, the recognition that learning has an important social dimension provides one justification for dedicated physical provision, and economies of scale, for example in the provision of facilities for extended hours, may also justify investment in a learning centre. Flexible design will provide some reassurance that space will not become unusable.

The major issue for the future use of space is likely to relate to the boundaries between teaching and learning space, rather than a justification of centralized provision. The educational changes which underpin the learning centre model also have implications for teaching sessions, where alternatives to lectures are actively being developed. Teachers are looking for different models of interaction with students, and approaches such as the use of break-out groups, practical sessions and problem-based learning require accommodation other than tiered lecture theatres. Some of the required accommodation will be in teaching areas, but learning centres will also have space designed to support these activities – with or without the presence of a teacher.

Virtual learning environments have at last created the opportunity for the widespread application of technology to learning and teaching, following a number of false hopes in earlier years. Many higher education institutions are now developing sophisticated electronic environments and there has been an enthusiastic response by tutors to products such as Blackboard and Web-CT. The ambition of these systems is to create electronic equivalents of learning centres, where it is possible to carry out the same range of activities electronically as in a real learning centre. Real and virtual learning environments are complementary and it should be possible for students and tutors to move between the two in a seamless way.

It is worth emphasizing that the majority of students are likely to prefer a combination of face-to-face contact with other people and working with new technology. Even the most occupied distance learner welcomes real contact with their host institution and with their peers, and the most enthusiastic computer users enjoy the facilities and contacts offered on-campus.

The importance of the social dimension of learning has been emphasized by a task force of the Foresight programme, which advises the UK government on strategies for the future. Even though the focus of the group's work has been on identifying opportunities to exploit new technology, its report says 'It is the view of the Group – and research studies reinforce this – that effective learning takes place in a social environment' (Foresight, 2000). The same point was made more directly by a student interviewed as part of a study on technology-enabled learning. Given an option of a course entirely based on networked content, his reaction was clear: 'Like the Open University, where you never see anyone … it's all done by computers … no thanks!' (SHU, 1999).

Virtual learning environments are developing at a fast pace. The first materials to be added have usually been electronic versions of locally produced teaching material and course information; conferencing and messaging systems are also well established. Electronic information content provided through library and information staff often provides the most highly developed part. One major area for development is the integration of a wider range of computer-based systems, such as student tracking, finance and assessment, to create truly comprehensive managed learning environments. However, it is the creation of electronic learning materials which is likely to prove the most challenging.

Much of the content that has been produced so far has been different in character to the multimedia, interactive learning materials which are required to fully exploit the potential of electronic environments. As teachers begin to experiment with virtual learning tools, it is natural that existing material, such as teaching notes, handouts and course guides, should constitute the majority of the content. This is an important first step in the development of teachers' skills and provides immediate improvements in the accessibility of course material (although there is some concern that the burden of printing out documents has been passed to the student). Much of the success of virtual learning environments is the way in which teachers retain control of their work: the flexibility offered by these systems allows individual teachers to work in ways which suit them and their students.

At the other extreme, there have been a number of major projects, such as those funded through the UK Teaching and Learning Technology Initiative, which have created substantial multimedia products. However, these projects have had considerable sums of money invested in them, far beyond those available to course teams working in universities. Although many of these materials have been produced by groups of staff drawn from a number of institutions, the evaluation study which examined their impact found that the material had been adopted by a very limited number of institutions and generally had not had a lasting impact (THECG et al., 1999).

Given the investment of time and resources that is required to produce interactive material, the development of appropriate materials which lie some way between these two extremes – of well-funded multimedia programmes and course handouts – is likely to be a major challenge. Clearly, new approaches need to be found to provide material of an appropriate level of quality to meet the expectations of new generations of students who have grown up with a wide variety of entertainment media.

This work will need to draw on the skills of a variety of staff who will need to work together to exploit the potential of the new environment. Librarians will be able to draw from existing information material, which may provide an appropriate base for interactive learning experiences, such as those which involve the use of information to solve problems. There will be an increasing emphasis on the adaptation and reuse of existing material, which will also require information professionals' skills of indexing to create metadata, and bibliographic searching to track down appropriate content.

Media production staff, such as graphic designers, television producers and photographers, will need to work with multimedia designers to create new content. As technology develops, this will allow for the combination and integration of different media elements in new ways to engage students in more exciting and effective learning.

Virtual learning environments are opening up new territory. It will therefore be necessary to create strong quality frameworks to guide developments, drawing on the excellent practice which has already been established; and also to underpin this new work with rigorous research and evaluation. It will be important to develop our understanding of how students interact with material presented electronically, to understand how we maximize the effectiveness of their learning in this new environment, and to see how to make the most of real and virtual learning. How long will it be before students characterize their course in terms of the portal which they use as a reference point for their activities day by day rather than the lecture room?

STAFFING

In staffing as much as in learning environments, flexibility is likely to be the key factor in meeting the challenges facing educational institutions. Experience in other sectors shows that the traditional boundaries between jobs are breaking down, and this is likely to be a key requirement for staff working in higher education. The key to successful educational innovation in the future will lie in creating mixed teams of staff who can bring together a variety of skills and experience.

Course teams provide a good focus to draw staff together. The team provides a forum for debate on the key academic issues which underpin course design. There is a long tradition of learning centre staff representation on such groups and sound experience in many institutions of teachers and learning centre staff working together.

Working with course teams is often challenging for staff who do not have a teaching background: teaching is a demanding activity and many academic staff are understandably wary of staff without teaching experience being in a position to influence the professional territory which they regard as their responsibility. Learning centre staff may sometimes place too much emphasis on the development of information skills in such meetings (important as these skills are), rather than contributing their knowledge of information resources and their experience of supporting students when they are working independently.

The increasing use of problem-based learning and technology-enabled learning means that the skills of a wide range of learning centre staff are relevant to the work of course teams. In addition to information staff, multimedia designers, educational developers, curriculum specialists and educational researchers will need to be drawn into the design, planning, delivery and review of courses. This involvement will be crucial if these staff are to work effectively. The key to successful relationships will continue to be academic staff being hospitable to the involvement of other staff, and learning centre staff striking the right approach with academic colleagues.

Support for students is likely to be one area which will increasingly draw on a variety of staff, with opportunities for learning centre staff to provide more learning support. The long opening hours offered by learning centres have meant that students have often turned to information staff for help with their work – and on occasions they seek help which goes beyond advice on information sources and technology. Some of this extra advice may be characterized as generic learning support – help with learning problems, study skills and institutional procedures – which does not require expertise from a specialist teacher. Students frequently require motivation, reassurance and confidence-building, and it would be possible for learning centre staff to help with these areas, too, recognizing that specific difficulties may need to be referred to other staff.

The increasing flexibility of study patterns, the increasing pressure on academic staff time and the common complaint from students that they do not have sufficient access to teaching staff, make it appropriate to consider new ways of providing student support. Although any shift between teaching staff and learning centre staff would need to be handled sensitively, it is likely that the latter would quickly develop the necessary skills; and they would welcome the challenge of an extended role.

The support requirements of students working in virtual learning environments may also be met by teams of staff working with students in the same learning space. This approach provides an excellent opportunity for individuals with a variety of skills to contribute to the discussion and to develop their own expertise. Virtual environments may also be regarded as neutral ground where new approaches may be developed without the preconceived roles and responsibilities found in conventional work.

There is a similar issue to be explored in relation to the development of learning materials. The writing and production of teaching materials is a well-established part of teachers' work and is likely to be carried into work in electronic learning environments. The production of multimedia and interactive learning material is, however, more intensive and will require new skills.

There is a tradition of enthusiastic academic staff developing more sophisticated teaching and learning materials, partly as a result of the emergence of user-friendly software and hardware. Many teaching staff took up new software as it came onto the market: desk-top publishing software is a good example. However, graphic design skills are still required to produce high quality material and it is clearly necessary to ensure that working arrangements are in place which make best use of individuals' time and skills. A graphic design studio is likely to be the most cost-effective solution to the production of large quantities of material. The key issue, of course, is ensuring that the support that teachers require is easily available.

This tension is likely to be a greater issue in virtual learning environments, with the need to develop new learning materials as courses of study develop. It will be necessary to develop arrangements which focus on meeting the needs of teachers and their students, which encourage cost-effective use of time and skills, and which produce material of an appropriate quality.

The future development of learning centres will be determined by changes in teaching and learning, and a high level of educational expertise needs to be available to guide and support the work of their staff. At Sheffield Hallam University, the Learning and Teaching Institute is an integral part of the Learning Centre department along with the Learning and Teaching Research Institute. These two units constitute, in effect, the research and development arm of the University's core teaching activity. Maintaining close working relationships with teachers is essential for this work and this provides a major opportunity for staff across the Learning Centre to engage with schools of study.

It is important to develop working arrangements that allow learning centre staff and teaching staff to work together. In addition to the institutional links through committees and teams working on projects and developments, flexible staffing schemes that allow staff to work across central and teaching departments will help to encourage them to extend their experience and will foster sound working relationships. Secondments into the learning centre, for example, provide the time and space for academic staff to develop new approaches to their teaching and will develop a network of practising teachers who have the credibility to promote new thinking in colleagues. Secondments of learning centre staff into schools of study provide specialist expertise close at hand and can provide centrally-based staff with experience of mainstream teaching.

Investment in a wide range of staff development activities is essential if institutions are to develop the capability to succeed in the future. Significant amounts of time and money are likely to be required given the pace of change and the proportion of institutional budgets devoted to staffing. Staff development activities need to be maintained as a high priority and may need a degree of protection when budgets are under pressure.

The focus of much development work will be on keeping staff skills up to date in their core area of expertise. A useful benchmark here would be that individuals should be able to satisfy the continuing professional development requirements of their professional body. However, there is a need to develop the range of skills held by individuals in order to develop creative solutions to teaching and learning challenges, and so that staff can adapt easily to changing demands at work.

Two examples may serve to illustrate this point. Firstly, students working independently will turn for help to learning centre staff, and are not concerned about their professional background – they simply require an answer to their current problem. Secondly, multimedia developers are likely to produce better solutions to learning problems if they have an understanding of teaching and learning.

A staff development framework is required which allows individuals to develop skills and experience in professional areas that are adjacent to their existing expertise.

Typically, the key areas in learning centres will include information work, computing, multimedia production and education – all underpinned, of course, by good management skills. To follow up the examples cited above: librarians will wish to develop their computing knowledge so that they can deal with the questions raised by students; multimedia designers will be interested in gaining some understanding of teaching and learning.

A distinction should perhaps be made between this approach and multi-skilling, which has been attempted with varying degrees of success. A risk with multi-skilling is that high-level expertise is lost as many staff attempt to gain the broad range of skills necessary to operate across a wide range of activities. The alternative suggested here is that individuals should develop a profile of skills which is appropriate to their current work as well as to their aspirations for future work. A common staff development programme encompassing all of the key professional areas would provide a sound basis for new staff to develop the broader understanding required for developing their future roles.

Learning centre staff face a number of challenges as they plan for the future. The role of staff in central support departments is often difficult, since it is teaching and research departments which have the major influence on their institution's core business. It is all too easy for academic services staff to feel at the margins of institutional activity; particularly, on occasions, when they are reminded that they are an 'overhead' that has to be carried by teachers and researchers!

The increasing pace of change is a further challenge for learning centre staff. New technology has already transformed areas of work dealing with the creation of materials and with information systems, and it is evident that learning is at the first stage of a similar transformation. Changes in student expectations of learning centre provision will also require new approaches to the organization and delivery of services.

A strong culture which values staff and encourages them to take responsibility for their work is an essential ingredient for success as learning centres prepare for the future. Sound organizational frameworks are also required which encourage staff to work flexibly to meet the needs of students. Investment in staff development activities provides the third key element which should enable staff to develop the self-confidence to embrace – and lead – educational change.

Of course, all learning centre activities depend on professional networks and on creating partnerships with colleagues. This is where learning centre staff come into their own. Learning centres have their roots in the strong traditions of libraries and academic services, and a focus on working with people to find solutions is where they excel!

REFERENCES

Carlson, S. (2001), The Deserted Library. *Chronicle of Higher Education: Information Technology*, November 16, at: http://chronicle.com/free/v48/i12/12a03501.htm

Enright, B.J. (1970), Non-book/media materials and the library: a note. *Library Association Record*, **72** (12), December, pp. 368–9.

Foresight (Information Communications And Media Panel. The Learning Process In 2020 Task Force) (2000), *Point and click: learners in the ICT driving seat: a consultation document*, at: http://www.foresight.gov.uk

Fothergill, R. (1971), *A challenge for librarians*. London: National Council for Educational Technology in association with ASLIB Audio Visual Group.

National Committee of Inquiry into Higher Education (1997), *Higher Education in the Learning Society* (Dearing Report). London: HMSO.

Sheffield Hallam University, Learning and Teaching Institute (1999), Evaluation study.

Sheffield Hallam University (2000), *Learning effectiveness*.

THECG et al. (1999), *Communications and information technology materials for learning and teaching in UK higher and further education: Summary report* [commissioned by the four UK HE funding councils, the Further Education Funding Council and the University for Industry]. Higher Education Funding Council for England, 1999. at: http://www.hefce.ac.uk/pubs/hefce/1999

Appendices

This section contains the job descriptions, employee specifications and similar material referred to in Chapter 3.

APPENDIX A
SHEFFIELD HALLAM UNIVERSITY LEARNING CENTRE: JOB DESCRIPTIONS – INFORMATION SERVICES POSTS

INFORMATION ASSISTANT/INFORMATION ADVISER/SENIOR INFORMATION ADVISER

1. **Department** — Learning Centre
2. **Post title** — Information Assistant (scale 2/3)
   Information Adviser (scale 4 bar 5/6)
   Senior Information Adviser (scale SO1/2)
3. **Grade** — Scale 2/3 bar 4 bar 5/6 bar SO1/2
4. **Responsible to** — Designated member of staff
5. **Responsible for** — Supervisory duties may be associated with posts at 4 bar 5/6 bar SO1/2
6. **Holiday and sickness relief** — Designated member of staff
7. **Function of post**
   To work as part of a team providing and supporting information services.
8. **Main duties and responsibilities**
   These will encompass, at an appropriate level:

   - answering enquiries relating to the use of information services, systems and software, referring complex enquiries to other staff as appropriate;
   - providing practical help and guidance on the use of facilities and equipment;
   - contributing to the management and administration of collections, services and systems;
   - undertaking duties associated with the selection, acquisition, maintenance, use and promotion of information resources;
   - supervising staff and service points;
   - providing guidance on the use of learning materials;
   - supporting academic liaison.

INFORMATION ASSISTANT (SCALE 2/3)

Staff at this scale will be expected to:

- carry out duties associated with the issue desk;
- answer reception, directional and routine operational enquiries relating to the use of information services, systems and equipment, referring complex enquiries to other staff as appropriate;
- carry out duties associated with the acquisition and maintenance of collections of books and other materials;

- carry out clerical and administrative tasks associated with the provision of information services.

Qualifications

Good general level of education, normally 4 GCSEs or equivalent.

INFORMATION ADVISER (SCALE 4)

Staff at this level will undertake a wider range of duties and responsibilities and will be expected to undertake at least one of the following categories of work:

User support:

- undertake first-line enquiry work under supervision; referring complex enquiries to other staff as appropriate;

Administration:

- support other staff with the administration of departmental services;
- assist with the training and supervision of other staff.

Qualifications and experience

Appointment within the scale will be according to experience and qualifications.

Staff eligible for progression to Scale 4 would be able to demonstrate knowledge of one or more of the following: departmental information resources; the use and application of software packages; the organization of university and departmental services.

Recently qualified persons at degree or equivalent level, whose substantive post is graded at Scale 5/6 but who do not have a minimum of one year's appropriate experience, would normally start within Scale 4.

INFORMATION ADVISER (SCALE 5/6)

Staff at this level will be expected to undertake one or more of the following:

- carry out a wide range of user support activities without supervision, referring only complex subject-based or specialist software enquiries to more senior staff;
- take responsibility for specific projects or take a lead role in the administration and provision of a major functional area of the service;
- assist with the selection, organization and exploitation of information resources;

- prepare documentation, guides and promotional material;
- contribute to induction and training programmes;
- support academic liaison activities.

Qualifications and experience

Normally there is a requirement for a degree *or* recognized qualification in information science or librarianship *plus* a minimum of one year's experience at an appropriate level. Full consideration will be given to other qualifications and experience.

Staff eligible for appointment or progression to Scale 5/6 would be able to demonstrate in-depth knowledge of one or more of the following: a range of external information sources; the application of software packages and networked services; the purpose and methodology underlying relevant departmental services.

SENIOR INFORMATION ADVISER (SCALE SO1/2)

Staff at this level will be expected to undertake one or more of the following (and may also be expected to contribute to duties relating to Information Advisers):

- manage, on a day-to-day basis, a specific service or campus facility;
- assume responsibility for the deployment, supervision and support of allocated staff;
- contribute to policy formulation and service development;
- represent the service area or campus facility within the University and to external bodies.

Qualifications

Normally there is a requirement for a degree *or* recognized qualification in information science or librarianship *plus* a minimum of three years' experience at an appropriate level.

Full consideration will be given to other qualifications and experience.

NOTES

1. The department will encourage staff to undertake appropriate training and development and to develop interests associated with the needs of the organization, including membership of professional bodies.

2. There will be an agreed number of posts at each level which will determine the number of opportunities for personal progression through the bar and, which will be reviewed annually with staff representatives according to service requirements.

3. Further details of the duties associated with specific appointments will be provided in supplementary information prepared in consultation with the staff concerned.

APPENDIX B
LEEDS METROPOLITAN UNIVERSITY: JOB DESCRIPTION AND EMPLOYEE SPECIFICATION – SENIOR INFORMATION OFFICER

JOB DESCRIPTION

Division	Learning and Information Services
Post Designation	Senior Information Officer
Post to which directly responsible	Learning Centre Manager/Bibliographic Services & Support Manager/Weekend Services Manager
Post for which directly responsible	Any temporary or permanent staff assigned by the Head of Learning Support Services

Purpose of the job

1. To be responsible for supporting students in using the full range of facilities and resources of the University's Learning Centres. To be responsible for maintaining essential learning support services in the Learning Centres and to be actively involved in the development of new services and facilities.
2. To be responsible for the acquisition and organization of information resources acquired through the Bibliographic Services Unit and for supporting the operation and development of digital systems and electronic services within the On-Line Learning Centre.

RESPONSIBILITIES

Note: The duties of Senior Information Officers will depend upon:

*   whether they are assigned to work in one of the Learning Centres, in the Bibliographic Services Unit/On-Line Learning Centre, or working between the two areas;
*   the number of hours worked each week;
*   the skills and competencies of the postholder.

Learning Centres

1. To provide help and enquiry services in the Learning Centres in person, by telephone and by e-mail and to assist learners in using the facilities and resources of the Learning Centres effectively.
2. To advise users on how to navigate through the range of printed and electronic information sources available and to assist users in exploiting resources both

219

within the Learning Centre collections and elsewhere to meet their information needs.

3. To assist with the use of standard information technology (including the library automation system), microform, and audio-visual equipment. To advise on the use of IT software installed on PCs in the Learning Centres (for word processing, spreadsheets, and databases) and to act as a first-line source of expertise on at least one specialist software package.

4. To maintain booking systems for equipment, facilities, and services.

5. To collect charges, sell consumables, and handle other financial transactions.

6. To produce publicity for users of the Learning Centres.

7. To participate as necessary in training and education schemes aimed at maximizing the ability of students and staff to use the facilities and resources of the Learning Centres.

8. To assist in maintaining and operating Learning Centre services which may include taking responsibility for the Learning Centre in the absence of other senior colleagues.

9. To follow established procedures for the operation of the Learning Centres' services and to assist with maintaining security and ensuring compliance with acceptable behaviour guidelines within the Learning Centres.

10. To assist with the opening and securing of the Learning Centres and with the general supervision and security of Learning Centre resources.

11. To carry out duties associated with the maintenance of the collections of learning resources in the Learning Centres including being responsible for systematically reclassifying and retrospectively cataloguing learning resources on the Learning Centres' catalogue following project guidelines and established procedures.

12. To provide essential support to the Learning Advisers including assisting with workshops/briefings and with producing documentation and self-instructional materials.

13. To be responsible for a budget for a designated area of information provision and to be responsible for developing information access in accordance with agreed information access strategy for the area.

Bibliographic Services Unit/On-Line Learning Centre

14. To work with other colleagues to ensure the speedy acquisition of information resources and to participate in the monitoring of the speed of throughput as required.

15. To follow established procedures for systematically cataloguing, classifying and indexing recently acquired learning materials on the Learning Centres' catalogue, to be involved in initiatives to improve the quality of cataloguing

and classification, and to participate in maintaining the quality of the catalogue database.

16. To be involved in the routine operation of digital systems and electronic services to support access to electronic information and the operation of the Learning Centres and to provide essential back-up support.

17. To be responsible for the production and setting up of relevant WWW pages for Learning & Information Services.

18. To assist the Senior Learning Advisers, the Digital Services & Systems Manager, and the Documentation Coordinator in their duties.

19. To be involved with digital projects to develop electronic services and information access.

Other

20. To participate in relevant staff development activities and to develop new skills and competencies to meet the changing needs of the service. To assist in the mentoring and training of new and existing staff.

21. To supply reports and statistics as required by LIS management and to participate in the evaluation of services in support of the LIS Service Level Agreement.

22. To be responsible for the promotion of good customer care practice.

23. To participate in and contribute to the work of various project groups and quality improvement teams as required.

24. To undertake any other duties commensurate with the grade of the post as requested by the Learning Centre Manager, Electronic Services Development Manager or the Head of Learning Support Services.

EMPLOYEE SPECIFICATION

Criteria

- A degree/professional qualification in information management.
- Experience of providing computing help or library enquiry services in a pressurized environment.
- Previous supervisory experience/demonstrates aptitude for supervising staff.
- Good IT skills evidenced through qualification or experience.
- Experience of managing resources and a budget.
- Previous involvement in quality improvement projects or initiatives.
- Appreciation of the role of learning support services within the University and demonstrates awareness of the value of converged services.

- Advanced information searching skills in a hybrid print and electronic environment with a good spread of knowledge of subject information sources.
- Willingness to train and mentor colleagues. Willingness to pursue staff development opportunities.
- Experience of team work and of working within an interdisciplinary framework.
- Reference to the importance of equal opportunities and health and safety policies.

APPENDIX C
LEEDS METROPOLITAN UNIVERSITY: JOB DESCRIPTION AND EMPLOYEE SPECIFICATION – INFORMATION OFFICER

JOB DESCRIPTION

Division	Learning and Information Services
Department	Learning Support Services
Post Designation	Information Officer
Post to which directly responsible	Learning Centre Manager/Bibliographic Services & Support Manager
Post for which directly responsible	Any temporary or permanent staff assigned by the Head of Learning Support Services

Purpose of the job

1. To assist learners in using the facilities and resources of the Learning Centres effectively and to provide support for the maintenance of Learning Centre services.
2. To be responsible for the acquisition and organization of information resources acquired through the Bibliographic Services Unit and to support the operation of digital systems and electronic services within the On-Line Learning Centre.

RESPONSIBILITIES

Note: The duties of Information Officers will depend upon:

- whether they are assigned to work in one of the Learning Centres, in the Bibliographic Services Unit/On-Line Learning Centre, or working between the two areas
- the number of hours worked each week
- the skills and competencies of the postholder

Learning Centres

1. To assist in the provision of help and enquiry services in the Learning Centres in person, telephone, and e-mail and to assist learners in using the facilities and resources of the Learning Centres effectively.
2. To help students and staff with the use of information technology including the equipment and standard software, using CD-ROMs and the Internet, and the library automation system.

3. To assist with the use of photocopiers and printers, replenish them when necessary, and deal with paper jams, and to assist in the use of microform and audio-visual equipment.
4. To maintain booking systems for equipment, facilities, and services.
5. To collect charges, sell consumables, and handle other financial transactions.
6. To assist in the production of publicity materials for users of the Learning Centres.
7. To assist in maintaining and operating Learning Centre services which may include taking responsibility for a designated area of service or operations.
8. To follow established procedures for the operation of the Learning Centres' services and to assist with maintaining security and ensuring compliance with acceptable behaviour guidelines within the Learning Centres.
9. To assist with the opening and securing of the Learning Centres and with the general supervision and security of Learning Centre resources.
10. To carry out duties associated with the maintenance of the collections of learning resources in the Learning Centres including stock editing, removing old editions, repairing damaged stock, display of new acquisitions and current journals, and arranging binding. To systematically reclassify and retrospectively catalogue learning resources on the Learning Centres' catalogue following project guidelines and established procedures.
11. To provide essential support to the Learning Advisers including assisting with workshops/briefings, budget expenditure, and producing documentation and self-instructional materials.

Bibliographic Services Unit/On-Line Learning Centre

12. To work with other colleagues to ensure the speedy acquisition of information resources and to participate in the monitoring of the speed of throughput as required.
13. To follow established procedures for systematically cataloguing, classifying and indexing recently acquired learning materials on the Learning Centres' catalogue, to be involved in initiatives to improve the quality of cataloguing and classification, and to participate in maintaining the quality of the catalogue database.
14. To assist with the routine operation of digital systems and electronic services to support access to electronic information and the operation of the Learning Centres and to provide essential back-up support.
15. To undertake the production and setting up of WWW pages for Learning & Information Services.
16. To digitize printed information resources and make them available electronically.

17. To assist the Digital Services & Systems Manager, the Digital Resources Coordinator, and the Documentation Coordinator in their duties.

Other

18. To participate in relevant staff development activities and to develop new skills and competencies to meet the changing needs of the service. To assist in the training and mentoring of new staff.
19. To supply reports and statistics as required by LIS management and to participate in the evaluation of services in support of the LIS Service Level Agreement.
20. To be responsible for the promotion of good customer care practice.
21. To participate in and contribute to the work of various project groups and quality improvement teams as required.
22. To undertake any other duties commensurate with the grade of the post as requested by the Learning Centre Manager, Electronic Services Development Manager or the Head of Learning Support Services.

EMPLOYEE SPECIFICATION

Criteria

- Education to degree level and, ideally, a professional qualification in information management.
- Experience of providing computing help or library enquiry services in a pressurized environment.
- Good IT skills evidenced through qualification or experience.
- Demonstrates a commitment to customer care with evidence of good service skills face-to-face and by telephone.
- Appreciation of the role of learning support services within the University and demonstrates awareness of the value of converged services.
- Good information searching skills in a hybrid print and electronic environment.
- Experience of teamwork and of working within an interdisciplinary framework.
- Excellent interpersonal skills and an ability to explain technologies and complex topics simply and clearly to non-specialists.
- Demonstrates commitment to the provision of a high quality service to meet customer needs.
- Appreciation of digital library developments and a willingness to be involved in developing/supporting electronic services and digital information access.
- Appreciation of the importance of keeping up to date with University developments and with developing new skills.

APPENDIX D
LEEDS METROPOLITAN UNIVERSITY: JOB DESCRIPTION AND EMPLOYEE SPECIFICATION – LEARNING ADVISER

JOB DESCRIPTION

Division	Learning and Information Services
Department	Learning Support Services
Post Designation	Learning Adviser
Posts to which directly responsible	Deputy Learning Centre Manager
Posts for which directly responsible	Any permanent or temporary staff assigned by the Learning Centre Manager

Purpose of the Job

1. To stimulate effective communication and encourage partnership with faculty colleagues, to raise the profile of LIS services and facilities in faculties, and to increase awareness of how facilities and services offered by LIS can support academic provision and innovation in teaching and learning.
2. To provide support to the academic programme of the University through the identification and acquisition of appropriate learning resources, the provision of high quality information and advice services, the preparation of documentation and self-instructional materials, and the design and delivery of courses and workshops on information literacy skills.
3. To take responsibility for liaison with designated Schools.

RESPONSIBILITIES

Academic partnership

1. To be responsible for encouraging partnerships between LIS and academic, administrative, technical, and managerial colleagues in a designated School or Schools.
2. To initiate and develop close working relationships with academic staff in the development and exploitation of learning resources to support the academic programme.
3. To participate in scheme/pathway/course/module development, to guide academic staff on the availability of resources, and to advise LSS management on resource needs and priorities.
4. To participate in scheme/pathway/course/module review, to report on the use of LSS services and facilities, and to advise LSS management on the adequacy of LIS facilities and resources to support academic objectives.

5. To participate in validation, review, and assessment events (including Teaching Quality Assessments) and to prepare and collate appropriate documentation about LIS facilities and services for them.

6. To participate and contribute to the work of course/pathway/scheme committees and other relevant academic meetings including supporting curriculum development.

7. To be a member of a Faculty Support Team and to work closely with a Senior Learning Adviser, the Academic Services Manager, and other Learning and Information Services colleagues in providing support to the academic work of the Faculty/School.

Learning resources

8. To be responsible, in cooperation with academic staff in the Faculties, for providing and developing access through the Learning Centres to learning, information, or computing resources to support a specified School or Schools.

9. To develop an understanding of learning and research resources relevant to specified subject areas and, in association with the academic staff and LSS management, to develop statements of policy on developing information access/ IT resources and facilities through the Learning Centres to meet the needs of the academic community within the specified School or Schools.

10. To manage efficiently the budget(s) for which responsibility has been delegated and to develop spending plans which follow the agreed statements of policy on developing information access/IT resources and facilities.

11. To work with other staff, as necessary, to ensure the speedy acquisition of, or access to, learning resources.

Information literacy skills

12. To encourage independence in learning by developing and participating in schemes aimed either at maximizing students' ability to find and exploit information held in printed, electronic or other forms or enabling the effective use of IT facilities and software.

13. To develop and teach modules for courses on information literacy skills as appropriate.

14. To introduce students and staff to Learning & Information Services and to raise awareness of the range of resources, facilities, and services available to meet their needs.

15. To prepare documentation and self-instructional materials to raise awareness of LIS facilities and resources and to guide students and staff in how to optimally use the facilities and resources. To work closely with the Documentation

227

Co-ordinator in the production of the documentation in the Learning & Information Services style and in its effective dissemination.

Information services

16. To assist in the provision of help and enquiry services in the Learning Centres in person, by telephone, and by e-mail and to assist learners in using the facilities and resources of the Learning Centres effectively.

17. To advise users on how to navigate through the range of printed and electronic information sources available and to assist users in exploiting resources both within the Learning Centre collections and elsewhere to meet their needs.

18. To advise on the use of standard IT software installed in the IT labs (for word processing, spreadsheets, and databases) and to advise and provide specialist expertise and support for named software (e.g. word processing, spreadsheets, databases, data analysis).

19. To develop expertise in, and to undertake searches of electronic information sources available on-line, on CD-ROM, or via the Internet.

20. To create computerized databases or produce information services as appropriate. To prepare navigational pages to digital resources on the World Wide Web for LMU students and staff.

Other duties

21. To follow established procedures for the operation of Learning Centre services and to assist in maintaining and operating Learning Centre services, which will involve some enquiry work.

22. To raise awareness among Faculty staff of *Skills for Learning* resources, to lead sessions on how *Skills for Learning* can be used in the development of key skills, and work with LSS colleagues in developing, extending, and encouraging use of the resources as appropriate.

23. To participate in relevant staff development activities, to develop new skills and competencies to meet the changing needs of the service, and to assist in the mentoring of staff and placement students as required.

24. To participate in and contribute to the work of various project groups and quality improvement teams as required.

25. To supply reports and statistics as required by LIS management and to participate in the evaluation of services in support of the LIS Service Level Agreement or other quality assurance initiatives.

26. To ensure compliance with appropriate legislative requirements including licensing, data protection and copyright.

27. To be responsible for the promotion of good customer care practice.

28. Performance of other duties commensurate with the grade of the post as directed by the Head of Learning Support Services or the appropriate Learning Centre Manager.

EMPLOYEE SPECIFICATION

Criteria

- A degree or a professional qualification in librarianship or information management.
- Appreciation of the role of learning support services in a University, preferably possessing previous experience of an academic library.
- Awareness of the issues affecting higher education and their significance for academic libraries.
- Advanced information handling skills with previous experience of enquiry work and, preferably, some knowledge of information sources in the subject areas serviced by the Learning Centre.
- Experience of working in partnership with a range of colleagues with, preferably, particular experience of liaising and working with academic colleagues in supporting students' learning.
- Evidence of using a proactive approach to meeting user needs.
- Ability to teach groups of students and, ideally, previous experience of teaching/ training. Ability to design teaching materials and self-instructional learning materials.
- Good IT skills with an ability and keenness to support the use of a wide range of electronic information sources and services for students' learning.
- Knowledge of learning resources in a subject relevant to the University and knowledge of software or information sources to support research and students' learning.
- Demonstrates enthusiasm and interest in the job.
- Experience of teamwork and of working within an interdisciplinary framework.
- Reference to the importance of equal opportunities and health and safety policies.

APPENDIX E
UNIVERSITY OF LINCOLNSHIRE & HUMBERSIDE: JOB DESCRIPTION – LEARNING ADVISER

JOB DESCRIPTION

Job title	Learning Adviser
Department	Learning Support
Reports to	Senior Learning Adviser
Grade	Scale 5/SO2
Date	August 1996

Overall Purpose

To provide assistance to University subjects in the areas of curriculum development, materials production, support for unit delivery and assessment, scholarship, research and consultancy.

PRINCIPAL ACCOUNTABILITIES

To contribute to the achievement of the following Departmental objectives:

- *To assist students to achieve Independence in Learning:* by (for example)
  - encouraging subjects to develop appropriate curricula
  - developing with subjects, appropriate unit delivery/assessment methods
  - assisting with unit delivery/assessment
  - developing appropriate teaching and learning materials/products
  - providing specialized skills/knowledge to support Service Advisers.

- *To be the preferred provider of Learning Services:* by (for example)
  - supporting Schools Undergraduate Modular Scheme Office with named award support
  - providing subjects with support for teaching and learning materials/product development
  - providing specialist support to students
  - facilitating user access to information sources
  - providing support to subjects for unit development/delivery/assessment.

- *To provide a quality service to customers:* by (for example)
  - supporting access to relevant technology and software
  - providing user access to appropriate media facilities
  - training and supporting Service Advisers
  - monitoring the service provided to customers
  - providing access to appropriate information sources.

230

- *To give value for money service:* by (for example)
  - monitoring the use of Learning Support facilities against targets
  - matching the supply of products, facilities and services to the emerging demands
  - identifying the means of continuous improvement against past performance
  - ensuring that subjects are aware of competencies available within Learning Support
  - ensure that Schools Undergraduate Modular Scheme Office are aware of Learning Support potential to support named awards.

ORGANIZATIONAL POSITION

Learning Support Manager
|
Team Leader(s)   Senior Learning Adviser (SLA)
|
Learning Adviser (LA)

DIMENSIONS OF THE JOB

Students
Academic departments
Subjects
Named awards
Units

IMPORTANT WORKING RELATIONSHIPS

Internal: Subject staff (academic)
Learning Support Managers
(Senior) Service Advisers
(Senior) Learning Advisers
Students
Administrative, technical and manual staff

External: Suppliers/Publishers of products and services
Examiners

DECISION MAKING AUTHORITY AND CONTROL

- Freedom to act within defined areas of authority determined by the Senior Learning Adviser (SLA).

- Responsible to individual team/project leaders for particular aspect of the workload. Experienced Learning Advisers with appropriate levels of competence are required to take on team leadership responsibilities.
- Prioritization of tasks and individual workload.
- Handle cash, requisitions, delivery notes and invoices.
- Maintain appropriate collection of information (electronic and paper) and access to them.
- Control User access to the University IT environment.
- Report violation of Learning Support user regulation regarding the use of facilities, equipment and products (normally to SLA). Eject customers in breach of regulations.
- Invoke University disciplinary procedures and exercise judgement in referring students to appropriate subject tutors.
- Support students undertaking learning packages or independent studies.

NATURE AND SCOPE

The specific responsibilities and tasks of the post will be determined by the SLA after consultation with the postholder and linked to the performance review process. The postholder will monitor and evaluate his/her own performance through the appraisal and performance review processes and undertake approved training and development which may include scholarly and/or research activities.

The postholder will be expected to work such hours as are reasonably necessary to fulfil his/her duties, which will mean working a designated number of sessions each week, in a flexible, efficient and effective professional manner. Duties may include all or some of the following:

- Ensure that all Service Advisers are aware of developments in the delivery and assessment of units, which are the responsibility of Learning Adviser associated with that subject.
- Use relevant software and technology as appropriate.
- Operate set up, assist and train customers in the correct and safe use of equipment and facilities. Engage in first-line fault diagnosis and reporting of faulty equipment.
- Ensure that health and safety policies and practices are implemented including any regulations governing the use of facilities or conduct of users.
- Produce and update publicity materials and user documentation.
- Assist in the collection of data and its analysis as required.
- Assess equipment and product needs and liaise with suppliers and publishers.
- The postholder should have a specialism in at least one University subject and at least one of the knowledge competencies. He/she should work with at least one

subject team and support curriculum development, research and consultancy, assist in the acquisition/development of teaching and learning material, and assist in the delivery and assessment of units.

- Learning Advisers will attend subject meetings (including Boards of Examiners) as appropriate.
- Provide guidance and advice to customers on sources of information, facilities (computer, media and language) learning packages, workshops and demonstrations.
- Evaluate new equipment and products for purchase, liaising with subject staff as appropriate.
- Assist in the production of the IT environment capability statement and the procurement of both IT and non-IT capital equipment.
- Assist in maintaining the security of premises, equipment, products and facilities.
- Assess security needs and implement accordingly.
- Maintain accurate and up-to-date records of work undertaken.
- Work to high levels of accuracy and to strict deadlines.

APPENDIX F
UNIVERSITY OF LINCOLNSHIRE & HUMBERSIDE: JOB DESCRIPTION – SERVICE ADVISER

JOB DESCRIPTION

Job title	Service Adviser
Department	Learning Support
Reports to	Senior Service Adviser
Grade	Scale 1–5
Date	August 1996

Overall Purpose

To provide an individualized quality service to the customers of Learning Support (predominantly students but also staff) and to undertake designated tasks in support of this activity.

PRINCIPAL ACCOUNTABILITIES

To contribute to the achievement of the following related Departmental objectives:

- *To assist students to achieve Independence in Learning:* by (for example)
  - putting requests/enquiries into context
  - establishing the nature of the required outcome
  - establishing the current skills/knowledge of the customer
  - providing an appropriate response
  - actively listening.

- *To be the preferred provider of Learning Services:* by (for example)
  - adding value to each customer interaction
  - being prepared to deal with a range of customer requests/enquiries
  - being sensitive to customer needs
  - responding successfully to an agreed percentage of customer requests/enquiries
  - making an appointment when referring customers to Learning Advisers.

- *To provide a quality service to customers:* by (for example)
  - structuring messages logically
  - ensuring a prompt response to meet required outcomes
  - communicating clearly and precisely
  - remaining courteous and polite at all times
  - keeping himself/herself up to date with service developments.

234

- *To give a value for money service:* by (for example)
  - organizing tasks and managing time effectively
  - being self directed
  - using resources effectively
  - monitoring performance
  - identifying areas for improvement

ORGANIZATIONAL POSITION

Learning Support Manager (LSM)
|
Team Leader   Senior Service Adviser (SSA)
|
Service Adviser (SA)

DIMENSIONS OF THE JOB

Students
Subjects
Named awards
Units

IMPORTANT WORKING RELATIONSHIPS

Internal: (Senior) Service Advisers
Shelvers
(Senior) Learning Advisers
Learning Support Managers
Students
Subject staff (academic)
Administrative, technical and manual staff

External: Suppliers/Publishers of products and services

DECISION MAKING AUTHORITY AND CONTROL

- Freedom to act within areas of authority determined by the Senior Service Adviser.
- Prioritization of tasks and individual workload.
- Handle cash, requisitions, invoices and discharge debts.
- Implement the loan/reservation of equipment and products.

- Exercise judgement in referring students to appropriate Subject Tutors or Learning Advisers and to support Learning Advisers in helping students to use learning packages or undertake independent studies.
- Invoke University disciplinary procedures and eject customers in breach of Learning Support user regulations.
- Report violations of Learning Support user regulations regarding the use of facilities, equipment and products (normally to SSA).
- Experienced Service Advisers, with appropriate levels of competence, are required to take on team leadership responsibilities.

NATURE AND SCOPE

The specific responsibilities, activities and tasks of the post will be determined by the SSA and linked to the performance review process. The postholder will monitor and evaluate his/her own performance through the appraisal and performance review processes and undertake approved training/development.

The postholder will be expected to work such hours as are reasonably necessary to fulfil his/her responsibilities in a flexible, efficient, effective manner.

The postholder will be responsible for organizing and executing his/her own workload and to be responsible to individual team/project leaders for particular aspects of his/her workload where appropriate. Other requirements may include all or some of the following:

- Ability to use relevant technologies and software as appropriate.
- Set up and operate equipment; train and assist customers in the correct and safe use of equipment; engage in first-line fault diagnosis; and repair/replace faulty equipment or report to CNS.
- Provide guidance and advice to customers on the sources of information and computing, media and language facilities available within Learning Support.
- Ensure that health and safety policies and practices are implemented including any regulations governing the use of facilities or the conduct of users.
- Monitor enquiries and the access and/or departure of customers as directed by the SSA.
- Assist with reception duties over the counter and over the telephone IT networks.
- Undertake additional supportive tasks as directed by SSA.
- Administer questionnaires to customers and collect other data for the performance measures relating to departmental objectives and quality assurance procedures as directed by SSA. Maintain accurate and up-to-date records.
- Monitor the use, and advise upon the effectiveness, of publicity materials (displays, posters, leaflets, guides, etc.) used within Learning Support.
- Assist in maintaining the security of the premises, equipment, products and users.
- Work to high levels of accuracy and to strict deadlines.

APPENDIX G
UNIVERSITY OF ABERDEEN (DIRECTORATE OF INFORMATION SYSTEMS AND SERVICES, CONSULTANCY & CLIENT LIAISON DIVISION) – HELP DESK OFFICER

FURTHER PARTICULARS

The University of Aberdeen

The University of Aberdeen was founded at King's College by papal bull in 1495. There was a second, Protestant, foundation at Marischal College in 1593 and the two colleges were amalgamated in 1860. The main campus is now in Old Aberdeen which retains its medieval layout, its village atmosphere and its fifteenth-century University chapel, yet is within the modern city. The University estate extends to some 263 hectares containing 150 000 sq m of academic related buildings mainly located on three separate major campus areas, with some remote outstations. Catering and student residential accommodation extends to some 100 000 sq m with some 4500 bed spaces. The annual turnover of the University is in excess of £90 million, and the University staff total more than 2500.

The Directorate of Information Systems and Services Library and computing services at the University of Aberdeen are provided by a single organization: the Directorate of Information Systems and Services (DISS), formed in September 1996 by a merger of the University Library, Computing Centre and Administrative Computing.

Library services

The University Library is one of the largest and best equipped in Scotland and employs the latest technology for both staff and student use. It operates on five closely integrated but geographically separated sites, linked by a networked computer system. The Queen Mother Library, in Old Aberdeen, is the headquarters of the University Library and offers nearly 700 study spaces on six floors. Another 700 seats are available in the other branches: the Medical Library at Foresterhill; the Taylor Library and European Documentation Centre, for legal studies, also in Old Aberdeen; the Education Faculty Library at Hilton; and the Special Collections Department at King's College, housing the Library's rare books and manuscripts.

In addition to the Library's computerized catalogue, CD-ROM databases are available and clusters of PCs connected to the campus network provide Internet access to on-line databases and other information resources.

Computing services

The Directorate is responsible for the provision and support of computing facilities throughout the University. This includes academic and library computing and file servers, administrative computer systems, computer classrooms and clusters, and the campus network. Individual departments purchase their own equipment, but the Directorate provides advice and support, coordinates the central purchasing and provides them with network services.

Organization

The Directorate is organized into eight divisions.

- The *Library Division* has inherited many of the Library's core functions, providing the site-based counter and reference services, and learning resources.
- The *Consultancy & Client Liaison Division* provides support services in the form of liaison with users, help desk services, teaching and training, and documentation. This division is also responsible for the management of the University's WWW service, the Audio Visual Unit and the Learning Technology Unit.
- The *Infrastructure Systems Division* maintains and supports the information processing, data storage and data transmission resources of the University. This includes PCs, file servers, central servers, the campus network and the telephone network.
- The *Applications Support Division* procures, licences, installs, maintains and supports software for academic, administrative and library use and installs and maintains teaching materials mounted on the classroom and other file servers.
- The *Corporate Systems Division* provides systems for administrative functions at institutional, faculty and departmental level throughout the University, and the software tools for efficient processing of management information obtained from these systems.
- The *Management Services Division* is responsible for the management of the Directorate itself, as a business unit, with overall responsibility for the administration of the Directorate finance, personnel, internal support services and logistics.
- The *Enterprise & Business Unit*: provides services in the areas of Photographic, Reprographic and Binding and identifies, negotiates, implements and maintains other income-generating projects and agreements both within and outwith the University; this function incorporates the maintenance and provision of the Business Information Service.
- The *Historic Collections Division* is responsible for preserving, promoting and conserving the University's collection of rare books, manuscripts and archive, its art collection and the collections of the Marischal Museum.

Consultancy & Client Liaison Division

The Consultancy & Client Liaison of the Directorate provides liaison and support services for users of University library and computing facilities. This includes liaison with staff and students, publication of a wide range of guides and documentation in both electronic and paper format, a programme of IT training courses and workshops, managing the University's World Wide Web services and providing Help Desk services for both staff and students. The University's Audio Visual Unit and the Learning Technology Unit are also part of this division.

The DISS Help Desk Service The Directorate's Help Desk services underwent a major restructuring during 1997 and 1998. The information and advisory services – formerly run separately in the Computing Centre, University Office and Libraries – have been combined into a single, integrated helpdesk service, providing information and advice on all aspects of the Directorate's services. A central helpdesk, specializing in IT-related help, operates within the Computing Centre and satellite helpdesks are located in the Queen Mother, Taylor, Medical and Education Faculty Libraries.

JOB DESCRIPTION

The Help Desk Officers provide first-line support to users contacting the Help Desk service. They are part of a larger team providing both first-line and back-up support to users of information systems and services. The Help Desk Officers are based at the IT Help Desk in the Computing Centre, but also spend part of their time working on the University Library helpdesks on a rota and shift basis.

RESPONSIBILITIES AND DUTIES:

- Receiving and processing queries and requests directed to the DISS Help Desk service, including:
  - dealing with personal and telephone callers, and with queries delivered electronically, through electronic mail and the helpdesk software system.

- Providing information and advice, at a basic to intermediate level, on the use of:
  - computer systems and the University network
  - commonly used applications software (e.g. Microsoft Office, Eudora e-mail, Netscape)
  - administrative applications (e.g. student records, finance system)
  - Library on-line catalogue, CD-ROM databases, subject searches
  - Library resources (e.g. location of stock)
  - electronic information resources available over the network (e.g. BIDS, EDINA, WWW)

239

- Library services (e.g. inter-library loans, interbranch requests, heavy demand, binding)
- training courses and documentation available to staff and students.
- Referring more complex queries to technical and specialist staff within DISS.
- Logging queries and keeping track of referrals using the Help Desk software system.
- Logging hardware, software and network fault reports, and referring these to the appropriate support team.
- Accepting service requests for software installation and upgrades and passing these on to the software support team.
- Dealing with some user administration tasks, such as registration queries and requests, filespace quota allocations, budget queries.
- Dealing with course bookings and queries.
- Selling documentation, computer consumables, copycards, Library publications, external publications, etc. (range varies with helpdesk location).
- Monitoring supplies of sale items.
- Operating a loan system for computer and software manuals.
- Supervising student-bookable PCs.
- Assisting in the delivery of training courses and workshops.
- Assisting in the authoring and reviewing of user documentation and training materials.
- Providing feedback on user needs to the other teams within DISS.
- Occasional delegated supervision of (student) helpers.
- Undertaking similar work, as allocated by the Help Desk Services Manager.

The Help Desk Officer is responsible to the Help Desk Services Manager who allocates the duties within the team. Appropriate training will be given and opportunities for gaining experience in the use of information systems will be provided.

QUALIFICATIONS AND EXPERIENCE

Applicants should preferably have a degree or relevant further education qualification, but this is not essential. Applicants with a good level of school qualifications, including Higher English or equivalent, will be considered. Experience of using an academic library is highly desirable. Good IT skills are essential. Applicants should be familiar with using a PC, working with a range of Windows software, and with using Microsoft Office applications, such as Word.

Good communication skills are essential. Applicants should have a good command of both written and spoken English, the ability to explain things clearly to other people, and have some practical experience of advising customers or tutoring students. A cheerful, pleasant manner is needed. You must enjoy working with different types of people and be able to work both on your own initiative and as part of a team.

Hours are currently Monday to Friday, 9 am to 5 pm but applicants may be required to work shifts – 9 am to 5 pm and 11 am to 7 pm – on a rota basis.

UNIVERSITY OF ABERDEEN: PERSON SPECIFICATION – HELP DESK OFFICER

GRADE SCO 3

Title Help Desk Officer

Department/Faculty Directorate of Information Systems and Services

	Essential	Desirable
1. Education/Qualifications Academic, technical and professional education and training	Good level of school qualifications, including Higher English or equivalent	Degree (highly desirable) or relevant further education qualification. Some numerical qualification, e.g. Higher Maths
2. Work and other relevant experience (including training) For example, specialist knowledge, level of experience, skills, supervisory experience, research	Familiarity with PCs and a range of software applications Experience of working with Windows and MS Office applications Experience of assisting and advising customers or tutoring students Some clerical experience	Familiarity with e-mail and WWW Some familiarity with software installation and PC configuration Experience of using other computer systems Experience of working on a Help or Info desk Experience of tutoring or teaching Experience of writing guides/instructions for others Library experience
3. Personal qualities and abilities For example, initiative, leadership, ability to work on own or with others, communication skills	Good command of written and spoken English Ability to explain things clearly Quick on the uptake – able to grasp problems quickly Cheerful, outgoing, pleasant manner – enjoys working with people Ability to deal with different types of people Ability to work under pressure Ability to work on own and as part of a team Likely to fit into Help Desk team Flexible, able and willing to adapt to change	Ability to write user documentation Teaching ability Initiative, creativity Good organizational skills Ability to gain satisfaction from doing a job well even when the work is routine Enthusiasm for information resources
4. Other For example, special circumstances (if any) appropriate to the job such as unsocial hours, travelling, physical requirements, etc.		Show interest/enthusiasm for integration of library and computing services. Able to work shift times as required by DISS

APPENDIX I
SHEFFIELD HALLAM UNIVERSITY: PERSON SPECIFICATION – INFORMATION ADVISER

Post Information Adviser
School/Department Learning Centre

	Details	E*	D*
Attainment Evidenced achievements: e.g. relevant qualifications (or equivalents), training	4 GCSEs or equivalent	✓	
	Degree or equivalent qualification in information science, librarianship, or IT		✓
	At least six months' training in library, information or IT support work	✓	
Experience Type and amount of experience and specific knowledge required for this job	One year's experience in library, information or IT support services, or of University learner support, at an appropriate level		✓
	Experience of working with IT	✓	
	In-depth knowledge of a range of information sources, or the application of software packages and networked services	✓	
	Basic knowledge of Windows environments	✓	
	Practical experience of applications software, including MS Office products	✓	
	Experience of supporting users with IT		✓
Aptitudes Skills and abilities required for effective performance: e.g. presentation skills, interpersonal skills, numeracy	Ability to work as part of a team	✓	
	Ability to explain technical subjects clearly to users	✓	
	Basic numeracy skills	✓	
	Ability to organize and prioritize workload and to use own initiative	✓	
	Ability to work under pressure and to deadlines	✓	
	Projects a professional image	✓	

E = Essential   D = Desirable

243

Appendix I concluded

	Details	E*	D*
Personal attributes			
Disposition and characteristics relevant to the job: e.g. ability to cope with pressure, ability to work with others, ability to motivate/ influence, ability to work on own initiative	High standard of interpersonal skills, including clear and concise oral communication	✓	
	Ability to work flexibly in a changing environment	✓	
	Commitment to high quality services for users	✓	
Circumstances			
Special demands of the job that have direct impact on performance: e.g. if job involves shift work or unusual hours, travel abroad, etc.	Flexible working arrangements according to the needs of the service	✓	
	Regular evening duty	✓	

UNIVERSITY OF LINCOLNSHIRE & HUMBERSIDE: LEARNING SUPPORT DEPARTMENT – COMPETENCY FRAMEWORKS

BEHAVIOURAL COMPETENCIES

	Level 1	Level 2	Level 3	Level 4
Communication	Polite and helpful manner when communicating with others	Provides clear, concise information and checks to ensure understanding	Influences the thinking, decisions and actions of others to achieve departmental objectives	
Continuous improvement	Makes suggestions to improve processes	Initiates change to improve processes	Positively challenges fundamental aspects of approach and provides viable alternatives	Promotes internal and external relationships which benefit the department
Enthusiasm	Self-motivated and works towards achieving his/her own outcomes	Self-motivated and supports others to achieve their outcomes	Self-motivated and able to motivate others to achieve departmental objectives	
Personal development		Is committed to his/her own personal development	Is committed to his/her own personal development and the development of others	
Planning and prioritization	Manages own routine activities	Schedules routine activities	Sets and communicates new priorities to meet new objectives	Develops a vision for the future in the context of the university and departmental visions
Positive regard for others	Works in a constructive way with all staff	Works as a team member	Promotes team working within the department and the university	Promotes new working alliances across the university
Problem solving and analysis	Identifies and solves simple problems	Identifies and seeks solutions to complex problems	Identifies current and potential problems and develops creative and effective solutions	
Service	Treats customers with politeness and respect to gain a positive response	Reviews and adapts service provided to customers	Identifies and develops best practice	

SKILL COMPETENCIES

	Level 1	Level 2	Level 3	Level 4
Subject	Can contribute to secondary delivery of university subject(s)	Can contribute to primary delivery of university subject(s)	Promotes and develops subject(s) within the university	Contributes to the research activity within one or more subject
LS technologies	Can describe and demonstrate the normal operation of Learning Support equipment and facilities	Promotes and develops technology within the university	Provides advanced technology expertise in support of Learning Support activities	
Information handling	Can describe and demonstrate the use of information sources	Promotes and develops independence in information access	Contributes to the department's information strategy and provision	Contributes to the university's information strategy and provision
Facilitating learning	Participates in the support of student learning		Initiates and leads student learning activities	
Curriculum development	Participates in the development of services and resources to support curriculum development	Contributes in the development of services and resources to support curriculum development	Initiates the development of services and resources to support curriculum development	
Product development	Participates in product development for secondary delivery	Develops products to specification for primary and/or secondary delivery	Initiates and manages product development projects	
HE environment			Represents the department within the university	Represents the university and/or department externally
Service procedures	Follows policies and procedures	Implements policies and procedures	Contributes to the evaluation and development of policies and procedures	Initiates the development of policies and procedures
Organization	Responds to immediate needs within existing resources	Ability to supervize the use of resources at a local level	Ability to supervize the use of resources at a tactical level	Manages the deployment of resources at a strategic level

KNOWLEDGE COMPETENCIES

	Level 1	Level 2	Level 3	Level 4
Subject	Familiar with the range of subjects offered by the university	Understands the range of subjects offered by the university	Understands the subjects offered by the university	
LS technologies	Understands the role of technology in supporting his/her own and student learning	Understands the role of technology in supporting the university operations	Understands and appreciates technological developments within the corporate context	
Information handling	Understands the role of information in supporting his/her own and student learning	Understands the role of information within the university operations	Understands the university's formal and informal information strategy and systems	
Facilitating learning	Familiar with approaches to teaching, learning and assessment	Understands different approaches to teaching, learning and assessment	Understands and appreciates innovations in teaching, learning and assessment	
Curriculum development	Familiar with curriculum development processes	Understands curriculum development processes	Understands innovations in curriculum development processes	
Product development	Familiar with project activities in the department	Understands project activities in the department	Understands the contribution of projects to the achievement of departmental objectives	
HE environment	Familiar with the university mission and the departmental contribution to the university's activities	Understands the university mission and academic plan, and the departmental contribution to the university's activities	Understands the university's strategic plan and its position in the national and international context	Understands the complexity of higher education issues
Service procedures	Familiar with policies and practices	Understands policies and practices	Understands strategy in the development of policies and practices	
Organization	Familiar with systems and procedures for resources	Understands systems and procedures for resources	Understands strategy in the development of systems and procedures for resources	

247

Index